Samuel Rawson Gardiner

The Fortescue Papers

Consisting Chiefly of Letters Relating to State Affairs

Samuel Rawson Gardiner

The Fortescue Papers
Consisting Chiefly of Letters Relating to State Affairs

ISBN/EAN: 9783337268053

Printed in Europe, USA, Canada, Australia, Japan

Cover: Foto ©Suzi / pixelio.de

More available books at **www.hansebooks.com**

THE

FORTESCUE PAPERS;

CONSISTING CHIEFLY OF

LETTERS RELATING TO STATE AFFAIRS,

COLLECTED BY JOHN PACKER,

SECRETARY TO GEORGE VILLIERS, DUKE OF BUCKINGHAM.

EDITED,

FROM THE ORIGINAL MSS. IN THE POSSESSION OF THE HON. G. M. FORTESCUE,

BY

SAMUEL RAWSON GARDINER,

DIRECTOR OF THE CAMDEN SOCIETY.

PRINTED FOR THE CAMDEN SOCIETY.

M.DCCC.LXXI

WESTMINSTER:
PRINTED BY J. B. NICHOLS AND SONS
25, PARLIAMENT STREET.

[NEW SERIES. I.]

COUNCIL OF THE CAMDEN SOCIETY

FOR THE YEAR 1871-72.

President,

SIR WILLIAM TITE, C.B., M.P., F.R.S., V.P.S.A., &c.

WILLIAM CHAPPELL, ESQ. F.S.A.
WILLIAM DURRANT COOPER, ESQ. F.S.A.
F. W. COSENS, ESQ.
JOHN FORSTER, ESQ. D.C.L.
SAMUEL RAWSON GARDINER, ESQ.
ALFRED KINGSTON, ESQ.
SIR JOHN MACLEAN, F.S.A.
SIR FREDERIC MADDEN, F.R.S.
FREDERIC OUVRY, ESQ. Treas.S.A.
EDWARD RIMBAULT, LL.D.
EVELYN P. SHIRLEY, ESQ. M.A., F.S.A.
WILLIAM JOHN THOMS, ESQ. F.S.A.
THE VERY REV. THE DEAN OF WESTMINSTER, F.S.A.
SIR THOMAS E. WINNINGTON, BART.
SIR ALBERT W. WOODS, Garter, F.S.A.

PREFACE.

FOR the papers in this volume the Camden Society is indebted to the liberality of the Honorable G. M. Fortescue, who, "on coming into possession of Dropmore in 1864, under the will of Lady Grenville—the heiress and sole representative of the Pitts of Boconnoc—found in the carpenter's shed an old box which had apparently belonged to Governor Pitt, containing a large quantity of papers in excellent condition, mixed up with the family papers of Mr. Van den Bempde, who died in 1725."[1] If I may judge by an indorsement in the handwriting of the 18th century, on the back of one of the letters, the collection narrowly escaped a still worse fate than that to which it was temporarily exposed. It is as follows, as far as it can be read, part of the paper on which it is written having been torn away:—"Marq. of Bucks on State affairs. .... ers to others, &c. Eliz. & Ja. — useless."

The selections which I have made include many papers which will only be of interest to the professed historian, many which, had the originals been in a public library, so as to be easily accessible to the inquirer, I should certainly have omitted. But there are others

[1] I quote these statements from Sir Erskine Perry's communication to the Philobiblon Society on the Van den Bempde Papers, of which he has kindly sent me a copy, accompanying it with information acquired by him in preparing them for the press.

which will no doubt attract more general attention. Such for instance is the important letter of James I. (No. XXXIV.) clearing up as it does a question about the procedure in Raleigh's case after his return from Guiana, upon which no light has hitherto been thrown, and showing that, at least in James's eyes, it was proved that he had recommended an attack upon the Mexico fleet very early in his voyage. After this may be mentioned the letters of Sir Robert Dudley (No. III.), giving an account of his improvements in naval architecture; of Lord Arundel of Wardour (No. X.), bringing forward a charge against Bacon, which happens to be capable of disproof; of Sir Thomas Wentworth (No. XI.), supplying a missing link in the correspondence on the office of *custos rotulorum* published in the Strafford Papers; of Sir Sebastian Harvey (Nos. LII. and LIII.), throwing light on Christopher Villiers' courtship; and of Charles I. (No. CLXI.), giving an account to Prince Rupert of his victory over Essex in Cornwall. Letters more or less on business matters will also be found from Buckingham himself, from Lord Keeper Williams, from Secretaries Naunton and Calvert, from Sir Lionel Cranfield, the Earl of Suffolk, and other notabilities of the Court of James I. Of a different kind of interest, though if it be read in connection with the remainder of Eliot's correspondence, its historical importance is considerable, is No. CXLV. From it we learn what sort of French Buckingham could write, when he tried his hand at original composition in that language.

The whole of the collection placed in my hands consisted of five hundred and eight documents. A calendar of the whole has been prepared for the Historical MSS. Commision, and will no doubt appear in their second report. It is a collection which has evidently been brought together from at least two, and perhaps from more sources.

The three last papers, all of them in print already, two letters of the first Earl of Clarendon and one of Madame de Maintenon, do not call for any comment. They may have been acquired by anybody at any time. Before these comes the letter of Charles I. mentioned above, which is believed to have been purchased by Lord Grenville, who was interested in it as being dated from Boconnoc. The remaining papers, five hundred and four in all, form the old collection, in which the last dated one was written in May 1627, and the first in June 1568. These papers seem to have found their way into the possession of the Pitt family from Mr. John Van den Bempde, who had purchased the estate of Hackness, in Yorkshire, from the Sydenham family, in 1707.[1]

How they passed into the hands of the Pitts does not appear, but it is certain that they were in Mr. Van den Bempde's possession at the beginning of the 18th century, partly because no one else, as will be seen, was in a position to unite so heterogeneous a collection, and partly because twenty-two holograph letters of Lord Bacon, which form its most valuable portion, were printed by Stephens in his second collection. Mr. Spedding, who examined the papers two years ago, found not only many of those printed in the present volume named in a MS. catalogue by Stephens, but a note (Add. MSS. 4258, fol. 95) in the handwriting of John Locker, "who edited Stephens's second collection after his death," in the following words :—

Mr. Bemde, a g[entleman] of D[utch] extr[action], gave Mr. Stephens those

[1] The Van den Bempde Papers, 22.

things which were made use of in a 4to. edition of letters and pieces, which L[d] Oxford is now possessed of.

In this note, after the word "which," was originally written "his lady gave to the R. Hon. the E[arl] of O[xford]." Mr. Van den Bempde's lady's maiden name was, as Sir Erskine Perry informs me, Temperance Packer, no doubt a descendant of John Packer, secretary to the Duke of Buckingham, whose name occurs frequently in this collection; a man of whom, considering the position which he held, we should have expected to know more than we do. He was probably one of those businesslike unobtrusive men who, as Charles II. said of Godolphin, are never out of the way and never in the way. Another side of his character is, however, revealed by some of these letters, from which he appears as a munificent supporter of the clergy, apparently rather of the Puritan type.

To Packer therefore we may without doubt attribute the mass of the collection, that is to say, the papers from amongst which the letters selected for the present printed volume have been taken, except the first three and the last. It is a series which begins with a letter from James I. to Caron, dated in 1616, not printed here. Another series of 52 papers, dated from 1600 to 1614, have only yielded three letters worth being printed. Many of them are written to Somerset, and they may all very well have come through the hands of a person who occupied the same position in Somerset's household which Packer occupied in Buckingham's. And if Packer was the sort of man which I suppose him to have been—a man of business, who would not trouble himself with Court parties—it is very possible that Villiers may have taken him on from his predecessor in James's favour, and so all this part of the collection would come through him.

There remain 68 papers to be accounted for. Of these the first 33 are almost, if not exclusively, from Sir Francis Walsingham's cabinet, and it is worthy of remark that whilst Buckingham allowed papers of the utmost importance to lie about and to fall into his secretary's hands, Walsingham took good care that the gleanings from his correspondence should be of so formal a nature that not one out of the 33 documents is worth the trouble of printing. Such being the case it is of the less importance to conjecture through whose hands they passed, a point on which I have no evidence warranting even a guess. The other 35 papers, from No. 34 to 68 in the original collection, are of a very different character. They are all, with one exception, letters relating to the marriage and family affairs of Sir Thomas Hoby and his wife, and though I have not admitted them to a place amongst the State Papers of the present volume, the picture which they afford of the progress of a courtship at the end of the 16th century may not be thought out of place here.

Before entering upon this topic, however, let me say a few words about the pedigree of these 35 papers. As Mr. Van den Bempde must have got the Packer papers from his wife, so he must have got the Hoby papers from his estate. He purchased Hackness, as we have seen, from the Sydenham family in 1707, and the first proprietor of the name, John Sydenham, succeeded to the property upon the death of Sir Thomas Hoby in 1640.[1] Sir Thomas Hoby acquired it by his marriage with Margaret the daughter and heiress of Arthur Dakins.

The correspondence opens with a letter from the Earl of Huntingdon, the Puritan Earl whom Elizabeth had made Lord President

[1] Van den Bempde Papers, 22.

of the North. It is written to Walter Devereux, husband of the heiress of Hackness, the brother of the second Earl of Essex, whose paternal grandmother had been a sister of the Earl of Huntingdon's father; Huntingdon being thus a first cousin of Devereux' father, the first Earl of Essex. The lady, before her marriage, had been taken into the service of the Countess of Huntingdon, and had been regarded, possibly through some connection between the Earl and her father, as under the special protection of the family. In this letter, which is dated Jan. 13, 1590, Huntingdon advises the young man "to call in tyme for the assurance of Hackenes," which advice appears to be connected with the birth of Essex's son and heir, and is grounded on the argument that if Essex were to die Walter could not expect anything good to be done for him during his nephew's minority. In point of fact the original arrangement had been that of the £6,500 for which the estate had been purchased as a provision for the young couple, £3,000 should be paid by Essex, £3,000 by Arthur Dakins, and the remaining £500 by the Earl of Huntingdon. As, however, neither Dakins nor Huntingdon had completely fulfilled their obligations, the estate was involved until the whole of the purchase-money could be paid.[1]

Of Walter Devereux we hear no more in this correspondence. He was killed in a skirmish near Rouen, on the 8th of September.[2] In those days marriage was regarded far more as an affair of business than it is now, and the scruples which prescribe a decent interval of widowhood before a second alliance had scarcely any existence. There was one young man, at least, who had no idea of allowing such feelings to stand in the way of the Hackness estate.

[1] For further particulars see Note at the end of the Preface.
[2] Lives of the Devereux, i. 158.

Thomas Posthumus Hoby, the younger and, as his name imports, the posthumous son of Sir Thomas Hoby, now a youth of some four-and-twenty years, had chances other than personal, of which he was resolved to avail himself. His mother, now Lady Russell, the widow of Lord Russell, second son of the Earl of Bedford, was, through one sister, aunt to Francis Bacon, and, what at that time was of far greater importance, was, through another sister, sister-in-law to the great Lord Burghley. No time was lost, and the courtship was opened by the following letter from the Lord Treasurer himself, written on the 21st of September, less than a fortnight after Devereux' death :—

My very good Lord : The harty love and dutyfull goodwyll that I knowe to be borne your Lp. by my good La. and syster in lawe the La. Russell, maketh me bowlde to joyne with her, as a mother for hir sonne, and my self for my honest servante and nephewe, to commend to your Lps. favore his intentione to seeke, by your Lps. both meanes and advyce, to be a suter to a late yonge wyddowe that was wyfe to Mr. Walter Devereux. And yf your Lp. shall please to geve my La. comforte therin. I wyll joyne with hyr in prosecutione therof both to the wyddow, and any other her freynds she may be advysed by. And I doubt not but the yonge gentlemane, thogh he be Posthumus by his father's death, beyng borne after, yet my La. hath such respect to hym, and he soe well doth and wyll deserve yt, as he shall be made able to be a father of lyvelode. And I can assure your Lp. by the proofe that I have had at his good nature and conditions, he wyll prove a good and corteous husbande, and a keeper and noe spender. And soe wyshynge to heer of your Lps. good recovery of your broose, from Elvetham the xxith of 7^{ber} 1591.

Your Lps. moste assuredly at com.

What answer was given to this request does not appear. On the 29th of October Burghley wrote again, this time to the lady's father :—

After my very harty commendations. Thogh yt may be that some have already moved you to understande your dyspositione for your assent to have suyte made to your daughter Mrs. Devereux, wyddowe of Mr. Walter Devereux deceased ; yet, I beynge in mynde, for a speciall particuler freynde of myne, to have, within some tyme after the death of the sayde Mr. Devereux, to have sought to have knowne your mynde, and to have alsoe obtayned your assent to my desyre : yett for some respect of the reputacione of your daughter, whome I accompted woolde rather myslyke of any that shoulde make suyte unto her soe suddeynly after her husbands death, and therefore have dyfferred my purpose untyll nowe that I ame informed that some have or wyll shortly attempt to make some request both to you and the yonge gentlewomane your daughter, and not knowynge what success they may have, I beynge very loath to be prevented by any delay, have presently fownde yt very necessary for me to delay noe farther tyme, and therfore, havynge a great desyre to preferr a yonge gentlemane of good byrth, honesty and understandynge, beynge allyed unto me, and of neer kyndred to dyvers my chyldren, I doe lett you knowe, the party is the sonne of Sir Tho. Hoby deceased and the La. Russell nowe lyvinge, syster to my late wyfe, and his name is Thomas Hoby with an addition of Posthumus, because he was borne after his father's buryall, whoe dyed in Fraunce, wher he was Embassador for hys Ma'y to the then French Kynge, havynge but one brother lyvinge named Sir Edw. Hoby, knyght, whoe hath noe children, soe as this gentlemane is lykely to inherytt all his lyvelode. And besyds that, my La. Russell, his mother, hath provyded a good portione of lyvelod to be left to hym, yf he shall content her in his marryadge, and wyll deal very honorably and kyndly with hym, to enhable hym to make to his wyfe a convenient joynture, in case she shall lyke of his choyse. And accordyngly, her La. and I have of late conferred heerupon, and wee both woolde be glade to procure a maryadge for hym with your daughter, and to that purpose I doe by thes present lettres sygnify to you both hys and my request, prayinge you to accept the same as proceedinge from our harty goodwylls, and of the allowance of your daughter's vertues and conditiones soe reported to us very credybly. And heerunto we both requyre your answer of your inclynatione heerto, soe as the party may have comforte to repayre thyther, to see and acquaynte hymselfe with your daughter, and to make his suyte to herself, to obtayn heyr love; and I shall moste kyndly accept your speedy answer. 29 Octob. 1591.

The reply, when it came, was not such as Burghley probably expected. Immediately on the receipt of the letter Dakins wrote thus :—

May it please your Lo. to understande that your lettres, dated at Westmynster the 29th of Octob. laste, wer delyvered unto me heer at Hackenes, neigh Scarborough, by a gentlemane one Mr. Peerse Stanly, this present day the xth of Novemb. the which to answer as I woolde I noe ways can, which breedeth some greefe in me for that my daughter toke her jorney towards London the 2. of this instant November laste with my lettres to the Right Honorable therle of Huntyngdon, and the Countess his wyfe, her owlde mistress; yeeldynge therby my consente to theyr honors for the disposynge of my daughter in her maryadge, which God knoweth is meane, and farr unworthy the proffer your Ho. doth make by your sayde lettres. Yf I wer able to gratify your honour by any meanes, I stande moste bownd soe to doe for your former goodness towards me, the which as your Ho. doth not remember, soe shall I never forget them, but shall dayly yeelde my harty thanks to Almighty God, whome yt hath pleased to prepare you a stronge pyller for this owre common weal. The L. preserve you, and sende you longe contynuaunce amongst us. Thus I moste humbly take my leave; from Hackeneys aforesayde; the sayde x[th] of Novemb. 1591.

Your Lo. honour's moste humble
at com. with his service,
ARTHURE DAKYNS.

There is nothing upon the surface of Burghley's letters beyond a desire to do the best for his wife's nephew. But it is not unlikely that political reasons mingled with his desire for the advancement of one so closely connected with his own family circle. Hackness was in the centre of a population which still held firmly to the creed and church of their ancestors. Lurking priests found warm protectors alike amongst the landowners and the people. The pursuivant who attempted to execute a warrant from the High Commission ran a good chance of coming back with a bloody head, and even the officials of the Council at York knocked in vain at the doors of houses which were prepared to stand a siege.[1] Under these circumstances Burghley may well have thought it politic to recommend a man whom he could thoroughly trust to hold what he must have regarded as the command of the Protestant garrison at Hackness.

In the meanwhile Hoby had been feeling his way towards making personal advances, as appears from the following letter written by Lady Perrot, who, as a sister of Walter Devereux, might have some influence over his widow:—

Mr. Hoby; I sent a man of myne who long served her to see my Lady of Huntington from me, who as of hime selfe did inquier of the gentill woman you

[1] J. Ferne to Sir R. Cecil, April 27, 1599. S. P. Dom. Eliz. cclxx. 99.

knowe of ; but coulde learne nothing of her coming up. If you will have me send to know as from my selfe, I will, or what else I may to do your liking ; I pray you remember me humbly to my Lady, and so I leave you to all good happs, this first of November.

Your frend that wisheth you well,

D. PERROTT.

A second letter of the 13th conveys the required information, that "the gentillwomane you know of is come to my Lorde of Hunttington's." By this time it was known that there was another suitor in the field. The Countess of Huntingdon was one of two sisters of the favourite Leicester, the other having been the wife of Sir Henry Sidney, and mother of Sir Philip and his two brothers. The youngest of these was Thomas Sidney, and his aunt Lady Huntington had made up her mind that the heiress should be his. According to information which subsequently reached Hoby, it was at the Earl of Huntingdon's request that Dakins had sent his daughter to the Earl's house in London, and where, as soon as she arrived, she was conducted to her chamber, "which she closely kept until she was maryed."[1] Thomas Sidney had a special claim upon the Earl as well upon the Countess, having been left as a minor to his guardianship by his father's will.[2]

As yet, however, Hoby was not aware how invincible were the obstacles opposed to him. The next letter we have is from his mother, Lady Russell :—

Posthumus. I have sent you what I have rec[eived]. Shew Mr. Stanley's letter to me unto my Lord your master.[3] Now, chyld, it standeth yow uper for your owne

---

[1] See p. xvi.

[2] Collins' Sidney Papers, i. 96.

[3] Burghley.

ereditt's sake to trye your frends. My La. Perrott the wisest, surest, and fittest to your good, who, after she hath fownd her dispositycn tooching Sidney, may, on some tyme of the gentlewoman's comming to visitt my La. Dorothie,[1] let you understand of the tyme when yowrself may mete her there. Yf this prove a matche, I will be bownd to leave to yow that which shall be worth v c li. by yere, wherof iii c li. of it joynter to her after my death, and a howse presently furnished to bring her to. Yf in affection she be gon to Sidney, it is one thing: if by reason she be willing to be ledd to her owne good, yow will be fownd the better mache of bothe.

I have promised your brother to defray the charges of assurances for the entayle of Bisham, which I consent to for feare of sayle. He sayth it will cost me 40 li. I pray God it be worth so much to yourself.

Your most loving mother,
ELIZABETH RUSSELL.

I woold you coold so use the matter that the widdow be here this Christmas. I have appoynted your brother's musi-tyons; have hard them and given the master v s. earnest.

Let Anthony Cooke[2] help to steale her away. She hath her father's consent to match where she list.

It soon appeared, however, that Hoby had no chance. Sidney's marriage to Walter Devereux' widow took place some time before the 31st of May, 1592, as appears from a letter of Huntingdon's to him of that date. On the 23rd of July, 1592,[3] Arthur Dakins died, leaving the young couple to take possession of Hackness. But this second marriage, like the first, was not of long duration. Thomas Sidney died in the summer of 1595,[4] probably about the end of July or the beginning of August, and her old suitor lost no time in making another stroke for the prize. A fresh application was made to the

[1] Lady Perrot.

[2] Lady Russell's nephew, son of Richard, the eldest son of her father Sir Anthony.

[3] I give the date from the Inquisition p. m. Chancery Inquisitions, 35 Eliz. part 2, No. 32. Sir Erskine Perry (Van den Bempde Papers, 13) gives it in the following year, without stating the authority.

[4] The first letter relating to Hoby's renewed suit is dated Sept. 12, 1595, whilst his marriage took place between June 26 and Sept. 4, 1596. According to Lady Hoby's epitaph in Hackness church, quoted by Sir Erskine Perry, she was a widow this time for thirteen months.

Earl of Huntingdon, who, knowing that the lady had not listened to Hoby on the last occasion, contented himself with giving him the following letter to Mr. Edward Stanhope, a member of the Council of the North, of which Huntingdon was President. Stanhope was in some way or other related both to Mrs. Sydney and to Hoby, who, as will be seen, had been knighted since we last heard of him :—

Mr. Stanhope. This gentleman, Sir Thomas Hobby, taketh a longe jorney into the North for a good cause, as himself will shewe you. My Lady his mother did first write unto me to give him my best freindly meanes in the matter. And since my Lo. Trea. hath also required the same of me, both by his letters and speaches to me, which I am willinge to performe; but, as I have said to the Knight himself, I take it to be verry sone for me to deale therein, yet; and, to speake the trewthe, though I be verry willinge to do any good office towards him that may lye in me, yet so bad hath bin my successe that yf I might be spared I would never deale that way agayne for any such matter. And for this tyme I am spared to write, but he requireth that I would assigne some man to accompany him to the place that he may the redilyar have a sight of the gentlewoman. And because you are his kinseman, I hope shortely to see you in Yorkesheire, and for this tyme, with my harty commendacions, I do comitt you to our Lord.

Your loving freind,
H. HUNTINGDON.

At Highgate the xii[th] of Septemb., 1595.

The result of Hoby's diplomacy appears in the next letter, which is Stanhope's reply to the Earl :—

My humble ductie to your good Lp. premysed. It may please you to be advertised that of Saterday last the xx[th] of this moneth, I receyved your Lps. lettres by my cosen Sir Thomas Hobby, and understandinge that night at Yorke that the gentlewoman was newely removed to Hull, wee spent the Sabbath at Yorke. The next daye, good Mr. Cotrell's funerall beinge to be solemnized, in respecte he put me in trust as a supervisor, wee staid ther till that afternoone, and then went towarde Hull, accompanyed also with Mr. Peres Stanley, whither we came upon Tuesday by one of the clocke, and went to the manor, where my cosen Sydney after a while admitted mee to her chamber. I founde her layde complayninge of payne in her eyes and heade, which I founde to procede of greate lamentacion for the losse of the worthy gentleman her late husbande, for she coulde not then speake of him without teares.

After some speches of curtesey and entertaynment, I recomended your Lps. favor unto her, appereuge by your lettres which I shewed her, whereby finding the occasion of my cominge, she shedd teares againe, sayinge that thoughe she helde her selfe bounde to your Lp. to whom[1] she was wholly devoted, yet the tender love she bare to him that was dead, made yt grevous to her to hear of any newe; and much more to be thought of the gentleman that she were to be delt with in any suche matter soe soone, which I excused, as I had receyved from himselfe before, that he had that reverend regard of her, as that in his owne opinione he might be thought to blame; but that two respectes ledd him.

One, in desier his eyes to witnes that which publicke reporte had delivered him, that the guyftes of nature had in some sorte equalled her vertues.[2]

Thother, havinge bene longe drawne to affect her for thes guyftes, he was desirous to be made knowne to her, as the first that shoulde seeke her, though he after forbore for some tyme to entertayne or prosecute his suyte.

In theud, unwillingly, but in duetifull regard of your Lps. recomendacion, and to avoyd to offer that discurtesey, not to be sene to a gentleman of his worth that came soe farr for that purpose, in very modest sort she yelded that after some tyme of my withdrawinge from her, she woulde admytt him to doe your Lps. comendacions to her.

In which meane while my cosen Alred's wief cominge thither, after some half hower, my self was required to bringe Sir Thomas and Mr. Peres Stanley into her chamber, where curteousley and modestly intertayning him with fewe speeches, she retired to the gentlewomen, and, after smal tyme spent in the chamber, wee left her, I sayinge to her that if your Lps. cominge downe were not very shortely, this gentleman woulde be boulde in his cominge up, to knowe if she woulde comaunde him any thinge to your Lp. and my good Lady.

That eveninge I acquainted my cosen Aldred and his wief both with your Lps. favor to recomende the gent. to this match, and with the licklyhoode how well, by the naturall affeccion borne him of his honorable mother, his owne indnstry, his educacion in soe good a schoole of experience as my L. Threasorer's chamber, and his alyence and kindered, he might prove a very good match to the gentlewoeman.

They both cheifely respectinge that it was mocioned with your Lps. speciall liking, which they doubted not but woulde be seconded by my Lady, when tyme had overworne the great grefe she takes for the losse of a kinsman of soe greate good parts and expectacion, did not onely yeelde to geve there best furderance to the match, as occasione might be offered them, but my cosen Alred entred into consultacion with us, what course might be helde in prosecuting of yt, best beseminge the reputacions of them boeth.

Whereupon, although Sir Thomas at the first was desirous to have procured some

---

[1] "wheu" in MS.

[2] So that he had never yet seen her.

place in or nere the towne of Hull, to the which, within a weeke or thereabouts, he might have repaired the better to take oportunitye to intertayne the gentlewoman; yet, upon better advisement, he yeelded to this counsell, that he woulde retyre himselfe for v or vi dayes, and if in that tyme he harde not of your Lps. presente cominge into the cuntry, he woulde take his journey by Hull to your Lp. and there salutinge the gentlewoeman, woulde let her knowe that he was so fully satisficed by sight of her, that all things was answerable to the goode reporte he had receyved of her before, as he ment to settle himselfe upon her favor. Nevertheles, tenderly regardinge her reputacion, he woulde for a tyme retyre himselfe into the southe, and there eyther awayte your Lps. cominge downe, or if it were not soe soone as he wished, hoped to receyve your Lps. recomendacion to her as well of himselfe, as by his freendes, for his state and haviour.

And this course he meaninge to observe, and apperinge to as desirous to be onely behouldinge to your Lp. and my Lady for this matche, which, chefelie in regard of the gentlewoeman's vertues, whereof he heareth by all that speake of her, he will accompt a greate preferment to him, we came of Wedensday from Hull soe farr together towardes Doncaster as I comytted him to Mr. Stanley nere his house at Womersley, and I repaired to Doncaster, where I was in respect of my place ther to attende the next day the eleccion of the [mayor],[1] where by foresight and good meanes, without contradiction or shewe of faccion (not usuall heretofore), William Hansley, one in ductie and service towards your Lp. was chosen there maior.

* * * * * * * *

I humbly cease to trouble your Lp. 27 7^{br} 1595.

Your Lps. humbly to command,

E. S.

This intervention of Mr. Edward Stanhope, which in the present day would have been enough to ruin any one's suit, was well received by the man who was chiefly interested in its success. The great Lord Treasurer wrote at once to Stanhope, and to his "cozen Alred," to thank them for their assistance. Hoby's next step taken seems to have been to collect letters in his favour from persons of note, much in the same way as a candidate for an appointment would now-a-days furnish himself with testimonials of his merit. The following letter from Sir Robert Cecil to Huntingdon looks very much as if Hoby suspected the Earl of being lukewarm in his interests:—

[1] This must be the word intended; but it is written "manor."

My good Lorde. I have ben so ernestlie intreated by my cosin Sir Tho. Hobbie to acknowledge in his behalfe the great obligacion for your favour already extended towards him, as I could do no lesse then by this lettre yeld your L. most humble thanks, and in regarde of myne owne affection towards him, further ingage my selfe towards yoer Lo. by beseeching your continuance as a favour which I will accomt my selfe bounde to deserve and requytt by anie service I can. And thus for this tyme I doe most humblie take my leave. From the Corte this xxviii[th] of Octobre 1595.

Yo[r] L. poore friend at com[mand].

In the next letter Hoby recounts to Huntingdon his ill success :—

R[ight] H[onorable]. Beynge very loath to neglect the fytt opertunity of this bearer, I have presumed by hym to troble your Lp. aswell to manyfest my dutyfull desyres to become thankfull for your honorable favoure shewed in your furtherynge of myn endevours, as to lett your Ho. understande howe I have proceeded, synce your Lps. departure. And because I can not my self render unto your honour due thankes for your honorable coorses helde in the cause, I wyll referr that unto thos honorable persons that fyrst recomended myself and cause to your favoure, and wyll be bould to relate unto them at large withowte any omyssyone the honorable care you have pleased to have of my suyte. Now, concernynge the state wherein I nowe stande, yt ys soe weake that I fynde noe reasons as yet to hope for better, neyther wyll my affectione be drawne altogether to despayre; for the favourable access which your Lp. obtayned for me ys soe unwyllyngly performed as, had I not learned a former lessone of *audaces fortuna juvat*, wherby I ame ledd contynually to exceed good manners in beynge more ruled by my love then reasone, it woold have been longe synce absolutely denyed me. But as I came not soe farr to be dyscouradged with some fewe repulses, soe wyll I not departe untyll I have performed the uttermoste of my strengthe in seekynge her, styll referrynge the sequell to God's good pleasure and her own self; and to that ende, God wyllynge, I wyll remayne heer untyll your Lps. retourne from the North parts, and then I wyll my selfe wayte upon you; and soe for this tyme I wyll humbly leave to troble your Lp. any farther. This xx[th] of Novemb. 1595.

Your Lps. moste humbly to commaunde.

Hoby's judgment of the lady's feelings towards him was justified by the event. She wrote to Huntingdon to decline her importunate suitor. But, as appears from the Earl's reply, Hoby had also made up his mind not to take no for an answer :—

Mrs. Margarett. Beare with me whatsoever I wryte, for I was not in a greater payne synce my laste jorney then I even nowe ame in. I did acquaynte hym with the contents of your lettre, and at the laste I dyd geve hym the lettre to peruse, but yt moved him not to that purpose you desyred. And soe he toulde me he woolde tell your self, yet withowte my lettre he wooldc not returne. He doth not beleeve that you wyll geve such a denyall as your lettre mentioneth. For God's cawse have care of all our credyts, and soe handle the matter as his commynge agayne may be neyther offensyve to you nor dyspleasynge to hymself. And so with wysh of all good and happynes to you, for this tyme I ende and commytt you to the L. Jesus. At Yorke this 9th Decemb.

Your lovynge freynde,

H. Huntyngdon.

Huntingdon's "greater payne" was the precursor of his death, which took place on the 14th of December, and Hoby had no help to look for from his brother and successor. On the 3rd of February, 1596, we have a letter from Hoby to his cousin Anthony Bacon, written to influence the Earl of Essex, who appears to have been offended with his brother's widow on account of her haste in marrying Thomas Sidney:—

Sir. Beynge more then desyrous to compass a matter that doth not a lyttle import me, I have been boulde (in respect of our neernes in nature, and our mutuall love,) to entreate your kyndest freyndship for the better effectynge therof, hopynge therin to fynde you as wyllynge as I have juste cause to thynke you able, fully to contryve yt. Soe yt ys, good cosyne, that my La. my mother shewed me a lettre sent unto her from my L. of Essex; wherin I founde very greate reasone to holde my selfe exceedingly bownde unto his Ho. for his favourable conceite therin expressed of me. And because I muste confess my selfe therof altogether unworthy, I wyll ever heerafter by all dutyfull endevours seeke to deserve the same. But wheras his Lp. seemed in the same lettre to be highly offended with the gentlewomane with whome I seeke to match, my earnest request unto you ys that you wyll be an humble suter to his Lp., that his Ho. wylbe pleased to heer some reasones that wyll suffyce (I hope) to move hym to remove all former dyslyke from his honourable breaste. And (because I wyll not name any thynge that his Lp. is wyllinge to forgett) I wyll only seeke to excuse the gentlewoman's suddayne marryadge at the tyme of her first wyddowhoode, wherof noe mane can better speake then my self, whoe was then desyrous to be a suter (as I nowe ame) unto her. And to delyver playnly what I thynke therof, I muste truely confess the actione in yt self to be meerly evyll, but all cyrcomstances ryghtly consydered, his Lp. (I doubt not) wyll see some cause to myttegatt his former displeasure commytted agaynst her. But to speake shortly of the matter, thus yt then stoode; I my self beynge then very desyrous to seeke her best affection, procured my La. my mother, to move the matter to my L. of Essex, which she dyd by lettre delyvered by my self; and, that done, I had my L. Thre. letters to break the matter to my late L. of Huntyngdon, and to the gentlewoman's father, the better to effect my purpose. This done, my sayd L. of Huntingdon seeynge my earnest persecutione of the cause (fearyinge to be prevented) sent Mr. Sydney presently downe; whoe (by his Lps. meanes) prevayled soe fare with owlde Mr. Dakyns, then lyvynge, as that he sent his daughter to London forthwith, unto my La. of Huntyngdone, and at her fyrst comynge she was brought to her chamber, which she closly kept untyll she was maryed. Nowe what I coolde say farther is fytter for my L. to imagyne, then for me to relate, and therfore leavynge her close prysoner in her chamber, whyther none wer suffered to come, withowte especiall admyttance, I wyll retourne unto my sute, which I ame humbly to make to his Lp. which ys that his Ho. wyll fyrst rightly conceave of the state wherin she then stoode, and then, yf she seem not altogether excusable, yet that he wylbe pleased at my humble suyte to forgett all former oversightes, because I wooldе be very loath to match with one that lyves in his Lps. dyslyke, and I shoulde be more loath by much to have her contenywe in his Lps. dysgrace after maryadge. And soe, leavynge my cause to your wyse mediatione and to my Ls. moste honourable dyspositione, I wyll take my leave this 3. of Feb. 1595.

On the 14th of March we have an appeal to the widowed Countess of Huntingdon, who had been the prime mover in the last marriage, and an undated letter, received on the 4th of April, from Sir Robert Sidney, Thomas Sidney's only surviving brother, stating that he had "not fownd fit time to move my Lady of Huntington," but would do so at his "next coming from the Court." Another letter received on the same day from the Countess of Essex, the widow of Sir Philip Sidney, ran thus:—

Sir,—I have receaved your letter, the contentes wherof being honest and honorably, doe so fullie free you, in my conceit, from all imputation of presumption, as that I would willinglie have testified both my approbation and furderance of the matter to your Mrs if I had not of late beene much importund to writte in the same argument by some that perswaded them selfes I hade small reasson (besides my will) to denie them (as they thought) so reasonable a request, and, if I would have bene an achtor in marege mattars, I wonld not have refust them my best fourdrans. Let thes excus my not sattesfieing your request, not bnt that I holde you worthe of har you desir, but that in honnor I cannot be for you sens I have promest an othar not to be aganst him. I comett you to the protection of the Higheyst, and

Your loving frend,

FR. ESSEX.

The next month a new phase of the affair presented itself. The new Earl of Huntingdon, looking over his brother's accounts, found, as he asserted, that he was himself the real owner of the Hackness estate. A long letter, written on the 28th of May to Mrs. Sidney, by Edward Stanhope, whom we have heard of before as Hoby's supporter, informed her that she had a Chancery suit before her. The story of Mrs. Sidney's business difficulties need not detain us here, all that is necessary to be known being given in a note at the end of the Preface. But the conclusion of the letter is in every way too noticeable to allow of its omission :—

Now, my good cosen, what course for you to take in the meane while to make yt [i.e. the chancery suit] sure, I cannot so well advise you, as if I were voyd of suspicion that my advise tended not to serve some other's turne, which I protest I am free from intencion, and therfore will let you simply know what I thinke for your good; which is that having thes great folks to stand against you, (and you having none greater, that you may make account as sure to you, that may sway with my L. Keeper to cast the ballance being indifferent of your syde,) if you would so farr use your faithfull servant Sir Thomas as dyrect him by your appointment to trye his credytt with my L. Threr. for you, I know his Lp. may sway the matter wholly, and I am assured he so much affecteth his kinsman, as if he fynde that the motion proceedeth from your self, and that Sir Thomas shall have kynde thanks of you for yt, he will stryke it sure for you.

Herein use your owne discrecion, for if I were not assured that the speciall favour I wish you to afford Sir Thomas for his long service and entyer affeccion should not fall out as much to your good and comfort hereafter, as his, and that I know his estate shall be so well supplyed by his honorable mother as that he shall be able (without that which you bring) to maintaine you according to his degree, I protest to you, by the faith of an honest man, I would not use thes speeches unto you, or seeke any way to draw you to your hinderance, and knowing the trust you repose in me, which I will never deceyve; and therfore what I have ingaged my creditt unto you for, I doubt not but be able always to maintaine, and even so referring you to your owne good wisdome and honorable government, which hitherto you have caryed of yourself to your great creditt, I leave the report of the rest of the buysines to Mr. Mease, and so betake you to God.

It is not necessary to believe that Lord Burghley and Sir Thomas Egerton would have lent themselves to such a scheme as this. But that their names should have been mentioned in connection with it is certainly startling. But returning to a less important subject, it looks very much as if it was this letter that effected the marriage, and that the widow granted, to the fear of losing a suit in Chancery, what she had denied to her wooer's importunity. At all events Stanhope's letter is dated May 28, and on the 26th of June we have the following letter from Hoby to Lady Huntingdon, couched in terms which show that he considered himself in a fair way to obtain the object of his desires:—

R[ight] H[onourable]. Fyndynge by sundry reports howe greatly I ame bownde unto your Ho. for youre favorable coorse helde in my present sute unto my Mrs, wherin your Lap hath pleased neyther to advyz her unto me, nor to geve her counsell agaynst me, but, with some favourable speaches not a lyttle tendynge to my good, your Ho. hath suffyciently publyshed the same to be a matter by you helde very indyfferent, and soe have[1] her to her owne free choyce, I have at this tyme presumed to troble your Ho. with thes rude lynes, that in them I myght both yeeld unto your Ho. moste humble thankes for your soe greate and by me altogether undeserved favoure, and alsoe that I myght the better manyfest my dutyfull desyres to become moste servyceable for the same. And although I have hitherto been but a meer stranger, and soe have wanted meanes to merrytt your Ho. favourable conceyte, and much less to deserve the leaste furtheraunce in my present proceedinges; yet shall your Ho. heerafter fynde me moste ready in all dutyfull endeavours to doe you all dutifull servyce. And when I shall prove soe happy as to possess the happynes I doe nowe seeke for (wherof my self-unworthynes myght make me dyspayre) I wyll be fownde as dutyfully servyceable, as if I wer a naturall braunch of the stocke yt self, whereto I shall then be but grafted. But I wyll leave at this tyme to be further troblesome unto your Ho. and wyll humbly submytt my servyce to your Ho. commant. This 26th of June, 1596.

The marriage was not long postponed. We have a letter of the

[1] "leave her" no doubt, in the original letter, of which the MS. is a copy

4th of September from Burghley to the new Earl of Huntingdon, inquiring after "certeyne hanginges" to be found amongst "the things that were at Yorke of the late Erle of Huntyngdon's," which his nephew, Sir T. Hoby, has informed him are the property "of his nowe wyfe, then Mrs. Sydney wydowe."

And so this diplomatic courtship had its ending. The letters from which its details have been gathered have transported us for a moment amongst men whose habits and modes of proceeding are different from our own, and they may perhaps help the historian to realise that the characters with which he has to deal are not to be judged by the standard of the manners of the 19th century. The affair of the marriage of Sir John Villiers, for instance, has, before this, been told by writers who have ascribed to Bacon feelings on the subject of the marriage-tie which it is certain that he never possessed, and the reader of the present volume will be all the more likely not to misinterpret Buckingham's letter to Bacon (No. LXXV.) about his brother's marriage, if he has first pondered the meaning of Hoby's correspondence.

Of the marriage itself and of the future life of Hoby there is not much to say. His name occasionally occurs in the correspondence of the times, but not in any marked way. Sir Erskine Perry has printed[1] a letter from Lady Hoby to her husband, which is written in the spirit of an affectionate wife, upon which he comments in the following manner[1]:—

Sir Thomas P. Hoby, however, it would appear, by no means deserves to stand on the high pedestal where his affectionate wife placed him. According to the traditions still existing at Hackness, he accelerated her end by kicking her down stairs; and the late parish clerk, John Noble, used to relate that he and his father had often tried to efface the spots of his wife's blood in the old hall, but in vain. He

[1] Van den Bempde Papers, 17.

was as bad a neighbour as he was a husband, and Sir Hugh Cholmondeley, who was owner of the adjoining lordship of Whitby, thus speaks of him in his memoirs:—

He says, "That his father, Sir Richard, 1608, was much annoyed by a troublesome and vexatious neighbour, one Sir Thomas Hobby, who, having married a widow, the inheritor of Hackness lordship, having a full purse and no children, delighted to spend his money and time in lawsuits." Sir Hugh in another part calls him, "My father's old enemy, Sir Thomas Hobby," and says, "That he was of such a nature, unless a man became his very slave, that there was not any keeping friendship, for he loved to carry all things after his own way and humour, how unjust or injurious soever; and within a year, being at the sessions and differing in opinion with him, he thought to put an affront on me, by determining the matter after his own mind; but I, putting it to the opinion of the bench, had them all on my side, insomuch that he, turning about, said to the gentleman that sat next to him, 'His grandfather once crossed me thus on the bench, but I made him repent it, and so will I this man.' And truly, soon after he began a suit against me in the Star Chamber, and I against him in the Court of York; but finding himself to have the worst end of the staff, procuring the Lord Coventry, then Lord Keeper, to send for me to compose both; but after the check I gave him in the Sessions, he never appeared there more, nor was so active or formidable in the country as formerly. The Sydenhams, now possessed of Hackness, may in some sort thank me for it, for Sir Thomas Hobby, to make the Lord Coventry his friend against me, proposed his cousin Sydenham in marriage to my Lord's grandchild, and so settled Hackness on him, which in right belonged to Mr. Dakins, next to Sir Thomas's lady, whose land that was."

Sir Hugh Cholmondeley is wrong in details, though probably right in substance, as to the negotiations between Hoby and the Lord Keeper, for Sir Thomas's nephew, John Sydenham, did actually marry, not the granddaughter, but the niece of the Lord Keeper, Anne Hart, and succeeded to the property at Sir Thomas's death in 1640.

I am not concerned to defend the character of Sir T. Hoby, of which I know nothing, except that Burghley speaks of him as "of a tractable and kynde dyspositione." But it is only fair to say that a parish clerk's legend of the last resident landlord of an estate deserted from 1640 till 1792 must be received with caution, and that, as for the Cholmondeleys, their account was that of a family whose proceedings had probably much to do with enlisting Burghley's warmest sympathies on the side of his nephew.

Let us see, for instance, how the two names come out in a letter written on the 27th of April, 1599, by a member of the Council of York to Sir Robert Cecil. After speaking of his intention to attack a house near Whitby, John Fern goes on to say:—

"I must imploy as great strengthe of people as I can from Yorke, for Sir Tho. Hobby being now at London I do not knowe of any faithfull assistance in the cuntry; in which respect, for that the people are wholy defected from religion xx myles along the coste, and doe resist all warrants and officers that come amongest them, I doe resolve (althoughe it hath seldome bene so used) to be the same tyme within 4 myles of the howse, to prevent any rescues to be mayd by the cuntrye (following Mr. Henry Cholmeley) whose tenant Hodgesonne is, for in January last one Aslaby, another of Mr. Cholmley's tenants, did rescue a person, a recusant, from the pursevant to the High Commission, and uppon the 23. of this present the like was done by 40 persons all weaponed against 2 men, that had bothe warrant from this counsell and the High Comession to apprehend some recusants; affirming that yf there came never so many with whatsoever authority, they shold be slayne befor any towards Mr. Cholmley shold be caryed away (and yet Cholmeley is a justice of peace, by what means I know not) and threatned revenge against Sir Thos. Hobby.[1]

Two families thus severed from one another so completely on religious and political grounds are not likely to have comported themselves peaceably as neighbours, or to have appreciated one another fairly in their descriptions of character.

ORDERS AND DECREES. CHANCERY. [See note [1], p. vi.]

1597 A, fol. 88. ix die Junii [1597].

Thom: Posthumus Hobby Knight, and the Lady Margarett his wyef, plaintifes; Geo. Earle of Huntingdon and Henry Smythe defendts.

Forasmuch as upon the hearinge and long debatinge of the matter this daye in the presence of the Councell learned on all parts touchinge the mannor and parsonage of Hackneys in the countye of York, which the pl. clayme to belonge in equity to the sayd Lady Hobby and her heyres, and which the sayd Earle of Huntingdon supposed to apperteyne to him in equytye in respect of such money as the late Earl of Huntingdon, whose brother and heyre the nowe Earle ys, did laye owt for or in respect

[1] J. Ferne to Sir R. Cecil. April 27, 1599. S. P. Dom. Eliz. cclxx. 99.

of a marryage to be had betweene Walter Devorux, brother to the Right Honourable the nowe Earle of Essex, and the said Dame Margarett, beinge dawghter and heyre of one Arthure Dakyns Esquyer, which marryage was effected by the meanes of the sayd Earle of Essex, and the late Earle of Huntingdon. The sayd mannor and parsonage was purchased of Sir Henry Constable, Knight, for the some of 6500 li., whereof 3000 li. should have ben payd by the said Earle of Essex, other 3000 li. by the sayd Dakyns, and the other 5 C li. by the late Earle of Huntingdon, and that yf the said Dakyns had payd the sayd 3000 li. accordingly, then the premysses had gone, as this court conceaveth, to the behoof of the said Walter Devorux and of the said Dame Margarett and of theyr heyres. But because the sayd Dakyns would then undertake to pay but 2000 li., which he payd accordingly toward the sayd purchase, and C li. more as the pl. alleadge, the said Earle of Essex undertoke to pay the other 4000 li., and thereupon the said mannor and parsonage were assured to Richard Broughton and Thomas Crompton Esquyers, who became sewertyes for payment of that 4000 li. for theyr endempnytye in that behalf. After which tyme the said Mr. Devorux dyed without yssue, and then the said late Earle of Huntingdon procured the said Dame Margarett to be secondly marryed to his wyef's nephewe, Tho. Sydney, whose preferment the same Earle sought, and at the specyall request of the same Earle made on that behaulf to the sayd Earle of Essex, wherein the said late Earle perswaded the said Earle of Essex that yt should be an honourable parte in him, synce the sayd Dakyns had payd 2000 li. towards the purchase of the sayd lands, to yeeld that the sayd land should goe to the Dame Margarett, beinge the sayd Dakyns' dawghter. He, the same Earle of Essex, very honorably was content that the sayd Browghton and Mr. Crompton should make over all the premysses to Sir John Harrington, Knight, and Edward Mountagewe Esq., beinge put in truste by the seyd late Earle of Huntingdon therewith, to the entent that they, beinge satisfyed all such money as they should pay in respect thereof, should convey the same over to such person or persons as the said late Earle of Huntingdon should appoynt, who meant the same to the behoof of the said Thomas Sydney whom he desyred to prefer, and of the said Dame Margarett, as in her right, as two wytnesses doe depose, and to the use of them two and of theyr heyres as a third wytnesse doth of his owne knowledge alsoe depose; and in respect that the saide premysses weere soe conveyed to the said Sir John Harrington and Edw. Mountagewe at the said late Earle of Huntingdon's request made to the said Earle of Essex, as aforesaid, the said late Earl of Huntingdon or the said Sir John Harrington and Edw. Mountagewe Esqr. were to satisfye unto the sayd Earle of Essex all such money as he had layd owt about the premysses being 4080 li., and did also as yt seemeth by one deposycion cawse a tytle of a joyncture which the same Dame Margarett was to have had from the sayd Walter Devorux her fyrst husband to be yeelded up. After which tyme the sayd Tho. Sydney also dyed without yssue, and in respect the sayd Smyth, when the said Sir John Harrington and Edw. Mountagewe were unwillinge to deale any further abowt the premisses, did, at the request of the said late Earle of Huntingdon, ingage himself for the same Earle for such great summes of money which the sayd Earle was to pay for the premysses, the said Sir John Harrington and Edw. Mountagewe, by the appoyntment of the same late Earle, conveyed all the premysses to the sayd Smyth, that, by meanes of such money as he hath layd owt about the same which hath ben hitherunto kept from him to his great hinderance, greatly weakened his estate, and yet neverthcles submytteth himself to convey the premysses as this Court shall thinke meete and appoynt, so as he may be fyrst satisfyed all such money as he hath disbursed for or in respect of the premysses, and all such damages as this Courte shall thinke meete to be allowed unto him, for or in respect that the same money hath, contrary to his will, ben deteyned from him; so as then the questyon chyefly rested whether the premysses should be conveyed to the same Dame Margarett, or the said nowe Earle of Huntingdon. But forasmuch as yt appereth that the father of the same Dame Margarett payd 2000 li. at the least towards the purchase of the premysses for her good, and that, yf he had payd his full parte fyrst agreed upon, viz. 3000 li., then the premysses should, without questyon, have come unto her and her heyres, the sayd Tho. Sydney beenge deade without yssue; and because also 700 li. was paid by the said Mr. Sydney towards the sayd purchase, and 2260 li. hath ben raysed of fynes also of leases made of parte of the premysses towards the same purchase, whereof 2000 li. at the least was payd by the said Thomas Sydney towards that purchase, and the rest as yt is alleadged 160 or thereabouts rests in the tenants' hands unpaid; and further also the said Dame Margarett hath noe joyuture or preferment left to her by eyther of her two honourable marriages, savinge a howse and a smale quantyty of land was (as the said Sir Thomas Posthumus Hobby now deposed in open court) sould by him and the said Dame Margaret also *bonâ fide* to the best advantage, and yet they could have but 510 li. for the same, which hath ben payd also for the debts of the saide Mr. Sydney; and becawse yt standes proved as aforesaide, that upon her said second marryage the premysses were meant to her behoof and to her and her heyres, as one deposeth; and because noe proof ys made that the same premysses were ever meant to the use of the sayd late Earle of Huntingdon, other wyse then for securytye of such money as he or anye for him disbursed for or in respect of the same premysses; this Cowrt therefore, and upon consyderacion had of the other circumstaunces of the cawse, ys rather enclyned, that the premysses ought to be assured to the said Dame Margarett and her heyres, then the said nowe Earle of Huntingdon, the same Earle beinge fyrst satisfyed whatsoever the late Earle hath disbursed or payd for interest or otherwyse for or in respect of the purchase of the premysses, and the same Smyth beinge also fyrst and speedely satisfyed as aforesaide; It is therfore ordered that Mr. X^r Lewy and Mr. X^r Hone, two of the Masters of this Cowrt, shall with all convenyent speede examyne and fynde owt by all good meanes what and how much money the said late Earle of Huntingdon hath disbursed or ben prejudyced for interest or otherwyse, *bonâ fide* for or towarde the purchase of the premysses, which hath not ben synce repayd or satisfyed unto him or unto the now Earle, by receypt of any rents or profytts of the premysses, or by any other wayes and meanes, or sufficiently proved betweene them to be freely gyven by the said late Earle to the said Mr. Sydney towards the said purchase, wherein they are to have specyall regard by all good meanes to fynde owt whether the sayd late Earle payd the whole 500 li., or not, which originally was appoynted to be payed by him to the said Sir Henry Constable towards the said purchase, for that the said Sir Henry ys nowe sure, as the said Sir Henry deposeth, for 200 li. of the same 500 li., which the said late Earle was appoynted by the said Sir Henry to pay to two of his credytors, and the sayd Smyth is to be examyned upon interrogatoryes to be forthwith mynestred unto him on the pl. parte to fynde owt what and how much money he hath payd or dysbursed in interest or otherwyse for or towards the purchase of the said mannor and parsonage or eyther of them, and what and how much thereof he hath ben repayd or satisfyed by any mannor of meanes. And then the pl. shalbe bownden by the examynacion to allowe that his, the sayde Smyth's, chardge, besyde his damages for forbearinge of his money, amounteth to soe much as he shall soe depose, and the sayd Smyth ys also further requyred to sett downe in wrytinge upon his othe also, in as particuler a sorte as he may convenyently, what damages he hath susteyned for want of his money which he hath disbursed as aforesaid, and by whose meanes he hath susteyned the same, and then the Lo. Keeper wilbe pleased, together with the said Masters of this Court, to consyder thereof, and to allowe unto him such reasonable and competent damages as shalbe thought meete; and the foresaid Masters of this Cowrte are also appoynted to examyne and fynde owt whether the said Dakyns payd any more then the foresaid 2000 li. or not towards the said purchase and thereof, and of all other the recon[i]ngs to them two only before referred to make report to this Cowrt, together with theyr opynion towchinge the same, for further order to be taken thereupon accordingly. And yt is lastly ordered that all the fynes and arrerages of rents, which rest dewe in any of the tennants' hands of any of the premysses, shalbe speedely payd by the same tenants to the said Smyth towards the satisfaction of that which shalbe fownd dewe unto him, and then, upon such payment of the said fynes and rents, all the leases for which the same fynes shalbe soe payd shalbe forthwith delyvered to the tenants which paid the same, and soe lykewyse shall all the bonds soe delyvered up, which were made for or towchyng the payment of the said fynes, and those bonds also which one Wm. Carrington heretofore toke of any of the same tenants for or towching the delyvery of theyre leasses shall lykewyse upon payment of the fynes and arerages forthwith [be] delyvered unto them.

CONTENTS.

ERRATA.

Page 21. Heading of No. X. *for* Arundell *read* Arundel.

Page 53. Signature, *for* Sheflild *read* Sheffield.

Page 58. Note 6, two lines from bottom, *for* vol iii. *read* vol. v.

Page 192. Heading of No CXXXVIII., *for* XCVI. *read* CXXXVII.

Page 214. Heading, *for* CLXIII. *read* CLVIII.

Page 215. Heading, *for* CLXIV. *read* CLIX.

FORTESCUE PAPERS.

No. 1.

James I. to Henry IV. King of France.

[Draft.]

Mon Frère. Nous avons receu voz lettres[1] du vingt cinquiesme jour d'Aoust dernier touchant un de noz subjects nommé Forbis, qui passa par vostre Cour ; pour qui nous trouvons par vos lettres que vous avez usé de plus grande caution et jugement en le recommendant, que luy d'honesteté et sincerité envers vous, en vous informant de son affaire. Ce que pour vous faire plus clairement comprendre, vous entendrez que il y a environ deux ans que quelques ministres de nostre Royaume d'Escosse d'un esprit turbulent et repugnant à la discipline et forme de gouvernement establie au dit Royaulme pour les affaires ecclesiastiques, entreprirent (sans qu'ilz en eussent authorité ou pouvoir de par nous,) de tenir une assemblée generale[2] pour les affaires de l'Eglise. Et nonobstant qu'ilz fussent admonestez par quelques uns, ayans à ce commission de nous, de l'erreur qu'ils commirent en cest endroict, et leur fust defendu d'y proceder plus avant, ils continuerent toutesfois leur assemblée, soustenans que de leur propre authorité ilz le pouvoient faire sans 1607. Sept. ?

[1] Neither this letter, nor any reply from Henry are amongst the Lettres Missives de Henri IV.

[2] At Aberdeen, July 2, 1605 (Calderwood, vi. 279), when John Forbes was chosen Moderator, for which he was, with five other members, banished in November 1606. (Calderwood, vi. 590.)

1607. Sept. ? nostre congé et licence. Pour laquelle presomption ils furent convenus par devant nostre Conseil, et leur fut remonstrée la grandeur de leur forfaict, et qu'en cest affaire ilz avoient empieté sur nostre authorité regale, et par les loix du Royaume ilz estoient tombez en crime de Lese Majesté. Néantmoins ilz s'obstinerent á maintenir le dict acte, declinerent nostre authorité, et ne laisserent pas de prononcer en pleine assemblée, que en causes de l'Eglise nous n'estions pas leurs juges, mais que leur authorité dependoit d'eux-mesmes. Et combien que nostre pardon et faveur fust offerte, moyennant qu' ilz voulussent retracter leur erreur, ilz le refuserent obstinéement. Sur quoy fut donné sentence contre eux par nostre dit Conseil, par laquelle ils furent jugez selon les loix d'iceluy nostre Royaume coulpables de Lese Majesté. Du quel crime combien qu'il soit cogneu à tous quelle est la punition, si est ce que de nostre clemence nous leur donnasmes la vie, et ne fismes que les bannir seulement hors du pais, afin d'eviter par là la contagion que leur example pouvoit espandre parmy d'autres. Or ce Jehan Forbis qui vous a surpris d'escrire en sa faveur n'estoit pas seulement un de ceste compagnie, ains chef et premier d'icelle. Lequel aussy du depuis a si peu merité de faveur de par nous que tout au contraire il a fort aggravé son offence, premierement en ce qu'il vous a celé (pour le moins á ce que nous divinons de voz lettres) qu'il estoit ministre, ains se disant Géntilhomme; puis en l'information de sa cause, ne vous ayant dit pas une parole vraye des particuliers d'icelle: tiercement, qu'estant condamné et consequemment fors de nostre faveur et de la protection de nos loix, il a voulu prende telle hardiesse que de nous addresser sans nostre licence preallablement obtenue, aucunes lettres. Finalement au stile de ses lettres à nous mesmes tant s'en faut qu'il recognoisse sa faute, ou qu'il face signe quelconque de penitence, qu'il ne laisse pas de prendre à partie nostre Conseil pour la sentence donnée encontre luy et ses compagnons, allegant impudemment à nous mesmes qu'il ne doubte point que ne soions maintenant bien persuadez en nostre entendement de tort à eux faict, et satisfaict touchant ce poinct. Lesquelles siennes lettres nous furent baillées à mesme instaut et par la mesme main que nous rendist les vostres, scavoir est, par son frere. Pour la quelle presomption estant de naissance nostre subject, n'eust esté la protection qu'il a de vostre service, nous ne l'eussions pas laissé eschapper impuny. Mais pour amour de vous ayant à cest' heure deduict tout le faict de ce Jehan Forbis, il ne sera poinct de besoing de vous alleguer aucune raison pourquoy nous n'accordons pas ce que vos desirez, d'autant que nous nous asseurons que la narration mesme du cas vous aura satisfaict, qu'il n'est pas seulement indigne d'aucune faveur de nous, ains qu'il merite vostre mauvaise grace pour avoir ainsy abusé de vous. Car, quant à vous, vous vous asseurerez qu'il n'y a chose fondée aulcunement en raison la quelle vous vouldriez desirer, que nous ne vous accorderions aussi volontiers et d'aussi bon cœur que scauriez esperer de celuy qui est. Et pour ce qui est de nostre disposition envers nos subjects faillant en ceste sorte là, nous avons fait preuve suffisante qu'à telz d'entr'eux qui en ont esté penitents nous n'avons jamais denié mercy et grace, dont un de ceux qui furent bannis quant ce Forbis a bien en experience, le quel ne s'est pas plustot repenty de sa folie, qu'il n'a esté receu en nostre bonne grace. 1607. Sept. ?

Indorsed:—Fr. Vere. Full. Cast. Wilbr.
Myne. Delv. Hadd. Ch. Prog. Adm.
Buchl. Min. Ful.

No. II.

James I. to Henry IV. King of France.

[Draft.]

Tres hault, &c. Comme l'injuste procedure du Pape envers moy ne vous est pas incogneu, en deschargeant par ses brevets et 1609. May $\frac{15}{25}$?

[1] The date is given in the King of France's answer of June $\frac{4}{14}$ (*Lettres Missives de Henri IV.* vii. 731), as May 15, most probably O. S., as it would be in the letter itself. The notices in La Boderie's despatches, on the whole, favour this conclusion. On $\frac{\text{April 26}}{\text{May 6}}$ he writes (Ambassades, iv. 315) that he had sent a copy of the book,

1609. May $\frac{5}{15}$? defendant à aulcuns de mes subjects qui estoyent Catholiques Romains de faire le serment de fidelité envers moy qui fust ordonné en mes Estats sur l'occasion de la trahison de pouldre, environ de trois ans et demy passez, aussy ne me puis je souvenir de cest affaire que je n'aye occasion de vous tesmoigner combien je me sens redevable à vostre affection en ce point la. Car premierement, incontinent aprez que ces dits breves du Pape furent publiez, vostre Ambassadeur alors Resident à Rome remonstra au Pape l'inconvenient qui ne pouvoit faillir d'ensuivre par la publication d'icelles. Dont, comme il vous pleust m'en advertir par aprez par vostre Ambassadeur icy resident, le Pape en sa responce fist semblant d'estre marry de ceste si precipitée procedure, en remettant la coulpe sur l'importunité de ceulx de l'Inquisition qui l'y avoyent pressé quasi contre son gré. Mais depuis ce temps, mon Apologie ayant este publiée pour la juste defence du dit serment, estant assez bien recognen pour mien (encores que mon nom ny estoit pas mis) deux libelles diffamatoires l'un en Latyn l'aultre en Angloys ont depuis sorty de la boutique Romaine, lesquels estoyent non seulement remplys de mille injures contre mon dit livvre, mais aussi n'espargnoyent point ma propre personne. Sur laquelle occasion vostre Ambassadeur aprez resident à Rome en parla derechef au Pape, qui a ceste fois aussi fist semblant en estre marry, dont il vous pleust m'advertir par vostre resident icy, qui par vostre commandement

the second edition of the *Apologia pro juramento fidelitatis*, but that it "aussitôt qu'il eut vu le jour fut renfermé," in order to receive further corrections. On May $\frac{4}{14}$ (Amb. iv. 323) he says that it had not yet been sent back to the printer, which makes it unlikely that the letter to the King of France should have been written on the following day, which it must have been if the 15th N. S. is meant by Henry in his answer. On the $\frac{17}{27}$ La Boderie writes that the book was just ready to appear, and would be presented to the Princes to whom it was addressed by the English ambassadors at their courts. Some days before he had had a conversation with Salisbury, who had inquired whether the King of France would receive the copy and read it. To this the Frenchman had replied that his master would doubtless receive it, but that he would not answer for his reading it. The letter above was no doubt written shortly after this interview.

m'asseura que le Pape estoit content de promestre que doresnavant il ne se mesleroit[1] plus de mon gouvernement en mes dominions ny publieroit plus aulcuns tels briefs au prejudice de mon estat, et de l'obedience que mes subjects sont tenus me porter. Mais le coup estoit premierement faict, et la playe donnee, devant qu'on ouyst parler de cest emplastre. Vostre dict Ambassadeur m'a aussi declaré vostre advis et bon couseil qu'il ne m'estoit nullement honorable de faire responce a ces calumniateurs, et comme j'ay grand occasion de vous remercier tres affectueusement, comme à present je fais, de vostre aimable procedure envers moy en toutte cest affaire, aussy vous puis je asseurer qu'il n'entra jamais en mon entendement de me peyner de faire responce a ces gents la; seulement ay je prins à ceste heure occasion de publier de nouveau ma dicte apologie, en y mettant mon nom pour monstrer que je n'ay point de honte de l'advouer au monde, y adjoustant aussi un aultre traicté en forme de preface, par lequel je dedie mon dict livre à touts les Roys et Princes Chrestiens entre lesquels (puis que vous estes non seulement le Roy tres Chrestien, mais aussy avez tousjours maintenu comme touts vos Predecesseurs d'heureuse memoire la liberté de l'Eglise Gallicane à l'honneur immortel de vostre couronne, et consyderant aussi l'estroicte amitié et alliance qui est entre nos deulx personnes et couronnes) je ne puis si dignement faire present à aulcun de mon dit livvre qu'a vous, comme je le vous envoye quant à[2] la presente, vous priant diligemment et meurement de consyderer sur un si grand point qui concerne l'estat et la liberté de touts les Princes Chrestiens; et comme vos Predecesseurs ont tousjours maintenu la Pragmatique Sanction qui fust premierement institutė et estably par un d'iceulx si Catholique qu'il en eust le tiltre de Lodovicus Pius; aussy ne puis je doubter que Dieu vous fera la grace de maintenir (aveсq pareille constance et courage que vous avez acquis la possession, et encores jouissez de vostre royaulme,) le commun interest de la liberté et securité de touts Roys 1609. May 15/25?

[1] Mosleroit. MS. [2] "et." MS.

1609. May 15/25? et Princes Chrestiens contre les ambitieuses usurpations de l'Eglise Romaine qui n'a jamais faillye dez long temps passé d'attempter et s'empicter sur la liberté des Roys et Royaulmes Chrestiens, quand oncques ils pouvoyent trouver la convenience de l'occasion. M'asseurant doncques que ce mien livvre vous sera agreable, et que vous prendrez la peyne de le lire à vostre bon loisir pour l'amour de moy.

Je &c.[1]

No. III.

Sir Robert Dudley to [Sir David Foulis].

[Copy.]

1614. May 8. My very honorable and woorthye frende. I receaved your answer[2] tuiching his Majesty's aprehension of the forcible vessell

[1] Henry's reply to this letter, dated June 17/27, is printed in the *Lettres Missives de Henri IV.* vii. 731. "Je suis marry" writes the King, after announcing his reception, of the book, "qu'il ayt fallu que vous ayés pris ceste peine, car je n'ay pas opinion que vous en retiriés la consolation et les advantages que vous en esperés. Veritablement les actions des Roys sont subjectes à detraction comme les aultres, et quelques fois plus que celles des moindres, d'autant qu'elles importent et attouchent à plus de gens, et servent souvent de regle comme d'exemple à leurs subjects: c'est pourquoy elles ne peuvent estre trop justes ny trop eclaircies et justifiées entre les hommes. Neantmoins comme l'envie et la calomnie ont, en ce siècle depravé, plus de vogue souvent et d'authenticité que la verité mesme, il est perilleux de soubsmettre au jugement public ce dont l'on n'est responsable qu'à Dieu seul et à sa conscience; et une trop curieuse justification aussy engendre souvent des effects contraires à nostre expectation. Mais celuy qui en tel cas s'est contenté soy mesme a obtenu la meilleure partie de son desir. Je veux croire qu'il vous en est ainsy advenu, de façon que je ne vous en diray davantage; mais vous prieray tousjours d'attendre de la continuation de mon amitié fraternelle tous vrays et sinceres effects."

[2] This correspondence was opened by the following letter (S. P. Dom. lxxi. 35) written to Foulis, as Cofferer to Prince Henry, on the 14th of November, 1612:—

"Sir,—Althoughe I have had heretofore a sufficiente taste of your reddines in doeinge many good offices for mee, whereby I houlde my selfe obliged unto you verry muche, yet I have beene since advertised by some letters from Mr. Yates, of

I propounded for his gratious service as I am obliged being his Majesty's subject: wherein first I gave yow exceeding thankes for the freindlye office, in presenting my dewtye and service to my King, wherin I am sure by my offer not to fayle in the dewtye of my loyaltye, as I am confident not to erre in the performance, when tyme shall serve to make testymonye therof. And if in all 1614. May 8.

the increase of your extraordinary good respecte unto mee, which nowe at his cominge to Florence hee hath soe fully confirmed (affirminge you to bee a principall agente in the speedie effectinge of my busines with the Prince my master)," *i.e.* the sale of his estate at Kenilworth, afterwards transferred to Prince Charles. "I cannot devise howe to give fitte correspondency to this your exceedinge lovinge kindnes towardes mee; seeinge therefore that I neede not doubte of your constante perseverance therein, I will not bee dainty to make you a partie to my dessignes. I have sente unto his Highnes a litle treatise muche importinge his owne security and proffitte, the coppie whereof I have herewith sente unto you, that you may the better instruct your selfe to incurrage his Highnes to undertake a matter of that consequence for his owne safety and perpetuall good. It cannott bee unknowne to you that I have given his Highnes my estate of Killingworthe for a smalle matter, consideringe the worthe thereof. I have onely reserved the conistableshippe of the castle, that I may have somme commande there under his Highnes, whensoever I shall happen to comme into Englande; and allsoe that he will protecte mee (and that but justly,) in the sale of Etchington and Balsall, that I mighte setle my estate, to bee the better able to doe his Highnes service; for withoute the sale thereof I shal bee in farre worse case then I was before. I have given warrante to Mr. Yates to undergoe all my businesses whatsoever in my behalfe, in my absence; and hee hath soe confirmed mee in the assurance of your forwarde and readie assistance uppon all occasions, that I neede not any more solicite you therein; but hee munn likewise assure you that, uppon the sale of those landes, I have proportioned a thankefull gratuity for you, as a testimony of my exceedinge love and thankfullnes unto you."

The treatise which follows is composed of two parts, the first showing "the greate importance for soe greate a Prince as your Highnes, to bee master of the seas;" the second, explaining the construction of the Gallizabra.

Again, in January 1614, we have a letter (S. P. Dom. lxxvi. 16) written by Sir R. Dudley to a friend in London; perhaps, to Mr. Yates, not, as suggested by Mrs. Green, to Sir D. Foulis, who is referred to as a third person, speaking of a new kind of vessel which he had invented, and had called a counter-galliass, and which seems to be the same as the Gallerata in the text.

In May 1614, probably on the same day as the letter to Foulis, Dudley wrote (S. P. Dom. lxxvii. 16) to Somerset, commending the matter to his attention.

1614. May 8. my propositions of the lyke nature and some more difficulte, I have hetherto performed more then promesed to others, I doubt not but be able to shewe much more perfection in the service of my owne King. In fyne I am sure of doing it upon the frayme of demonstrable proofes I have made, applying all my experience and tryall of that mater in one perfect vessell, and wishe onelye his Majestye had somme store of them for his owne safetye, and prefer that wishe befor any other wishe to my selfe of performance.

It is trewe that it is not possible to give a perfytte demonstration of the thing without it doinge, and if I had my meanes maid over to me for certane lands to be sould by agreement in the bargan in Kennelwoorthe to the Prince, as yow well know and Mr. Yattes,[1] I would not fayle, uppon such orders as his Majestye would command me, to make one of my owne charrges, referring the recompence to his gratiousnes, in all wherin my honour nor honestye may not be taxed, and, wherof I am sure his Majesty's goodnes would have principall consideration, and to that I referre me. In the meane tyme, to give his Majestye some demonstrable reason that it is possible to make a vessell of dowble the force to his gallions, that is to saye, 10 for 20, I will argwe this by example of others, and proofes of some thinges I have doun.

First, for example, his Majestye maye informe himselfe that 10 of his owne gallions is well able to beate 20 of the King of Spaynes, as hathe bene proved, though they be bigger then his. And the reason is, the qualitye of shippe to be swyfter and there ordinance plaiced for more advantage, by which advantage they maye take the wynde of these huge gallions and sincke them, becaus in sincking consistithe the moderne secretes of fight, and not in boording as anticnlye they did. So by the lyke reason that arte which can make a vessell of suche qualytye to be much swifter then the Kinges Majesty's, and carye more ordinance and better to passe then theye arre able to doe, I maye conclude that

[1] His agent in England.

vessels of such qualitye and force are as much towe strong for his Majesty's shippes, as his Majesty's are proved and sayed to be towe strong for the King of Spaynes. 1614. May 8.

Secondlye, to conferme the probabilitye by the proofes I have doinge, this is manifest to be seene that I speake of at this hower. I maide a vessell of my owne invention, and the first I maide for the G[rand] D[uke] called the gallion *St. Gio*[*vanni*] *Babtista*, which is but 600 tonne, and not halfe in burthen to the famous shippe that the Prince maide; yett this small one caryethe as manye ordinance and of as much force as that greate one which caryethe 60 peices or thereaboutes, and so manye dothe this of myne, being the lower tyere demy cannones, and upper tyere demy culverin; by which force this small shippe being swifter of saille then the greater, as I take sure to be, is by that qualitye able to take the advantage of the wynde, and equall in ordinance hathe the advantages to beate the greater, and is of more force.

An other vessell I have made nearer by proofe this sorte of vessell I pretend for the Kinges service, that is but 300 tonnes or rather 250 tonnes, I call *gallizabra*, which by her proportion is farre swyfter then the other mentioned and caryethe but 50 peices. Yette her lower tyere being all demy cannones and better to passe, is as forcible as the other of 600 tonnes. I saye then that this lesser vessell being fare more swyfte then the Gallie *St. Gio*[*vanni*] *Babtist* (espetiallye uppon a tacke) by her qualitye, is of better sorte then the greater, and of much more service by her flatnes, not drawing above 8 feete water, and so maye offend or defend upon more advantages.

Touching the proofes of swyftnes, yow must understand that gallies and galliases are the swyftest of the world, by reason of there great lenthe and fleteness, so as theye are able to saille 2 feete for one with anye shippe. I have maide a vessell of my owne invention I call *gallerata*, different in proportion from a gallie, that is proved to saille ⅓ parte more, and wherin a gallie cariethe but 7 or 8 peices, this *gallerata* being no bigger then a gallie and so swyfte

1614. May 8. as I saye, caryethe neire 30 peices of brace and 20 bombardini or pederers, so as she maye be treble or 4 tymes the force of a gallie, &c.

Nowe I conclude from these proofes and experiences that I have maid, with dyvers others to longe to repeate, I have framed this vessell I propounded for the King's service, which for swyftnes I can promes shall alwaye the worst of these ought saill[1] the Kinges ships ⅓ parte: eache of these shall carye 100 peices of ordinance as good in service as anye the shipps of his Majestye can carye: I meane in any one shippe, not anye one peice.

That these sorte of vessels shall not pass 10 or 11 foote water at most, which is but ½ the draught of some ships of the navye.

That these vessell by a proved invention can hardlye be suncke by the enemyes ordinance.

That these shalbe sufficientlye secure for fowle weather.

That these maye in the symmer tyme be able to rowe lyke galliasses, albeit they have 2 whole deckes and the galliasses but one decke, in which consistithe much arte, and a great secrete of continewing.

That these vessels maye be kept under arches in an arsinall as galliasses be so kept drye, and no charge to kepte them, in respect of shippes.

That this vessell usithe square salles, with some difference from shippes.

That this vessell is not halfe the charge to make as a greate shippe, I mean for the building, and in lesse tyme.

That the use of these vessells is not so fitt for long viages to the Indies or such lyke, as to defend the State, thoughe they maye be able verye safelye in occasion to navigat to the West Indies.

This vessell I call a contre galliasse by reason of there exceiding force, swyftnes, and that they are able to rowe competentelye well, thereby to gayne manye advantages that shipps can not doe.

And this what I wryte I am able to make good by my owne experiences as securelye as anye of them I have maide and more :

[1] Outsail.

and if I had my monyes which I expect for Balsall and Ichington I would make one at my owne charge upon such conditions as his Majesty willbe pleased to offer me: wherin yow must consider what condition maye bring me home with my honour and honestye and honour of my birthe right, well deserving them to doe the State so memorable a service, and the derect waye to make it the happiest and greatest monarchie of the world being applyde as I knowe.

One thing I resolve yow, that if it please his Majesty to harkin to this greatnes to him selfe, I must pretend to desyrè to be generall (with that tytle) of such a squadron of these vesselles as his Majestye shalbe pleased to have, and to be a command and goverment by it selfe, not to be under the Admirall of England; but as the gallies is in France, a different command at sea, nor hazard the reputation of my owne workes under the discretion or skill of an other. His Majesty maye make as manye of these as he please for his safetye and strenthe, but lesse then 6 were no fitt squadrant, which maye be maide in one yeire, and having maide an arsinall after my fashion for these vessels, which his Majestye maye doe about London hedland or where he pleasithe, and kepe these vesselles drye alwayes above the water for litle charges yerelye.

This for the present is as much as I can saye to satisfye his Majestye in this poynt, which I am most willing to doe as his loyall and faithfull subject that hathe not spent his tyme idlye to serve him, and so I commit yow most affectionatlye to God's protection. From the Great Duke's Court at Pisa this 8 of Maye 1614.

Your most faithfull frende ever to command,

RO. DUD[LEY] ET W[ARWICK.][1]

Indorsed: A trewe copye of Sir Robt Dudlye's lettre, sent from Florence in Maye, 1614.

[1] On the 15th of July Dudley wrote again to Foulis (S. P. Dom. lxxvii. 65) to press the adoption of his project. "I thought it not amisse," he says, "at this preasent to writte you a worde of some importaunte matter for his Maties good, uppon the occasion of the thawartnes I understande of late the parlement useth towardes him, neather consenting to such subsedies accostomed or necessarie, but rather with much presumtion standing uppon worser termes; and I conseaving to under-

No. IV.

Sir George Villiers to Lord Howard de Walden.

[Autograph signature.]

1616. Feb. 4. My noble Lord. I have acquainted his Matie with the contents

stande something these naturs, I doubte in time may growe to a bad obstinancie, especially understanding there malice much pretendeth agaynst the Scotish nation to whome I have bene particularly beholding, maketh mee ought of gratitude wright this, which for a time I had thought to have prolonged; neather would I doe it to anye ther but yourselfe, knowing your fidelytie to the Kinge, and worth. Having longe suspected some mischeafes I see creaping one, I kepte in store a certeyne dissecne of mine, which followed in Englande by his Matie, I knowe may make him secure agaynst all these rubbs, for his profit, and make him safe to doe what he please with his owne, as an absolute monarche as he is, withought dangerous resistance, and as free from the possibilitie of foren invasions, if anie should eaver be attembted, and kepe the bridel in his owne hande, so stronge [?] and neaver Kinge had a greater in those parts; nay, I doubte not, by the same means I knowe he may increase his revenew to a much greater valewe, I hope duble, and I make noe question withought discontent of his poepel, and not to be vexed with the varietie of so manie men's minde[s] as the Parlamente afford[s]."

The scheme is to be unfolded if the King will give a commission to some Scottish gentleman to come to Florence to hear it, for he "will trust noe English" with his "design."

On the 12th of September Somerset wrote (S. P. Dom. lxxvii. 84) in reply, "If the offer made in your letters prove answearable [to] that you promise, I shalbe ready to employ myself to procure you such favour and reward as shall be sutable to the service as, uppon the returne of this messenger and his Maties satisfaction by his report of the businesse, you shall more particularly understand."

The scheme thus presented for James' acceptance must have been that which subsequently acquired notoriety by the Star Chamber prosecution of Sir R. Cotton in 1629, for having it in his possession. It is printed in *Rushworth*, vol. i. App. p. 12, and a full account of the affair will be found in the *Biographia Britannica, ed. Kippis*, Art. Sir R. Cotton. Note *\,*. The date, however, there given of 1613 is shown to be wrong by the extracts here printed; and the idea was evidently one which sprung from the events of 1614. Sir Robert Cotton, no doubt, got the paper into his hands from Somerset, with whom he was closely connected. It is to be noticed that the treatise about the Gallizabra forwarded to Prince Henry (p. 6, note 2) appears from its indorsement to have been laid before Charles I. on the 1st of January, 1630. The King was then reminded of Dudley's inventions in naval architecture by the affair of Sir R. Cotton's prosecution, and wished to refresh his memory.

of your LoPs letter concerning the affairs of the middle shires,[1] at the sight whereof his Matie rijoyceth to have played the prophet. For, allthough his Matie knew not till now of the taking back of that half of the garrison from residing in that part of the cuntry where your LoPs lands do lie, and where his Matie had ordayned them to remaine, yet as soone as he heard of the Earle of Cumberland's coming up, and having been informed of the daily growing of disorders in that cuntrie his Matie sent a dispatch (two daies agoe) to his Councail commanding them to call my Lord of Cumberland, your LoP, and my Lo. Wm Howard before them, and to examine you of the causes of those abuses, and especially what was become of that half of the garrison which his Matie had appointed to lie in your part of the cuntree: so as thereupon your LoP will have good occasion to relate what hath fallen out, wherein his Matie will not faile to take order accordingly. The notice your LoP takes of my service done to your sister,[2] is beyond my meritt, since his Matie hath taken it into his owne hands, who alone deserves thanks. 1616. Feb. 4.

Your LoPs servant,
GEORGE VILLIERS.

Newmarkett, the
4th of February, 1615.

No. V.

KING JAMES I. TO FREDERICK V. ELECTOR PALATINE.

[Copy.]

Mon tres cher filz. Le Colonel Schomberg vous apporte la responce ce qu'il m'a proposé de vostre part, à la suffisance du quel j'en remets la relation. Je suis marry d'avoir entendu de la dispute que vous avez eu aveques ma fille, touchant la presceance; mais je ne puis m'estonner assez que vous en ayez faict une si publique contestation sans avoir premierement sondé mon advis là dessus en privé, 1616. June.

[1] The borders.

[2] The Countess of Essex.

1616. June. mais je m'asseure que vostre bon naturel a esté abusé en ce poinct par quelque pernicieux conseil. Pour ma part, vous vous pouvez asseurer que jamais pere ne s'esvertuera plus que moy de faire sa fille humblement obeissante à son mary, mais en ce qui concerne sa qualité et l'honneur de sa naissance, elle seroit indigne de vivre si elle quitteroit sa place sans mon sçeu et advis. J'espere que de vous mesmes vous trouverez quelque moyen en vostre prudence d'esclaircir au monde vostre bonne intention et le respect que vous portez à la naissance de ma fille, mais si vous ne vous y pouvez resouldre de vous mesmes, je ne faudray point, Dieu aydant, de vous envoyer un des miens qui vous en dira mon opinion et vous assistera des meilleurs conseils de celuy qui demeurera à jamais

Vostre tres affectionné Père.

No. VI.

KING JAMES I. TO ELIZABETH ELECTRESS PALATINE.

[Copy.]

1616. June. Ma fille, mes comportements ont esté tels au Colonel Schomberg pour l'amour de vous, que je m'asseure il en a reçeu ample satisfaction touchant la dispute de vostre presance. Je vous remercie de tout mon cœur que vous, n'avez voulu ceder en ce qui concerne la qualité de vostre naissance sans mon consentement. Si vostre mary ne se peult resouldre de considérer mieux le respect qu'il me doibt, je luy envoyeray un des miens, qui vous assistera à tous deux de mes meilleurs conseils. Cependant consolez vous, ma chere fille, que je n'omettray à toutes occasions de vous maintenir et assister, tant par mes meilleurs conseils qu'autrement, selon ce que la nature a obligé celuy qui ne peult estre autre que

Vostre bon Père.

Indorsement to this and No. V., which are written on one sheet of paper:—June 1616. Copies of his Majesty's letters to the Count Palatine and the Lady Elizabeth, with his own hand.

No. VII.

Mr. Toby Matthew to Sir George Villiers.

[Holograph.]

It may please your Honour. I may have pardon if I take the boldnes either to trouble your buisines or to disquiet your leasure by these few lines, since I understand many waies that your Honour hath vouchsaft to keepe so poore a man as my selfe not only in your memoire but in your favour. My very enemies have never adventured to esteeme me ungratefull, and I must be so in the highest degree if I faile to professe the uttermost of my service to a person whome the greate favour of my Soveraigne hath not only made worthie, but founde worthie of all respectes, and whome the splendour of fortune hath not beene able to make either lesse vertuous nor less courteous. The world hath alreadie, in my hearinge, geven your H[onour] this due, that you have nobly obliged more persons in fewe monethes, then some others of like condition could be drawne to doe in many yeares. It will not, therefore, seeme straunge, if I runne towards your H[onour] with hope to be regarded, since I have winges geven to me, not only by the common fame of your goodnes, but by the knowledge I have of the favour your H[onour] was wont to doe me, and the notice which is come to me of late, that bothe you are pleas'd to wishe me well, and that you wilbe carefull upon just occasions to expresse it. 1616. July 16.

I have a suite unto his most excellent Majestie, which shall cost him nothinge, but shall rather make him the richer, since it will minister an occasion to the exercise of much royall vertue; and your H[onour] shall have made a purchase, at an easie rate, of as many humble and faithfull servauntes as I have frendes in the worlde, by vouchsafinge to move it. It is, that after the absence

1616. July 16. of so many yeares out of my countrey, in such a conversation as your H[onour] sawe in Paris (and I have cause to glory in such a witnes), I may be repatriated, and withall be obliged, whilest I live, to kisse that hande of yours which shall have derived such a benefite upon me frome his moste excellent Majestie. The reasons that may induce it are such as followe: That some[1] nine yeares since I was not bannished, but absented only, with this clause, that I should not returne till his Majesties pleasure were first knowne; That the Lordes of the Councell promised, as appeares by the order it self, to move his Majestie for my returne, upon notice had of my dutifull behaviour abroade; That I have lived these nine yeares abroade, without all tutche of disloyalty; That I have never accepted from any Prince or Prelate one peniworth of enterteynement; That I have upon all occasions published my self for the instance of his Majesties great clemencie and goodnes towardes me; That I have lived with great satisfaction of the great persons of my station, and his Majesties Ambassadours and Agentes whome I have had the honour to converse withall, wherein I remitte my self to theire testimony; That my estate in England is entangled, partly by a suite in the Chauncery, and partly by debtes, whereby, without my presence there, I am not able to make benefite of my poore estate, accordinge to that graunte which his Majestie hath beene pleasd to make me; That I have offended noe otherwise then in the errour of my judgmente, and noe otherwise then thousandes of my profession in England, who yet are suffred to breathe in the aire of theire countrey; nay, that I may be accounted to deserve more favour then they, rather then lesse, bycause I have made so long a probation of my fidelity and loyall affection to his Majesties sacred person and

[1] An extract from this letter commencing here, "Some nine years since" down to "die then feele," with some verbal differences, is calendered by Mrs. Green, next to a letter on the same subject of Sept. 6, under the date of Sept. ? (S. P. Dom. lxxviii. 74), there being nothing in the paper itself to fix the exact date.

the State in places of temptation and daunger; that, if it should be doubted whether in England I shall carry myself with that modesty and discretion as is requisite, it is to be answered, that I may instantly be sente out againe with so much scorne and shame as I had rather die then feele. 1616. July 16.

These are some of the many groundes whereupon I would hope that a greater buildinge then that of beinge restored to my countrey might be raised, nor can I feare but that my desire and hope will securely take effecte, if it may be putt in motion by so powerfull an intercessour to my most gracious Soveraigne, whose very person my conscience tells me that I doe so reverently and deerely love, and of whose fame it is well knowne I have beene a trumpett in the eares of great persons, protesting that I had, in many occasions, heard his Majestie make certaine proofes of greater partes then I thought any subject of his in the worlde could approache unto. I could speake of diligences which I have used to discover the authours of infamous libells at the instance of some Ministers of his Majesties, whereof I can make solide proofe.

I will not doe my Kinges clemencie, your noblenes, or mine own innocencie so much disadvauntage, as to enlarge myself upon this subjecte. It sufficeth towardes the strengthning of my hope, that you are yourself, and that the least shininge of your favour towardes me wilbe able to discharge all cloudes of misconceite, which may offer to interpose themselves betwene me and my returne into my countrey.

Nor am I so vaine as to make you a solemne presente of my service, bycause I am not worth so much; but although you are not capable (through your fulnes) of any substantiall addition from me, yet it is in my power to geve you the glory of praise, and you feede not that mouthe in the worlde which shall open it self to your H[onour] with more appetite of affection then this of mine, and that, whether you move this suite or noe, for I am not mercenarie, and you have already done me more honour and favour then I can

1616. July 16. answere for. I humbly doe your H[onour] all reverence and kisse your hand, continuing

Your Honour's most obliged humble servaunte,

TOBIE MATTHEW.[1]

Spa, this 16th of July 1616.

Indorsed: Tobie Mathew.

No. VIII.

SIR HENRY DOCWRA TO VISCOUNT VILLIERS.

[Autograph signature.]

Nov. 9. Right Honorable. It is not unknowne to your Lordship when I first became an humble suitour to the King for this place of imployment in his service which of his gratious favour it pleased him to bestowe upon me, my desire was to have had it in the same tearmes that he and many others that went before me had held and exercised it for many yeres together. But it seemed otherwise fitt to the Lordes of the Counsaile for his Majesties service, and so was concluded the office shold be divided in twoe, but with this speciall cawtion, that our charges shold be kepte aparte and so distinguisht as neither of us shold have power to incroache or invade eche upon other.[2] In defaulte of which order, it was even then easy to be seene, the service wold be prejudiced by a confused and preposterous course of paiementes, and that which his Majestie intended to me as a grace and singuler benefitt wold manifestly redownd to the diminution both of my profit and estimation. My L[ord], I speake not upon an uncertaine grownd; I am very well informed and assured

[1] He obtained the permission which he desired, and returned to England in the following summer. *Chamberlain to Carleton*, July 19, 1617, S. P. Dom. xcii. 96.

[2] Docwra was Treasurer at Wars in Ireland July 19, 1616, at which time Sir Arthur Savage became Vice-Treasurer of Ireland and Receiver-General. Sir Thomas Ridgway had previously held the two offices in combination.

of it: there are divers both here and in England that doe earnestly labour to gett themselves removed from the establishment to receive their entertaynmentes imediatly upon the revenues: a pointe once gained by one will followe by consequence to manie more; and then what will insue further is easy to be forseene. My humble desire therefore is this to your Lordship that, as I hold this place from the begyning by none other help or favour but your owne free and honorable intercession for me to the King (which as I shall ever be duly thankefull for, so let me speede and prosper and none otherwise), so you will nowe be pleased to contynewe and goe on in the same way to support and uphold me in it, which I dowt will verie hardly be done, except your Lordship vouchsafe me so high a favour as directlie to acquaint his Majestie with my case, and procure the signification of his gratious will and pleasure, that there be no suche alteration of the before-intended order, and to satisfie them at the full with reason (if that maie content them) that are the suitours for this innovation, if the former order may stand and be kept inviolable, that the Vice-Threasurer be directed to deliver unto me suche surplusage of the revenues as he shall at any tyme have in his handes. If then I give cawse to anie man justly to complaine against me for cunning or delaies in giving them their due, the sentence of condemnation shall passe out of myne owne mouthe against myself. Let me be dealt withall and handled according to my desertes: I ask no favour. My L[ord] I am not discouraged by any consideration of my owne defect of merit to presume thus farre to tender this humble suite of myne to your Lordship's favour, for it is with this knowledge and testimoney of the true intentions of my harte that I am in all thinges as becomes an honest and thankfull man for the same, 1616. Nov. 9.

Your Lordship's true and faithfull servant to commaunde,

HENRY DOCWRA.

Dublin, 9 November, 1616.

Addressed: To the right honorable my very good Lord the Lord Viscount Villars.

Indorsed: Sr H. Dockwra to my Lord.

No. IX.

Sir John Digby to the Earl of Buckingham.

[Holograph.]

1617. June 4.

My singular good Lorde. Finding that my Lords the Commissioners were not likely to take any speedye resolution in the businesse of the Pyratts, and that my instructions injoyned me to receave my derections therin[1] from them before my departure,[2] I thought it fitt to have recourse unto his Majestye for my dispatch, and to that effect have written to your Lordship with the rest of my Lordes, to move his Majestye that my going be no longer delayed, which I beseech your Lordship to further, for that his Majestyes service will receave prejudice by my further staye. For the solliciting hereof, as likewise for that I was desyrous to put his Majestyes cypher into a hande that might be answerable for the delivery of it unto your Lordship, I have sente downe my secretary to attende yow; and I hope that by him I shall receave my full dispatch, together with your Lordship's commandments, that I may within two dayes after his retourne beginn my journey.

My Lorde, it is written to me out of Irelande that the eyes of all the townes of that State are sett on the proceeding that is like to be held within the towne of Waterforde for the pointe of conforming of themselves. His Majestye hath bene pleased to thinke this interim whilest a match was in treatye with Spayne the fittest for the settling of those businesses there, and I am tolde by your Lordship to put his Majestye in myndc of doing so, for that I know (that uppon any difference that may happen) Spayne relyeth uppon noe advantadge against England but by Irelande, and it may be this treatye may administer to the Irish some hopes of mittigation

[1] On the plan for obtaining the co-operation of Spain against the Barbary pirates.

[2] For Spain.

which may make them backwarder in conforming of themselves: and therfore I humble offer it to his Majestyes consideration if it will not be fitt that order be given for a speedye and rownde proceeding with the towne of Waterforde,[1] leaste otherwise the advantadge which his Majestye intended by the interim of this treatye for the settling of Irelande be perverted to his disservice. 1617. June 4.

Her Majestye and the Prince, God be praised, are well; and all here is so quiet that ther is no newes to write unto yow, and I am loath to interrupt your Lordship's businesses with unnecessarye lynes, and therfore humbly intreating that my service may be presented unto his Majestye,[2] I give your Lordship thankes for all your favours, assuring your Lordship that you shall ever finde me a mindefull and a gratefull man for the good I have receaved by you, and so wishing you much increase of honor and happinesse, I rest

Your Lordship's faythfull servante,

JHON DIGBYE.

London, the 4th of June, 1617.

No. X.

LORD ARUNDELL OF WARDOUR TO THE EARL OF BUCKINGHAM.

[Autograph signature.]

My good Lord. I receaved your Lordshipp's letter, and finde thereby that the King is willing that the matter in controversye may bee peaceablye ended, but is much agaynst the delay of any proceeding in matter of justice, especially the Chauncerye. Truly, my Lord, I never intended by my petition to delay justice: all that I aske is but that justice may be observed, and that the just judgment of the late Lord Chauncellor given in the same cause and in the same court and confirmed by the greate Seale Sept. 3.

[1] The citizens of Waterford had for some time elected magistrates who refused the oath of supremacy, and the seizure of their charter was now in contemplation.

[2] The King, attended by Buckingham, was then in Scotland.

1617. Sept. 3.

of England may be kept, the contrary whereof would be great injustice. The president is strange: the continuance thereof wilbe insufferable. I am not ignorant how much I am bound unto your Lordshipp for some speeches to my Lord Keeper in this matter, wherein though his Lordshipp hath hitherto given little satisfaction, yet now I assure myselfe (for some reasons which hereafter I will make knowne to your Lordshipp) that if you shalbe pleased to use the same speeches once more unto him, it will worke a better effect in him; if not, then I desire to be soe much beholding to your Lordshippe as that eyther your selfe or the King by your procuring will talke with Mr. Attorneye-Generall concerning this businesse, charging him upon his alleagance to deliver his opinion not onely of the cause (wherewith he is acquaynted from the beginning) but of this new president allsoe of revoking of decrees; and I shall rest bound to your Lordshipp for soe great a favour, which though the justnes of my cause may well expect from a noble minde, yet, because myselfe have noe way deserved it, I must acknowledge my bond to be the greater, and shall ever rest

Your Lordshipp's ready to doe you service,

THO. ARUNDELL.

Wardour Castle,
this third of September, 1617.

I have sent your Lordshipp here inclosed certayne reasons to prove that a new tryall in Chauncery after a publike decree under the great seale is great injustice.[1]

Indorsed: Lord Wardour.

[1] A charge of this kind against Bacon deserves investigation. From the Chancery Order Books it appears that a suit had been instituted against Lord Arundell, nominally by the Earl of Worcester, but in fact by Thomas Arundell, the eldest son of Lord Arundell, and the husband of Worcester's daughter. It related to certain lands settled by Lord Arundell's father, which, as the young man contended, could not be alienated before they came into his hands. On the 11th of February 1615 Ellesmere (*Order Book*, 1614 A. fol. 740) directed Lord Arundell to pay his son an annuity of £600 a-year for his maintenance, and on the 26th of November 1616 he finally dismissed the suit (*Order Book*, 1616 A. fol. 233) on the ground that he could not come to a decision where the evidence was so uncertain. At the same

No. XI.

Sir Thomas Wentworth to the Earl of Buckingham.

[Autograph signature.]

Right Honorable and my very good Lord. Thes are to give your Lordship humble thankes for your respective letters dated 1617. Sept. 15.

time he expressed a strong opinion that the case was one for arbitration, and that it ought not to come into Court.

This decision Lord Arundell took as implying a revocation of the order of February 1615, and accordingly omitted at Lady Day 1617 to pay the half-yearly instalment of his son's annuity. Thomas Arundell at once filed a bill against his father, reopening the whole question of the right to alienate the lands, and specially demanding the payment of his annuity. Bacon, who had now succeeded Ellesmere, recommended Lord Arundell on the 1st of July 1617 (*Order Book*, 1516 A. fol. 1129) to pay the annuity, but reserved his decision on the main question, and a few days later made the following order (*Order Book*, 1616 A. fol. 1006), which is the one complained of by Lord Arundell:—

"Sabbati 12mo die Julii [1617].

"Thomas Arrundell, Esqre., plt.
Thomas Lord Arrundell, deft. } Forasmuch as the right honorable the Lord Keeper was this day informed by Mr. John Fynch being of the plts councell, that the deft by order of the first of this present July was wished and advized to continewe the payment of the annetye of 600li to the plt., and allso to pay the arrerage thereof, beinge 300li due at our Lady Day last, or to shewe unto his lopp good cause to the contrary before the end of the last terme, but hee hath shewed noe such cause; wherefore, and because the plts occasions are urgent and wanting meanes to support his chardge, it was desired, on the plts behaulf, that the deft might be ordered forthwith to pay the 300li due at our Lady Day last, and allso to pay 300li at Michas next, and soe to contynnewe the payment of the said annity every half yeare as the same shall from henceforth growe due. And forasmuch as the deft hath spent all the last terme in delayes; and nowe the very last day of the terme hath putt in a demurrer to the plts Bill, upon noe other ground but because the suit was formerly dismissed, the Lord Privy Seale being plt in the former suite; nowe the same is preferred onely by and in the name of the nowe plt; which demurrer his lopp will take into consideration, and give such order and direccion therein as shallbee meete. And whereas Mr. Sr Fynch of councell with the said deft alleadged that the saide plt is

1617. Sept. 15. from Warwicke the 5 of this instant September,[1] which I receaved the 13 of the same; the messinger told me your Lordship expected a speedy answear, in observance whearof I must crave your patience in reading a long letter.

Your Lordship was pleased therin to lett me understande, that wheras his Majestie is informed that Sir John Savill yealded up his place of *Custos Rotulorum* voluntarily unto me, his Majestie will take itt well att my hands that I resigne itt up to him againe, with the same willingnes, and will be mindfull of me to give me as good prefermentt upon any other occasion.

satisfied his anuity to a penny, that should accrewe at our Lady Day last, by reason the def[t] had satisfied his sonne to supply his wantes one half yeares anuity before hand, which whether yt were receaved before hand, or for presente mayntenaunce then, as was nowe alleadged by the pl[ts] councell, was overruled in the former suite, and the def[t] adjudged to pay the same half yeares anuitye which hee pretended was paied before hand, as by the said order of the 11th of February 12[mo] Jacobi R[s]. appeareth, and therefore his Lo[PP] thought fytt, this beinge for the sustentacion and liefe of the deft[s] owne childe, that the def[t] should paye whatsoever of the saide anuity is in arrere, and for direccion therein his Lo[PP] willbee guided by the said former order of the 11[the] of February; and doeth nowe order that the def[t] shall upon notice or sight of this order forthwith pay unto the pl[t] the 300[li] due at our Lady Day last, and at Mich[as] next 300[li] more, and soe contynewe the payment of the said anuity of 600[li] accordinge to the said order of the 11th of February, and the direccion thereof."

Against this Lord Arundell complained to Buckingham, timing his letter exceedingly well, as it was written just when every one supposed Bacon to be in deep disgrace on account of the part which he had taken about Sir John Villiers' marriage.

It is evident that it is untrue that Bacon reopened a case decided by his predecessor, Ellesmere having refused to decide it at all. As far as the annuity went he maintained his ground. On the 8th of November (*Order Book*, 1617 A. fol. 153) he peremptorily ordered it to be paid, adding, however, that he "thought not fytt now to heare or consider of the demurrer as touchinge the bodie of the cause." Of any further proceedings I can find no trace. Possibly Arundell and his son were induced to submit to that arbitration which Ellesmere recommended. At all events, if Bacon used his influence to keep the dispute out of court, he was only carrying out his predecessor's wishes. Lord Arundell's charge appears to have been entirely without foundation.

[1] The recovery of this letter fills up the missing link in the correspondence on the subject of the office of *Custos Rotulorum*, which is printed in the Strafford Letters. In his Life of Strafford (p. 199) Mr. Forster expressed his regret at its loss.

My Lord: I am with all duty to receave and with all humble thankfullnes to acknowledge his Majesties great favours hearin: both of his espetiall grace to take the consentt of his humblest subject, wher it might have pleased his Majestie absolutely to commaund, as alsoe for soe princely a promise of other prefermentt: and itt wear indeed the greatest good happ unto me, if I had the means wherby his Majestie would be pleased to take notice how much I esteem myself bownd to his princely goodnes for the same. 1617. Sept. 15.

Wher your Lordship is informed that Sir Jhon yealded up his place of *Custos Rotulorum* willingly unto me; under favour, I have noe reason soe to conceave; for first, he had noe interest to yeald, and further, I imagin he would not have done the same willingly att all, wherof this his desiring itt againe is a sufficientt argumentt. Butt, howsoever, voluntarily unto me I cannot be perswaded, both in respect he never acquainted me with this motion, which would have been done, had I been soe much behoulden unto him as is pretended, and in regard I had then some reason to misdoubt (which I have since found) he was not soe well affected towards me.

Butt if itt please your Lordship to be satisfied of the truth, you shall find Sir Jhon brought into the Staire-chamber for his passionate cariage upon the benche towards one of his fellow commissioners; upon a motion in that Court for his contempts committed to the Fleet, and, upon reading of an affidavit, thought unfitt to be continued in the Commission of Peace, to which purpose my late Lord Chancelour gave his direction about the 3. of December shallbe tow years; which Sir Jhon getting notice of, to give the better coullor to his displacing, writt some 3 dayes after to my Lord desiring his Lordship would be pleased to spaire his service in respect of his years; wher indeed he was in effect out of the Commission before, by vertu of that direction: and so consequently ther was nothing in him to resigne, aither voluntarily or other wayes. This will partly appear by a coppy of Sir Jhon's letter,[1] and my Lord's answear under the same, which this bearer hath to shew your Lordship.

[1] Savile to Ellesmere. Dec. 6, 1615, *Strafford Letters*, 3.

1617. Sept. 15. Presently hearupon itt pleased my Lord Chanceclour, I being att that time in the cuntry, freely of himself to conferre that place upon me, and as his Lordship did fully assure me, without any motion made unto him, directly or indirectly, by any frend of mine whoe-soever.

Being thus placed I have ever since, according to that poore talent God hath lentt me, applied myself, with all paines, dilligence, care, and sincerity to his Majesties service, both according to the common duty of a subject and the particular duty of my place, wherin if any man can charge me to the contrary, I wilbe ready to justifie my self.

Allbeitt I doe infinittly desire to doe his Majestie service, I may truly say that I am free from ambition to desire places of imploy-mentt whereby ether his Majesties service might not be soe well performed, or my owne ends better effected; yett, my Lord, to be removed without any mis-leamenour, I trust, that can be alledged against me, the like I thinke hath not been heard of; but thatt Sir Jhon should supply the roome in my place, the worlde conceaving generally and I having felt experiencedly to be very little frendly towards me, itt might justly be taken as the greatest disgrace that could be done unto me, and being that which his Majestie never offered to Sir Jhon during all the time of his displeasure against him, I might well conceave his Majestie to be (to my greatest greef) highly offended with me, by some indirect means of my adversaries.

Thes reasons give me assurance in my hope that his Majestie out of his accustomed goodnes to all sort of persons willbe pleased to deale graciousely with me, espetially when his Majestie shallbe in-formed of these reasons, which I humbly desire he may by your Lordship's good means, as alsoe if Sir Jhon be soe desirouse to doe his Majestie service (which is all our duties) he may doe itt as effec-tually, being Justice of Peace, as if he wear the *Custos Rotulorum.*

Howsoever with all due reverence and observance shall I waite his Majesties best pleasure, and willingly and dutifully submitt myself to the same, yett humbly crave to be excused if, out of thes reasons,

I say plainly as yett I finde noe willingnes in myself to yeald up my place to Sir Jhon Savill. 1617. Sept. 15.

Thus much am I bold to signifie to your Lordship to give you satisfaction, which I doe very much desire, and withall to move your Lordship very humbly that ther may be noe further procedings hearin, till I attend your Lordship, which shallbe, God willing, with all convenient speed.

Lastly, my Lord, myself never having nourished a thought that might in any sortt draw your Lordship's hard conceitt towards me, I fully rely upon your Lordship's favour, in a matter of this nature, that soe deeply concerns my creditt in the cuntry whear I live, which makes me now therof the more sensible; and shall give me just occasion still to indevour myself to doe you service, and beseeche God to blesse your Lordship with longe life and all happines.

Your Lordship's humbly to be commaunded,

TH. WENTWORTH.[1]

Gawthorp,
this 15th of September, 1617.

No. XII.

SIR THOMAS SAVILE TO THE EARL OF BUCKINGHAM.

[Holograph.]

My most noble Lorde. I presumed the reading of a letter would be less troublesome to youre Lordship then my owne attendance, which makes me the rather choose to write. For Sir Thomas Wentworth's allegations, I can saye no more then this, that if Mr. Bond, who was then my Lord Chauncelloures Secretarie and the messenger to me from his Lorde, do not justifie that my Lord was unwilling to put in anie to the place which my father had resigned, but whome he wished wel unto; and therefore he desired me to name one, and I named Sir Thomas Wentworth: let me Sept.

[1] Buckingham's answer closes the correspondence, Sept. 23, 1617, *Strafford Letters*, 4.

1617. Sept. forfett for ever my creditt with youre Lordship, which I would not doe for all Wentworth's estate.

I could alledge my father hath beene in it this forty yeeres and done the King continuall service; I could allso alledge that his deservings to the King (setting aside the wrangling in the Parlament which you, my noble Lord, I hope have reconciled,) would farr outweigh his. But my humble suite and weightiest argument at this time to your Lordship must be this, that the doing of this concernes me so much in my estate, as if your Lordship should give me two or three thowsand pownd a yeare; which, though none know, I make bold to let youre Lordship understand. The prejudice that comes to Sir Thomas Wentworth by it, is not worth two shilling, and, done fairelie, the disgrace none. I most humblie therefore desire, that this greate importance to me maye outweigh in youre Lordship's opinion the peevish and malitious humoure of him. My father doth expect everie hower my answeare, which I begg of your Lordship, and if I have anie more powerfull praiers then mine own, I add them to, for I presume I maye, and shall for ever rest

Your Lordship's most humble servaunt,

THOMAS SAVILE.[1]

Indorsed: Sir Th. Savile.

No. XIII.

SIR THOMAS LAKE TO THE EARL OF BUCKINGHAM.

[Holograph.]

Oct. 25. My ducty to your Lordship humbly remembred. This afternoone arrived here this gentleman Mr. Simon Digby, who hath lettres to his Majestie, and was desirous to deliver them as soone as he might. He hath also delivered me lettres directed to the

[1] The writer of this letter was the third son of the Sir John Savile whose restoration to office was in question; Sir John Savile was created in 1628 Lord Savile of Pontefract, in which title he was succeeded, in 1630, by this his then eldest surviving son Thomas.

Commissioners,[1] which cannot be opened till they meet, and, some of them being this after noon at Grenwich, their meeting is appointed to morrow after noon at two of the clock at my Lo[rd] Keeper's howse. But because Sir John Digby sent to me a copie of that which is written to my Lordship, and that I know not whether he have written at so much length to his Majestie, I thought it not unfitt to send the copie to your Lo[rdship] that his Majestie may be acquainted with it, and thereuppon consyder whether he will give any present direction before he doe further heare, or no. I doe not conceave of any point that will need advertisement, but that of the Nuntio's declaring himselfe adverse, whether it procead of truth or of art; in both cases it is necessary Sir John Digby be wary in his proceeding, least, when all other thinges be passed over, that may be reserved for a straw to stumble at, that the Pope will not consent. And although that Sir John Digbyes proposition to the Duke of Lerma be very provident that they should talke of the points of religion but by way of discourse, and not as in vertue of the commission till it might appeare how neere they shoulde come together, yet *caveat* from his Majestie uppon that point cannot but doe well. If his Majestie uppon his own lettres doe make any dispatch from theare, it may be remembred, or els I will writt as your Lordship shall direct. After my Lords have perused their lettres, if any thinge falle into their consyderation fitt to be advertised to his Majestie, your Lordship shall heare of it. 1617. Oct. 25.

I thought it not unfitt to send to your Lo[rdship] a lettre he hath written to my selfe, because of some wordes in it which have relation to Sir John Digby and my selfe, leaving it to your Lo[rdship's] judgment whether you thinke fitt to lett his Majestie know it. If a matter of this moment be liked by none but him and me,[2] it were

[1] The Commissioners for the Spanish business.

[2] If this, as is most probable, refers to the marriage, it shows that, in Digby's opinion, the approbation of the Commissioners to whom it had been referred was no indication of their real opinions, and also that Digby had, at this time, expressed himself in favour of the marriage.

1617. Oct. 25 pity there should be any more don in it. When your Lo[rdship] hath don with the lettres, I beseach you return them.

I have this evening receaved yours concerning the agent,[1] and though the Master of the Rolles and I have not yet spoken with him but purpose to doe sometyme to morrow, yet that much I can say for his Majesties satisfac[tion] in that clause which your Lo[rdship] sent by itself taken out of his last writing, that he meaneth his Majestie; and the avowing of the wordes *sentina* and *cloaca:* for when he was with me, I putt him to it uppon that place, and he told me that his Majestie at Woodestock had avowed them. For Sir John Bennett, I thinke he cannot produce profe, though he be stiffe in it that it was told to the Spanish Ambassador and him by some who now dare not stand to it, but we will speake with him together, and then your Lo[rdship] shall heare.

When your Lordship hath perused this minute of Sir John Digbyes lettres, it may please you to lett my Lord Fenton see it, being one of the Commissioners. So I humbly take my leave.

Your Lordship's humbly to command,

THO. LAKE.

From Charing Crosse,
this 25 October, 1617.

No. XIV.

SIR THOMAS LAKE TO THE EARL OF BUCKINGHAM.

[Holograph.]

Nov. 14. My ducty to your Lo[rdship] humbly remembred. I thought good to lett your Lo[rdship] know that yesterday at councell was effected in the matter of his Majesty['s] howshold[2] which I writt of to your Lo[rdship] to be don by his Majesty: that is, that my LL., after debating and disputing, finding[3] no other certain way,

[1] The agent for the Archdukes. The passage refers to a libellous book *Corona Regia*, which had been printed in the Low Countries.

[2] In his letter to the Council of November 21 (Cabala, ed. 1691, p. 337), the King writes, "Ye know what task I gave you to work upon during my absence." We have here a glimpse of the first steps in the economical reforms of the succeeding year.

[3] "finde," MS.

did command the officers in his Majesty['s] name to take it in hande, signifying to them that it was his pleasure to have his expenses of howse reduced to fifty thowsand poundes yearely, togither with the Queen's; onely omitting the stable, which is left to your Lo[rdship's] ordering; and there is fowrteen dayes given them to frame their project and send it to his Majesty. Notwithstanding I am of opinion it shalbe to good purpose that his Majesty writt to them a lettre to that effect which I desired by my last; for in truth they went very unwillingly about the busines, and his Majesty['s] authority will spurre them much. For the wardrobbe my Lo[rd] Hay[1] and my Lo[rd] Chamberlain[2] have taken the charge to make a frame thereof, and to give it as much expedition as they possibly can. So of the three greate heades there resteth but the matter of pensions, which we shalbe next in hand with, and how it shall proceed your Lordship shall heare. 1617. Nov. 14.

In the Navy we concluded yesterday with Sir Robert Mansell, uppon his offer that, if he might have ten thowsand pound presently his Majestie should save six hundred poundes a monthe for ever, which is about seven thowsand pounds by yeare, and the mystery was not great, though it have been long in suspence, for it was no more but where his Majestie keepeth now continewally at seas seven ships and pynaces he wold keep but fowre and discharge the rest, which this ten thowsand pound must full pay for their service past; but we have ordered he shall have the money.

In Ireland we can doe little till the officers come, who are not yet arrived. Wednesday next is appointed for the Border matters, where, if the garrison be discharged and the fees of Commissioners, his Majestie shall save one thowsand pound by yeare.

The Venetian ambassador[3] hath been with me, who, uppon these occasions which are conteyned in the lettres of Sir Henry Wotton[4] which I have sent to your Lordship, presseth still for a declaration of his Majesty, although his advertisement, as he delivered it to

[1] Master of the Wardrobe.
[2] The Earl of Pembroke.
[3] Pietro Contarini.
[4] Ambassador at Venice.

1617. Nov. 14. me, be farre short of that which Sir Henry Wotton writteth. I have given him good wordes concerning his Majesty['s] disposition to that State, and that when it shall appeare that the King of Spain breaketh through his own fault, his Majesty will not fayle to doe as his honnor shall require. This I did the rather because Sir Henry Wotton craveth tyme of a weeke more to advertise more certainly. If Mr. Comptroller [1] had spoken with me before his going I might have learned by him what opinion is in France about the observation of this peace with Venice,[2] or what their disposition is toward the maintenance of it, and have knowen better what to have sayd to the Venetian; but now he is there his Majesty may know it of him, and so give his directions as he shall see cause.

I have sent your Lo[rdship] lettres which I receaved even now out of France. When your Lordship hath perused these lettres which I send to you from tyme to tyme I beseach you that Mr. Packer may return them. So I humbly take my leave. From the Court at Whitehall this 14 November 1617.

Your Lo[rdship's] humbly to command,

THO. LAKE.

[1] Sir Thomas Edmondes, who had been, for many years, ambassador in France. He was now recalled and had arrived in London on the 11th. On the day on which this letter was written, he set out for the Court at Newmarket. *Chamberlain to Carleton*, November 15. S. P. Dom. xciv. 30.

[2] Articles to serve as a basis of peace between Venice and the Archduke Ferdinand, and also between Spayne and Savoy, were signed at Paris, $\frac{\text{August 27}}{\text{September 6}}$. The latter combatants signed the final treaty at Pavia $\frac{\text{September 29}}{\text{October 9}}$, the former did not come to terms till $\frac{\text{January 22}}{\text{February 1}}$, 1618. It was, no doubt, in consequence of this delay that the Venetians appealed to James.

No. XV.

Sir Thomas Lake to the Earl of Buckingham.

[Holograph.]

My ducty to your Lo[rdship] humbly remembred. I am very sory that his Majesty doth mistake my meaning in the matter of the pensions; for I did not intend his Majesty should be troubled with particuler abatements; but, wher[1] he had exempted such as I doe assure myselfe he will, as forrain Princes, his necessary servants, and some Privy Councellors, to deliver his pleasure straightly and in generall, that off all others he wold have abated a third part. But it seameth his Majesty will have it the worke of his Councell to abate uppon particulers, wherein I feare there wilbe so much diversity of opinion as there will not be much don to his Majesty['s] expectation. I doe not forgett, nor will not, my ducty in calling uppon it, but I beseach his Majestie to consyder that their LL. have so many thinges to doe, and the terme taketh up so many of the principall of them as they can meete but twice in the weeke. 1617. Nov. 21.

This afternoon shalbe read his Majesty['s] lettres by Mr. Comptroller[2] and those your Lo[rdship] sent me inclosed in yours, and after your Lo[rdship] shalbe advertised, what shall passe.

I have sent your Lo[rdship] the Warrant for Sir Thomas Dashington, and so humbly take my leave. From Whitehall this 21 November 1617.

Your Lordships humbly to command,

Tho. Lake.

[1] Qy. when.

[2] Sir T. Edmondes.

No. XVI.

Lord Keeper Sir Francis Bacon and the Earl of Suffolk to James I.

[Autograph signatures.]

1617. Nov. 24. It may please your Majestie. We have, accordinge to your Majesties command, taken into our consideration the offers made by Sir Richard Haughton[1] to your Majestie of his allome workes; and, aswell by our owne experience in generall as upon perticuler conference with divers your Majesty's officers and others, fourth of longe practice likelyest to have best knowledge in those workes, we fynde that your Majesty's owne allome workes are now already setled for the yearely makeinge of soe many tonnes of allome as (accordinge to a medium thereof formerly east upp) can possiblely receave vent eyther at home or abroade. Soe that if these workes of Sir Richarde Haughton's weare at this instant in your Majesty's handes, we doe not se to what purpose your Majestie should be at the charge to keepe them upp, beinge there is as much allome already undertaken to be made for your Majestie as can be vented. Besides, your Majestie haveinge byn already at soe greate a charge in setlinge these workes of your owne, how fytt yt may be to yssue more monies in these needefull tymes in a new worke unnecessarie, we humbly leave to your Majesties good consideracion. Yet beinge that the makeinge and sellinge of allome at Sir Richarde Houghton's workes may hinder the vent of the proportion now made at your Majesties, in that respect your Majestie may please to gratify him with some such convenient sute as he shall fynde out fyt for your

[1] The King visited Sir Richard's at Hoghton Tower in Lancashire, on the 15th of August. Assheton writes in his diary (Nichols' Progresses, iii. 399), under the date of Aug. 16, "About four o'clock the King went downe to the allome-mynes, and was ther an hower, viewed them preciselie, and then went and shott at a stagg, and missed."

Majestie to grant in lieu of the benefyt of his allome workes; and in the meane tyme, till such a sute be founde, if your Majestie shall please to lay some comande upon Sir Robert Bannister to forbeare to take the extremitie of the forfeture of Sir Richardes landes, yet soe as he may sustaine noe losse in the forbearance of his monies, we thinke your Majestie deales verie graciously with Sir Richard Haughton and yt cannot be much prejudiciall to Sir Robert Banister. We have sent some other certificates and reasons concerninge the state of this businesse to our verie good Lorde the Earle of Buckingham to give your Majestie further information therein. All which we humbly submitt to your Majesties good pleasure as 1617. Nov. 24.

Your Majesties most humble Servantes,

FR. BACON, C.S.
T. SUFFOLKE.

xxiiij°. November, 1617.

No. XVII.

SIR THOMAS LAKE TO [THE EARL OF BUCKINGHAM].

[Holograph.]

My duety to your Lo[rdship] humbly remembred. After I had made up myne other lettres I receaved these inclosed from Mr. Trumbull,[1] bringing me the discomfortable newes of my Lord Rosse[2] coorses, who is now certainly at Rome, and what further so unsettled and unconstant a brayn as he hath will doe I know not. That Diego, his Spaniard, is not with him, I doe beleave the cause to be that he stayeth somewhere hidden till his peace be made. I confesse I never liked Diego, for all his show of religion; howsoever my Lord of Canterbury had a great opinion of him, for I heard that Nov. 27.

[1] Agent at Brussels.

[2] Lord Roos, grandson and heir of the Earl of Exeter, and son-in-law of Sir Thomas Lake.

1617. Nov. 27. he had secret resort to the Spanish Ambassador, and I was uppon a coorse to have found some certainty of it, when we went into Scotland, but before his Majesty's return he was gon, and had caryed his master with him. All these revolters are suspicious to me till I see good proofe.

Now that it is knowen where he is I desire to know his Majesty['s] pleasure, whether my selfe in his Majesty['s] name or some of my LL. may writt to command his return, thereby to trye him, although I feare now the worst. If his Majesty like it I will finde some way to have it delivered. I thought it my ducty to lett his Majesty know what is become of him.

Touching Mr. Trumbul's motion for his return, I shall attend his Majesty tyme enough at Newmarkett, but for his increase of allowance, so as to putt his Majesty to a new charge, I know not how to doe it; but, if his Majesty like to have him stay there, I will, out of the allowance I have for secreat services, give him one hundred poundes or two hundred markes more by the year, rather then draw a new charge on his Majesty for example. And seing that he resteth there but in the quality of a private man,[1] if his Majesty thinke fit to continew him in that quality, he must have signification of his pleasure; if as an agent or publike minister, he must have some lettres of credence. So I humbly take my leave. From Charing Crosse, this 27 November, 1617.

Your Lordship's humbly to command,

THO. LAKE.

In the middest of your serious busines you may take ether learning or mirth out of this booke, specially being so neere allyed to you. The title is multifarious and the contents multiplicious. I have learned so much onely by looking on it.

[1] He had been recalled and had taken leave in June, but had been directed to remain at Brussels till further orders. He subsequently continued however at his post as agent for many years.

No. XVIII.

Elizabeth, Electress Palatine, to James I.

[Holograph.]

Sire. Monsieur l'Electeur envoyant le Baron de Winnenberg vers V. M. et aussy à la Royne pour l[uy su][1]pplier qu'avec mon cher frere il luy pleut [de lever][1] au bastesme le petit *black babie* que j'ay eu dernierement,[2] je l'ay voulu charger avec cellecy pour remercier tres humblement Votre Majesté your ces graticux lettres et beau present que Mons. Morton m'a apporté, et ce qui m'[a] resjouy encore extremement c'est de voir par la lettre de la main propre de Votre Majesté qu'elle y en agreable le desir que j'ay d'avoir l'honneur de la voir, et qu'aussy Votre Majesté paroist à le desirer en me donnant esperance que cela se fera, car il faut que je confesse que je ne saurois avoir un plus grand contentement que de revoir encore V. M. Ce porteur pourra dire à V. M. toutes les nouvelles d'icy; il nous laisse tous en fort bonne santé, je n'importuneray plus V. M. pour à cest heure, la suppliant de me conserver tousjours en ces bonnes graces comme estant à jamais. 1618. Jan. 3.

Sire, de V. M.

La tres humble et tres obeissante fille et servante,

Elizabeth.

D'Heidelberg ce 3 de Janvier.

Je remercie tres humblement V. M. qu'il luy a pleu de faire Morton son Agent, car cela servira beaucoup a mes affaires. Ma bonne mere Madame de Harrington se sent extremement honnoré qu'il a pleu à V. M. de la nommer en sa lettre; elle dit que, tant qu'elle aura un corps et des jambes pour la porter, elle me suivera par tout.

[1] Almost entirely obliterated by damp.

[2] Her second child Charles Louis, who succeeded his father in the Electorate. The term "black baby" ? = "black doll" was applied by Elizabeth also to her eldest child. See Mrs. Green's Princesses, v. 278.

No. XIX.

Sir Thomas Lake to the Marquis of Buckingham.

[Autograph Signature.]

1618. Jan. 12. My ducty to your Lordship humbly remembred. This lettre shall give his Majesty by your Lo[rdship] an accompt of such things at it pleasd him to committ to mee at Theobalds, or as do concerne his service.

First for the Lord Wotton, when I had delivered his Majesties message to him in such manner as I receaved it, his Lordship tooke thereby occasion to repeate from the beginning the course of proceeding in that businesse betweene him and Sir Henry Carey, inferring still that he never yeelded to deliver his staffe[1] and retire without some marke of his Majesties favor, and he hoped his Majesty had not beene otherwise informed. That, notwithstanding, he did not intend to capitulate with his Majesty, for he knew his staffe was in his pleasure, and he would lay it at his feete, if he would have it soe, but yet had confidence in his long service and in his Majestyes gracious acceptance thereof, and that he hoped his Majesty would not regard him lesse then he had done others of his ranke, and named my Lord Wallingford, who had not only an advancement of dignity, but a ward yearly by condition with his Majesty.[2] To that I awnswered that my Lord Walllingford's case and his differed, for from my Lord Wallingford his Majesty tooke the staffe for his service, and gave him no leave to dispose of it; and for the ward, he had it not by condition, but of his Majestyes favor some moneths after. My Lord Wotton said that he knew not that, and when I urged that he ought to have had the like confidence of his Majestyes

[1] Lord Wotton resigned the Treasurership of the Household, and was succeeded by Sir T. Edmondes, Feb. 1, 1618. The Comptrollership thus vacated was given to Sir Henry Carey, afterwards the first Lord Falkland. Lord Wotton is spoken of by Gondomar as being secretly a Roman Catholic.

[2] When removed from the Treasurership of the Household to the Mastership of the Wards.

grace towards him in any reasonable matter, as the other had had, his reply was, that he had no cause to doubt it, but asked mee if I would give my word that I would be carefull sollicitor for him. I said I durst not give my word (without I had warrant) in a thing depending upon his Majestyes will, but would advertise his Majesty of his awnswere, and for mee his Lordship needed not to doubt but that for myne ancient acquaintance with him I would be ready to do him any good office that lay in my power. I must not omitt to tell your Lordship that, among other things, I said to him that he was to accompt it for a great marke of his Majestyes favour that he had leave to nominate his successor, which he did acknowledge, but alleadged his auncient service, and that he thought his Majesty would not find it unreasonable he should expect his favour in his suite. I thinke that if he may have some hope thereof, though he do it not by way of capitulation, yet he will performe with Sir Henry Carey. But because I see him desirous to have some comfort of it, and to put in me some confidence for the furthering of it, I durst go no further than I have till I heare from his Majesty. I must not omitt also that in speaking of the reference of his suite to those who could judge of it, hee tooke exceptions to the Lord Treasurer[1] and Mr. Chancellor[2] as havinge beene adverse to him before, which I said his Majesty might easely helpe by adding some others to them. And this is as much as I can say for that part. 1618. Jan. 12.

I have acquainted my Lords with the suite of the Ambassador of Venice,[3] who do like very well of his Majestyes awnswere, and do appoint to speake with him on Wensday next. I receaved also lettres from Sir Henry Wotton, whereby he doth advertise that the State there have made the like motion to him. The lettres I have sent herewith and others from other places, which, though they bee many, I hope his Majesty will not be displeased with mee for discharging my duety, and yet there is no great matter in any of them. By this occasion I desire your Lordship to lett me know

[1] The Earl of Suffolk. [2] Sir Fulk Greville.

[3] See pp. 31 and 32, Note [2].

1618. Jan. 12. whether hereafter when like lettres come to mee I shall addresse them to your Lordship or Mr. Secretary[1] when he is there.

Yesterday my Lords heard the matter of Captaine Bayliffe,[2] and when so much had beene examined as concerned his leaving of Sir Walter Raleigh, I thinke, if nothing else had happned, my Lords would have beene divided in opinion about his committing, at least some of us should. But my Lord Admiral[3] produced two things whereof my Lords had never heard before; the one was a report made by Bayliffe, and delivered abroad in writing, wherein he doth lay foule imputacions on Sir Walter Raleigh, whereof there is no proofe, and of many the examinacions do cleare him, so that wee should all have agreed to have committed him for that.

But, that being done, my L[ord] Admiral alleaged that Bayliffe had, on Thursday last at a dinner, spoken that he could accuse Sir Walter Raleigh of treason, and some others greater then hee, and presently called in two men who advowed to my Lords that Bayliffe had so said, and likewise a third was sent for by Bayliffe's direction, one Captaine Chester, who did in effect affirm as much, and Bayliffe being urged to the particulars, awnsweared he knew them not; but that Mr. Hastings, my Lord Huntingdon's brother, had told him at Plymouth that Sir Walter Raleigh was a false unworthy fellow, and that he had said to him that which was treason. Upon this, my Lords have committed Bayliffe close prisoner, and given order to his Majestyes Councell to examine the witnesses and him, for if that be true which he saieth upon Sir Walter Raleigh, yet is it misprision of treason in him to conceale it so long. Of this my Lordes will write themselves to his Majesty, and so I am the shorter.

I have spoken with Mr. Chancellor of the Exchequer concerning the Earl of Somerset's motion, and my Lord Hay, and hee and I had some conference about it. He conceaveth it to bee indifferent for his Majesty, but cannot give a direct awnswere till he know how many yeares purchase my Lord will insist upon, for if he tye his

[1] Sir Robert Naunton, who had been just made Secretary.

[2] Bailey.

[3] The Earl of Nottingham.

Majesty to the uttermost valew, then is my Lord Treasorer and hee but my Lord of Somerset's bayliffes to make money for him. and perhaps his Majesty tyeing himselfe to a certainty at the highest rate, may loose. I thinke, for my opinion, it were good Mr. Chancellor had order to go speake with him and to understand him clearely and to conclude as he shall see cause. 1618. Jan. 12.

The Merchants Adventurers have delivered a very honest awnswere, which is that they will pay[1] . . . . . rent with[in] foure or five dayes, and within tenne dayes after tenne thousand poundes, and the whole before Shrovetide.

After I had written thus much I receaved a lettre from my Lord Wotton which I send your Lordship herewith, and thereby I thinke you will discerne that which I have delivered as my opinion that, upon a new charge of his bargaine, with some hope in the suite, he will make an end. And so I humbly take my leave.

Your Lordship's humbly to command,

THO. LAKE.

Whitehall, this 12th of January, 1617.

Indorsed:—Secr. Lake, 12 Jan.

No. XX.

SIR LIONEL CRANFIELD TO THE MARQUIS OF BUCKINGHAM.

[Holograph.]

Right Honorable my most Honnored Lord. My fellowe Commissioners and myselfe are laboringe daylye from morninge till night in that great buyssines of the Howshowlde wherin it hath pleased your Lordship for his Majesties service to ingadge me: and do hope within fewe dayes to give your Lordship such an accompt as wilbe most acceptable to the Kinge and pleasinge to your Lordship; for I do thincke wee shall do more then satisfie his Majesties expectation. Jan. 14.

I was yesternight with my L[ord] Chauncellor, with whom I spent som tyme in acquaintinge him with the manner of owr proceedinge,

[1] Paper torn.

1618. Jan. 14. who was pleased to approve therof, and is as full of hope and desire it maye succeed to his Majesties satisfaction as wee that are the laborers in it.

I shall ever with all thankfullnes acknowledge the many honorable favors I have received from your Lordship, and do humbly praye your Lordship to increase my obligation by mackinge one addition to the rest, which is to move his Majestie to bestowe on me the Chauncellor of the Dutchie his place, when hee dyes that now hath it,[1] who I hard this morninge is verry sicke. I shall in liewe therof leave to your Lordship's disposition my Master of Requestes place, and my Receivorship of the Lycences of wynes, which do equall that place in proffitt, or do any thinge besides your Lordship shall please to commaund. My desire beinge to conclude with that marcke of his Majesties favor (by your Honnor's mediation), that after my many and dangerous adventures in his Majesties service, I maye (notwithstandinge the mallice of my greate enemyes) reste saffe in so good a harbor. I humblye leave my selffe and this my suite to your Lordship's trewe noble disposition, and will ever rest

Your Lordship's humble and faithfullest
Servant to command,
LIONELL CRANFEILDE.

January 14th, 1617.

Addressed: To the Right Honorable my most honnored Lorde the Marques of Buckingham, Master of his Majesties Horse.

Indorsed: Sir L. Cranfield.

No. XXI.

SIR THOMAS LAKE TO THE MARQUIS OF BUCKINGHAM.

[Holograph.]

Jan. 21. My duety to your Lo[rdship] humbly remembred. This gentleman Mr. Scott used your Lordship's name to me in a busines which

[1] Sir Thomas Parry. He was succeeded by Sir Humphrey May.

may concern his Majesties proffitt, wherein Mr. Secretary Wynwood dealt while he lived. It is a matter of great difficulty and wherein good consyderation is to be taken, which maketh me goe warrily to worke. He will lett your Lo[rdship] understand the particulers, and so I shall not need to be more troublesome to your Lordship. 1618. Jan. 21.

I was this afternoon with the Lord Wotton to subscribe his resignation,[1] but he hath taken tyme till tomorrow, because it seameth he hath not full satisfaction from Sir Henry Cary about his moneys. I have sent doun my sonne Arthur to your Lo[rdship] to acquaint you with some thing passed here concerning his sister my daughter Rosse,[2] wherein I humbly desire your Lordship's favor for even and indifferent proceeding. I know your own nature is just and honorable, and I hope that to me or myne it will be kinde and favorable. So I humbly take my leave. From Charing Crosse this 21 January 1617.

Your Lordship's humbly to command,

THO. LAKE.

I have made bold to send to your Lo[rdship] herewith the true copies of two writings, one a declaration delivered to the Commissioners by my daughter, the other of the writing which he[3] gave her. I beseach your Lordship to take the paines to peruse them, and doe me the favor that his Majestie may peruse them, and then lett them be given to my sonne Arthur.

No. XXII.

SIR THOMAS LAKE TO THE MARQUIS OF BUCKINGHAM.

[Holograph.]

My ducty to your Lo[rdship] humbly remembred. I have sent to Mr. Secretary the resignation and commission concerning my Lord Jan. 24.

[1] Of the Treasurership of the Household.
[2] Lady Roos.
[3] Does this mean Lord Roos?

1618. Jan. 24. Wotton, and withall some forrain lettres; but this from Mr. Cottington I thought good to send to your Lo[rdship] because of the later clause concerning Sir John Digby. I hope within three or fowre dayes his Secretary wilbe here, for these lettres have been almost six weekes on the way. At his arrivall his Majestie shalbe able to conjecture of the successe of that busines.[1]

I did writt unto your Lo[rdship] concerning the office of the Dutchy, and directed my sonne to attend your Lordship about it. I cannot but still sollicite you as one that wold be glad to cary some testimony of your good will to me. I doubt there be some that may seeke to doe ill offices, which is common to thinges in Court, but I know your Lo[rdship's] judgement will not be caryed with others' passions; therefore I doe still beseach your Lo[rdship's] favour in it, and the chief cause is for that that place hath a good howse and standing conveniently for his Majesties service: besides a little ambition pricketh me that I might have that place which my master Sir Fra[ncis] Walsingham once had.

I did also will my sonne to acquaint your Lo[rdship] with the case between my La[dy] of Excester and my daughter, which when your Lo[rdship] shalbe truely informed of, you will, I doubt not, rest satisfied.

I have some cause to speake with his Majesty, though my stay be not long, and purpose to come abowt the middle of the next weeke, as I have written to Mr. Secretary Nanton, and therein I beseach your Lo[rdship's] favor, and rest

Your Lo[rdship's] humbly to command,

THO. LAKE.

24 January 1617.

[1] Of his negotiation in Spain for the marriage.

No. XXIII.

Elizabeth, Electress Palatine, to James I.

[Holograph.]

Sire. C'estecy est pour remercier tres humblement V. M. pour la belle bagne qu'il luy a pleu m'envoyer par le gentilhomme de Monsieur l'Electeur; l'assurance qu'il m'a donné que V. M. me faites l'honneur de me retenir tousjours en ces bonnes graces me resjouyt infiniment; je la supplie dont de m'y conserver toutes fois que je ne puis meriter tant de faveurs que je reçois journellement de V. M., laquelle je supplie tres-humblement de souvenir de l'esperance qu'elle m'a donné d'estre un jour si heureuse que de voir V. M.[1] et de luy pouvoir dire de bouche en tout humilité que je suis a jamais, 1618. Feb. 10.

Sire, de V. M.

La treshumble et tresobeissante fille et servante,

Elizabeth.

D'Heidleberg, ce 10 de Fevrier.

No. XXIV.

Sir Humphrey May to the Marquis of Buckingham.

[Holograph.]

My Lord. I do most willingly acknowledge that I have hereto- 1618. March?[2]
fore received greate favours and benifites from you, and that without

[1] See, on this projected visit to England, Mrs. Green's Princesses, v. 286.

[2] I take the date from the following extract. " Sir H. May is to bee Chancellor of the Duchye, but not Counsellor. Ben Rudyerd is to be Survayer of the Court of Wards, and Mr. Packer is to have 300li a yeare pension, which Sir Hum. May held in the Exchequer. It was thus agreed when the King came from Newmarket, but my Lord of Buckingham, being angry with Sir H. May, hath thus long kept it backe from bestowing, to lett him knowe that only for my Lord Hamilton's and the

1618. March ? any merit of mine, in a short space wherin I injoyed the benignity of your aspect upon me you were pleased to do more for me to the raysing and setling of my fortune, then any other frendes had donne in reward of the service and observaunce of many yeares performed unto them. This being trew and sincerely professed by me, your Lordship may easily conceive that the loss of your favour, if I have any sence of morall dutyes, must needes be matter of extreme greefe and discontentment unto me, and that as I have cause to æsteeme it one of the greatest infelicityes that ever befell me, so nothing could be more pleasinge unto me then the recovery thereof, which to the uttermost of my power I will indevour to effect, by all other meanes then such as would dishonest me to the world and you, and make me unworthy to be received by you. I have often heretofore attempted it by the best wayes I knew, and thoughe hetherto it hath bin without success, yet in duty and humility I do still persevere to seeke unto you, and do not dispaire but that I shall find you, bycause I know there is noblenes of nature, goodness and magnanimity in you.

I do confess that those ill impressions [received by[1]] your Lordship concerning me, and which fir[st took all] heart from me, were so appareled with [cunning false]hood that they would have wrought [in an]y [man li]vinge those ill effectes towardes me as they did in you. But, my Lord, I do infinitely desire your favour, and not to debate whether I have bin faulty or unfortunat only towardes your Lordship, being unwillinge to ravell into the memory of those

Lord Chamberlaynes sake, and to advance Mr. Rudyerd, he hath yeilded to him. The offence was that Humphrey May, to make sure of this place, had written to Mr. Packer that he wold resigne the Survayorship of the Court of Wards, and hys pension also to him, if he cold bring my Lord of Buckingham to advance him to the Chancellorship. He also acquaints Ben Rudyerd, that if he wold engage hys frends for his remove to that place, he wold give over the Survayorship to him; which made him allso use hys frendes, so that, by theyre importunacy on both sides, he assurd himselfe he cold not misse, which he doth not; but yett the Marques made offended with him." Gerrard to Carleton, March 6, 1618. S. P. Dom. xcvi. 48.

[1] Paper torn; the lacunæ filled up by conjecture.

offensive particulers which may stir up a fresh acrimony [in your] Lordship towardes me, and cannot conduce to the end I [aim] at, which is the recovery of your Lordship's good opinion, to [which] purpose I humbly desire your Lordship that nothing may be remembred of the times past, but only the favours and benifites which I have received from you, which in gratitude ought ever to binde me to serve you faithfully, and that your Lordship wilbe pleased to looke forward only upon me, and to valewe me as you shall find me to be just and upright in all my wayes and actions towardes you. M[y] Lord, this my desire to be received into the n[umber] of your servantes, is, without any temporary ar[tifice] sincere and cordiall, and if you shalbe pleased to accept of me, you shall find that I have a larger heart to serve you faithfully then a pen to express it. 1618. March?

Your Lordship's
In all humbleness to be commaunded
HUMFREY MAY.

Addressed :—
To the right honorable my Lord the Lord Marques Buckingham Lord highe Admirall of England.

No. XXV.

THE MARQUIS OF BUCKINGHAM TO SIR HUMPHREY MAY.

[Draft.]

Sir. I have receaved your letter by Sir Henry Rich, whome I (that by the tryall I have had of your frends and enemies, can best judge in that kinde) assure you to be your very true frend.[1] *And allthough you had made so great and powerfull meanes to me by his Highnes, who next after his Majestie hath so transcendent a command over me that I can deny him nothing, yet, seing so free an expression of your mynd in this letter which I have now receaved, I* March?

[1] The words in italics were no doubt omitted in the fair copy, and the following paragraph substituted.

1618. March? *am the more disposed to take you by the hand, assuring you that what I doe is reall and cordiall, and I doe it the more especially at this tyme when there is some thing in acting against you, that you may have proofe that I am as good an enemy as a frend. I finde some what in your letter which I doe not understand, but will tell you what it is at our meeting that you may be your own expositor.*

But before your lettre came I saw what powerfull meanes you had made by the Prince, who next after his Majestie hath so transcendent a command over me, that I could not but be very willing to take you by the hand; and the rather at this tyme because it was now in my power to act something which might make you see that I am as good an enemie as a frend.

And now seeing in your own letter to me the earnest protestation of your sinceritie, I can assure you of this on my part, that what I doe is very cordiall. Some thing I finde in your letter that I doe not well understand, which I leave to our meeting to be interpreted by your self.[1]

Indorsed: Coppie of my Lord's answeare to Sir H. May.

No. XXVI.

The Marquis of Buckingham to Sir Robert Naunton.

[Draft.]

June 16. Sy[r]. His Majestie commaunded me to write unto you that you should make ready an answeare to the Duke of Savoyes last lettre touching the rendring of Vercelli,[1] with all speed, containing

[1] "Sir Humphrie May," wrote Chamberlain on the 7th of March (S.P. Dom. xcvi. 50), "hath outstript his competitors and carried away the Chauncellorship of the Duchie, though yt be muche maymed by the renting of a speciall member, for the Lady Compton or Villers hath got a lease, and is in possession of the house belonging to yt at the Savoy."

[2] This place, taken by Don Pedro de Toledo from the Duke of Savoy, in July

these 3 points:—First, to thank him for his care in giving his Majestie so quick advertisement of that good newes; next, to congratulate with him the rendring of that town, and yet to lett him knowe that it is no more then his Majestie ever expected, both because his own Ambassador, then residing in Spayne, and his agent, gave him continull advertisementes that order was given in Spayne for the yielding of it up. And besides the Spanish Ambassador here gave his Majestie confident assurance therof, and bad him take himself to him if it were not done; and therefore his Majestie imputeth it to the ill nature of Don Pedro de Toledo that it was so long delayed, who hindred the performance thereof against the hart of his Master. Thirdly, to give the Duke of Savoye assurance from his Majestie that he is as glad as any man of this good beginning of the settling of his affaires, so he will in all occacions continue his affection for the finishing thereof. Now the reason why his Majestie hasteneth his aunsweare so much is this, because without there be speed made of it, it will lose the grace; and so I rest 1618. June 16.

Your very assured frend at commaund,

G. B.

Indorsed: 16 June, 1618. M. to Sir R. Naunton. Answeare to Duke of Savoye for the rendringe of Vercelli.

No. XXVII.

The Marquis of Buckingham to the Count of Gondomar.

[Copy.]

My very good Lord. His Majesty hath commanded me to signifie unto you, that whereas he is given to understand of the paynes June 18.

1617, was to be restored by the treaty signed at Pavia in $\frac{\text{September 29}}{\text{October 9}}$. Don Pedro had however delayed carrying out his part of the bargain till now.

1618. June 18. and care which M[ris] Timperley,[1] of Hintlesham, in the Countie of Suffolk, hath taken in procuring ease unto your Lordship in point of your health, he will cause such meanes to be used for the mitigation of any rigorous course to be taken against her for matter of religion, as that both herself, her husband, and family shall finde great comfort and ease in regard of the service she hath done unto your Lordship, so long as they shall make moderate use of this his Majestys gracious favor, and not presume so much thereon as to give any publike offence or scandall. God keep your Lordship many happie yeares, as I desire. From the Court at Theobalds this 18 of June, 1618.

Your Lordship's servant.

Indorsed: Coppie of my Lords l[ett]re to the Sp[anish] Amb[assado]r touching M[ist]ris Timperley. Mem. The 17[th] of June Sy[mon] Digby brought a lettre to be signed, which being shewed to the King, he said it was quite mistaken, and called in Sy. Digby, to whome he gave new directions according to this coppie, which his Majestie looked upon at Waustead, and said it was well.

XXVIII.

The Earl of Suffolk to the Marquis of Buckingham.

[Holograph.]

July 31. My Ho[norable] good Lord. I do acknowledg your noble favour in procuring leave for my servant Humfrees coming unto me, but I pray your Lordship to lycens me truly to acquaynt you what mesery yt hath produced unto me; for, searching the bottom of

[1] See a reference to this lady's case in a consulta by Aliaga and Gondomar, of which extracts are printed in the Appendix to Francisco de Jesus, 311.

my debt, I fynde my selfe forty thowsand pounds to pay upon bounds and morgages, wherin many of my frends and servaunts stand engaged for me, besydes the land that I lately sold to Williams the goldsmyth, for which I had fiveteen thowsand pounds, and fyve thowsand of Sir Nycholas Salter for land sold hym not long before. I report this mesyry of myne to your Lordship to no other end but to let you knowe how desierous I am to satisfye all men, because the fault of the expence was my folly. Now, my Lord, my state stands so as no body wyll bargayn with me for any thing untyll his Majestie be satysfyed that I am not endebted to hym, by which I may be freed to bargayn and deale with them. My desyer ys not so to hasten this as therby the Kyng's Majestie may have any prejudyce in concealyng one crown that I duely do owe hym; on the other syde, I appeale to your Lo[rdshi]p, my case were extreame hard yf this brute of my being much endebted to hys Majestie showld contynew long; therfore my humble sute to your Lordship ys that out of your noble dysposition you wyll take this into consederation, that some course in fytt tyme may be taken, that by your Lordship's favour I may be releeved in this reasonable sute of myne, which I wyll ever acknowledg to you for a great oblygation, which I presume the rather to do because yt pleased you to promyse me your kyndnes and favour in any fitting occasion; and so, kyssing your hands, I rest

1618. July 31.

Your Lordship's loving cosen and servaunt to commaund,

T. SUFFOLKE.

Audly End this last of July.

Addressed: To the right honorable my very good Lord the Marques of Buckyngham, Master of his Majesties Horse.

No. XXIX.

Lord Sheffield to the Marquis of Buckingham.

[Autograph Signature.]

1618. Aug. 1. My very good Lord. I understand by my Lord Scroope howe noblie your Lordship hath given furtherance unto my ends in his suite and mine unto his Majestie, of which I will allwaies have a thankefull remembrance whensoever I may doe your Lordship service. Notwithstandinge which I perceive that his Majestie, for some respects knowen to himselfe, is resolved to continewe my attendance in those places which I holde under him in the Northe,[1] of whiche (by reason of the many infirmities attendinge my yeares and constitution,) I desired to have beene eased, therbie to have given way unto some other more able to doe his Majestie service. Howbeit, since his Majesties pleasure is otherwise, I humblie submitt my selfe therunto. But by reason this his gracious purpose comes unto me only by reporte, wherbie it may seame presumption in me to resume them without the significacion of his Majesties pleasure, eyther from himselfe or some other by whom hee shall please to doe it, havinge formerly resigned them into his handes, I desire your Lordship that under such warrantie I may bee protected, otherwise I shall not adventure to doe his Majestie service in those places. And because this resignacion of my imployments falls out in a time when others doe the like out of other grounds (beeinge giltie of some miscarriage in their places), therby to avoyde question, by reason wherof some scandall hath fallne upon me as conceived to bee in the same predicamente, his Majestie shall bee very gracious unto me (and for the same I will thinke my selfe muche bounde unto your Lordship) if in my restitucion some such gracious passage bee incerted as wherbie the trewe cause of my offringe up of my imployments (wante of healthe and abilitie to doe his Majestie

[1] As President of the Council of the North.

service) may bee intimated, for the satisfieinge in some sorte of this calumniatinge worlde which lies in waite to blemishe my good name and honor. And thus, reliengе upon your Lordship's approved favor, I commend my love and service to you and reste 1618. Aug. 1.

Att your Lordship's commaundment,

E. SHEFFILD.

Att Lond[on] this firste of August 1618.

I desire your Lordship to returne your answere with all convenient speede, for I have nowe noe other cause of stay in towne.

Addressed: To the right honorable my very good Lord the Lord Marqueis of Buckingham, Master of the Horse to the Kings Matie these dd.
Indorsed: Lord Sheffeild. 1 August.

No. XXX.

LORD SHEFFIELD TO THE MARQUIS OF BUCKINGHAM.

Noble Lord. Your many noble respects towardes me (of which I am very sensible) doth imbolden me to commende unto your Lordship's favor a busines more particulerly concerninge me then any I have ever had occasion to use you in. It is not unknowen to your Lordship, that I have served the Kinge and the State now these 15 yeares in a greate, a chargable, but a poore place, by reason whereof I have soe muche prejudiced my estate, as, the Kinge not beeinge able or willinge to releeve mee, I have beene forced to desire sparinge from further attendance or publique imployment. Nowe, my Lord, findinge an opportunitie offred wherbie I may releeve myselfe and therbie bee enabled to serve the Kinge without pressure unto him, I desire your Lordship's favour and furtherance therin, which is no more but that your Lordship will bee a furtherer of me in beeinge a suitor unto the greate riche Aug. 4.

1618. Aug. 4. widowe of Sir William Craven,[1] and that your Lordship will make this my resolucion knowen to the Kinge, movinge him humbly from me for soe much favor and furtherance as hee may give me in this busines; then I doubt not but to carrie it against all men, and therbie bee made able to serve him without any charge to him in any his imployments (which I shall bee ever willinge and readie to doe as longe as I have life and healthe with all ductie and fidelitie) reservinge unto my Lord Scroope that right which your Lordship knowes me tied unto in honor, if it shall please his Majestie to give allowance therunto: and I shall likewise bee enhabled to bee every way thankefull to my frendes, of which number I doe especially accounte your Lordship one, whome I will for this and all your other noble favors ever honor and love, and soe reste

Your Lordship's moste faithfull frend,

Ever to bee commaunded by you,

E. SHEFFIELD.

Att London this 4th day of Auguste 1618.

Addressed: To the right honorable my very good Lord the Marquis of Buckingham these dd.

Indorsed: Lord Sheffield. Vid[ua] Craven.

No. XXXI.

THE EARL OF SUFFOLK TO THE MARQUIS OF BUCKINGHAM.

[Holograph.]

Sept. 13. My honorable good Lord. Hys Majestie drawing neer to the end of hys progress geves me meanes to have oportunitye to kyss hys hands, which as I do infynitly long for, so out of the hope of your Lordship's favour I desyer that you wolde be pleased to bring me to have access to hys Majestie. I purpose to wayte upon hym when he comes to Theobals, but thought fytt fyrst to acquaynt your

[1] According to Dugdale, Lord Sheffield's second and last wife was Mariana, daughter of Sir William Erwin, so that this stroke for a fortune came to nothing.

Lordship withall, by whose kyndnes I desyer to obtayne this hapynes, for which I wyll ever be 1618. Sept. 13.

Your Lordship's loving kynsman
And servaunt to commaund,
T. SUFFOLKE.

Audly End this 13 of September.

Addressed: To the right hon. my very good Lord the Marquis of Buckyngham, Master of the Horse to hys Matie.
Indorsed: Earl of Suffolk. Sept. With my Lord's answer.[1]

No. XXXII.

THE MARQUIS OF BUCKINGHAM TO SIR ROBERT NAUNTON.

[Copy.]

Sir. His Majestie hath commanded me to send unto you these two letters from the Countesse of Exeter, the one to his Majestie the other to myself, being graciously inclyned to showe her anie favor in this her desire that may according to lawe be yeelded unto hir; which not knowing how farre he may lawfully grant, hath commanded me to signifie his pleasure unto you that you call his Atturney-generall and Sollicitor both unto you, and advise with them what is fitt and convenient in lawe to be donne in this case either for any warrant from his Majestie or deliverie of any writinges or other thinges appertayning to this proces now in hand; and, whatsoever they shall thinke fitt, that you take speedie order for the performance thereof accordingly. Oct. 10.

October 10, 1618.

Indorsed: My Lord to S. Naunton, Ladie Exeter.

[1] Half of the fly-leaf, on which Buckingham's answer was no doubt written, has been torn off.

No. XXXIII.

Sir H. Carey to the Marquis of Buckingham.

[Autograph Signature.]

1618. Oct. 14. Infinitely noble Lord. I was in hope when his Majesty was att Hampton Courte that my Lord of Wallingforde had beene in peace with his affayres, because all was then husht upp in silence: but since my comminge to Lundon I fynd the cry broaken owt lowed and constant ageyne for his remove,[1] for which I must needes say (*ignotâ causâ*) I am veary sorry. Whatt fate dependes uppon that voice, or what vertewe there is in the people's ydle predictions to bringe eventes to passe, though I beleeve not much, yett to soe generall a concurrency as I doe discerne in that opinion, I cannot but yeald upp my dowbte of the worste which may befall him. And that dowbte begetts in my contemplacion the consideracion of what must ensew, viz. manifould desires and competitions to succeed him. Amongest which (pittiing that necessity his hard destiny may enforce) yf withowt the imputacion of irreguler ambition to prefer myselfe, or seemeing to overpress your noble inclynation to me warde, I might lawfully offer my desires, I would presente them to you for it. Yett if he cann stand in his Majesty's favor and your Lordship's good likeing by any vertew of his owen innocency, I ingeniously confess yt, I wishe it truly and shall be gladd of it sincerely. But yf his fate or faulte will have him fall, I knowe his gladd consent will goe with me to supply his place, might his Majesty's grace and your Lordship's good opinion concurr with it. In this playne forme I use you may discerne with what open confidence I proceed with you, whose faythfully I am, and he cannot justely accuse me to have dealte hollowly with him, whom he trusted to deale for him, for I have yourself to be my noble wittness for my intyre proceedeing. Now I have mentioned my name and my desires with my motive and reservations, I recommend the reso-

[1] From the Mastership of the Wards. He was a son-in-law of Suffolk, and his wife had taken part in the attempt of the Howards to overthrow Buckingham.

lution to your wisedome, and myself in all other considerations in yt to the absolute disposall of your election, as becomes him who hath allready receyved obligation more then sufficient ever to remayne in all the degrees of my fortune. 1618. Oct. 14.

Your Lordship's most affectionate honest servant,

H. Cary.

Cary Howse, this 14th day of October, 1618.

By Sir Dudley Digges himself your Lordship will receyve the relation of the present state of Muscovy.

Addressed: To the Right Honorable and ingulerly Noble Lord my Lord the Marquisse of Buckingham, at the Courte.
Indorsed: Sir H. Cary, Mr of Wards.

No. XXXIV.

James I. to the Commissioners for the Examination of Sir Walter Raleigh.

[Draft.]

Right trustie and welbeloved Counsellors, we greet you well.[1] We have perused your letter touching the proceeding with Sir Walter Raleigh, in both which courses propounded by you we find imperfeccion. As first we like not that there should be only a narrative sett forth in print of his crimes togither with our warrant for his execution. And for the other course of a publik calling him before our Counsell wee think it not fitt, because it would make him too popular, as was found by experience at his arraignement at Winchester, where by his witt he turned the hatred of men into compassion of him. Secondly, it were too great honor to him to have that course taken against one of his sort, which we have observed never to have been used but toward persons of great qualitie, Oct. 20.

[1] This is a reply to the letter of October 18, from the Commissioners to the King, printed in Bacon's Works, ed. Montagu, xii. 331.

1618. Oct. 20. as namely the Countesse of Shrewsbury, and some such. Besides it would make too great a stirre to have such sending of advice and directions to and fro as you mention in your lettre. We have therefore thought of a middle course. That he be called only before those who have been the examiners of him hitherto, and that the examinations be read, and himself heard, and others confronted with him who were with him in this action. And that our Atturney and Sollicitor be employed to informe against him [touching[1] his actes of hostilitie, depredation, abuse as well of our Commission as of our subjectes under his charge, his imposture, attempt of escape, and other his misdemeasnors]: only for the French, we hold it not fitt that they be named, but only by incident and that very lightly, as that he should have escaped in a French barke.[2] And then, after the sentence for his execution which hath been thus longe suspended, a declaration be presently putt forth in print, a warrant being sent down for us to signe for his execution. Wherein we hold the French Physitian's confession very materiall to be inserted, as allso his own and his consortes confession that, before they were at the Islandes,[3] he told them his ayme was at the fleet, with his son's oration when[4] they came to the town, and some touch of his hatefull speeches of our[5] person.[6]

Indorsed: October 20. His Majestie to my
Lo. Chancellor Sir W. Raleigh.

[1] The words in brackets are added as an interlineation.

[2] Here follows, erased by a penstroke, "without drawing them into the crime." That which was not to be mentioned was, doubtless, the intrigue with the Admiral of France for permission to return to a French port.

[3] This shows that the King's impression of the full evidence was that the proposal to attack the Spanish fleet was made before, and not after, the failure at the mine.

[4] "when" is substituted for "bef." *i.e.* before.

[5] "Our" is substituted for "his Matie's," erased.

[6] This letter not only shows what was the nature of Raleigh's trial before the Commissioners, of which all we know is taken from Sir Julius Cæsar's notes printed in the Camden Miscellany, vol. iii., but it fixes approximatively the date of that paper, which I had, as Mr. Spedding has kindly pointed out to me, assigned to the

No. XXXV.

Sir Thomas Lake to the Marquis of Buckingham.

[Holograph.]

My ducty to your Lo[rdship] humbly remembred. I have made bold to renew unto your Lo[rdship] a sute I moved in a lettre to his Majesty at Hampton Coort, uppon a clamor made by my Lady of Excester about a mayd of my daughter's who should speake strange thinges of me, and that I had given her money for lettres she delivered me. My sute then was and now is that it wold please his Majesty to be informed of those lettres, and what they were, for his own private satisfaction, and I have them ready if his Majesty wilbe pleased to see them or appoint your Lo[rdship] to see them and informe him; for, as I then gave my faith to God and my allegiance to his Majesty, he shall finde they doe no way concern this busines of my Lady of Excester, nor are fitt to be spoken of in the hearing of this cause, as his Majesty will judge when he shall know what they are. The same sute I doe humbly still renew to his Majesty, and to th'end that his Majesty may see how idle and in generall termes the accusation is, I have sent to your Lordship the deposition of the Lady Bamfield from whom the report came first, and likewise of the mayd, as she is deposed both on their part and on myne, exceedingly contradictory to the Lady Bamfield. And for the money, how it came to be payd to hir and uppon what occasion, this bearer can satisfie your Lordship, who knoweth more of it then ever I did till it came to be talked of. I beseach your Lordship that it may please his Majesty (if his affaires will give him

1618. Nov.

17th of August, on altogether insufficient grounds. The trial must evidently have taken place soon after the writing of this letter on the 20th of October. Mr. Spedding has also noticed the following errata in Sir J. Cæsar's notes, as printed by me: p. 10, l. 14, dele "King;" p. 11, l. 23, for "looked" *l.* "tooke a;" p. 12, l. 6, for "falt" *l.* "fact;" l. 9, for "had hee" *l.* "hee had;" p. 13, l. 1, after "deceaved" insert "him;" l. 4, for "confesseth" *l.* "confessed;" l. 6, before "July" insert "12;" before "counsell" insert "in the."

1618. Nov. leave) to peruse these depositions, and I hope he shalbe satisfied concerning me. If the money had been given hir for those lettres, or to conceale anything concerning my Lady of Excester, it wrought little effect, for the talke between hir and the Lady Bamfield was in August, and the money she had, as it seemeth, about Midsummer. So I most humbly take my leave, and remayn,

Your Lo[rdship's] in all true service and duety,

THO. LAKE.

Addressed: To the right honorable my singuler good Lord the Lord Marquis of Buckingham, Master of the Horse to his Majesty, of his Privy Councell, and of the most noble order of the Garter Knight.

Indorsed: S. Lake. 9ber. Examinacions.

No. XXXVI.

SIR THOMAS LAKE TO THE MARQUIS OF BUCKINGHAM.

[Holograph.]

Nov. 14. My duety to your Lo[rdship] humbly remembred. Seing it pleased your Lo[rdship] to say to me that, for any misconceipt you had taken of me, you were pleased to bury it, I hope that the same noble nature which moved you to remitt your own, will perswade you to be a mediator to his Majesty to forgive myne offence toward him, and I cannot beleave but that so gracious a nature as he hath, sollicited by so noble a meanes as you, shalbe able to effect it, and to procure me so much favor as to understand that his Majesty is pleased to forgive me. Your Lo[rdship] shall thereby oblige a disconsolate man to you, and shalbe assured to finde from me as much faith and assurance to your selfe as from an honest mynde can be expected. Your Lo[rdship's] last aunsweare to me at my being with you did so much distemper me, as I was never well since: for I finde that the long mist of his Majesty's displeasure, which hath lyen uppon my mynde, doth worke to fast uppon my body, except by your Lordship's favor and meanes some comfort be procured me. For the matter of the Starre Chamber, I must abide his Majesty's pleasure, although I doe not see why, if it shall please him to remitt his own offence, he might not shew me some testimony of his good opinion to keep me from despaire, whereof hoping to finde the comfort by your Lordship, I will rest 1618. Nov. 14.

Yours, in all duety and service,

THO. LAKE.

14 Nov. 1618.

Addressed: To the right honorable my singuler good Lord the Lord Marquis of Buckingham, of his Majesties Privy Councell and Master of the Horse to his Majestie.

Indorsed: Sec. Lake, Nov^ber.

No. XXXVII.

SIR LIONEL CRANFIELD TO THE MARQUIS OF BUCKINGHAM.

[Holograph.]

Right Honorable and my most Honnored Lord. I have signified his Majesties pleasure abowt the accompte of the chest belonginge to the maymed soldiers to my fellowe Commissioners, which wee will expedite, that Sir Wm. St. John maye be satisfied according to your Lordship's desire. Nov. 17.

For the buyssines of the Navye wee followe it daylie, wherin wee fynd all thinges to succeed better then wee could hope; only Sir Richard Bingleye excuseth his offer of one thowsand poundes for the two shipps, saying Sir Wm. Russell[1] was to forward to informe his Majestie therof, it beinge but cursorye speech withowt either meaninge or meanes (on his part) to mack good that offer.

Owr Commission[2] wilbe ready within three or four dayes, wherby your Lordship shall perceive wee have no other ende but

[1] Treasurer of the Navy.

[2] The permanent Navy Commission.

1618. Nov. 17. to do his Majestie service, and to restore the Lord Admirall's place to the auntient right and greatnes; and that wee intend to bee but your Lordship's servauntes, allthowghe some to gayn your Lordship's good opynion have indevored to mack yow believe otherwise.

I have attended the Lordes twise abowt those greate and importaunt buyssinesses of the strangers imployment, and allteration of the monyes, in which allthowghe I fynd that measure at my Lord Chauncellor's handes which I did not expect nor have deserved, yet I am not discorradged nor wilbe cowld in buyssinesses of that highe nature, consideringe not only my great master his honnor, but one sixt part of his Highnes revenue is in question.

I knowe your Lordship respectes no man in comparison of the Kinges service, which cawseth me with cowradge and compforte to spend my tyme and suffer that which I do. My humble suite for the present is your Lordship wilbee pleased to suspend your judgment (notwithstanding any informations or insinuations) till his Majesties Pryvy Councell macke their joynt reporte; and then your Lordship will fynd yf I ever did service acceptable to his Majestie or pleasing to your Lordship this wilbe it.

I humbly pray your honnor to give creditt to him in this who never did nor will abuse his Majestie or your Lordship with an untruth. And so, with my prayer for the continewaunce and increase of your honnor, I rest

Your Lordship's faithfullest servant and lover,

LIONELL CRANFEILDE.

Wardrake, the 17th November 1618.

Addressed: To the right honorable my singuler good Lord the Lord Marques Buckingham, of his Majesties Pryvy Councell.

Indorsed: Sir L. Cranfield. Nov.

No. XXXVIII.

Sir Robert Naunton to the Marquis of Buckingham.

[Holograph.]

My most noble Lord. I am exceedingly bound to your Lordship for your taking so much care of me as to dictate so long a lettre as you did touching the Lady Carre,[1] which I must aunswer, because your Lordship wisheth me so to do, and only to be rightly understood by your Lordship, which if I be, I have no further ambicion to give her Ladyship or many others any other satisfaction then will stand with the trust reposed in me by my dead friend. It is pore incouragement for one that hath so much buisines of importance charged upon him, as I have, to be put to write apologies for doing his ducty, upon every causeles complaint. One I was put to for Boote,[2] and now for this Lady. She sent an old instrument of her brother to me, whom I have knowen thes 20 years, and not one of all them that served her husband could she trust with her errand. He came to me to tell me that shee, out of her tryall of my faithfulnes to her father (who committed her and her porcion and all her moveable estate unto me at his death), had caused her husband to make me executor. Now his mocion was I wold help her to the wardship of her sonnes directly against her husband's will. Lettre from her he brought none. I answered him I beleeved not his message, nor that she wold oppose her husband's last will, and added how sory I was to heare of her fall to Poperie. He would have had me write to her. I tould him (as he might see very well) I was extremly sicke in my bed, and fitter to thinke of making myne own will then to execute an other man's ; but that I cold litle 1618. Nov. 21.

[1] Anne, daughter of Sir Richard Dyer, Knight, of Staughton, co. Huntingdon, second wife of Sir Edward Carr, Baronet, of Sleaford, co. Lincoln.

[2] A Dutchman in the service of the King, who had been arrested in Holland on a charge of an intrigue with the Archdukes. See Carleton Letters, 327–385, *passim*.

1618. Nov. 21. hope to have mine owne faithfuly performed if I shold breake my frend's will in such an important poinct as the bringing up his sonne and heyre: that it was against the King's instructions to thinke of any other executor, when the testator had named one without exception. My conclusion was, I pray'd him to commend me to her, and her to give me leave to be as honest a man to her husband as I had bene to her father. Some 2 or 3 weeks after she wrote me a lettre affirming she had made me executor to her husband, which if it had bene true, she had done me small honor in choosing me to be her fittest man to breake the trust he had reposed in me. I told her messenger, when she came to town I wold aunswer her lettre by word of mouth, which was all the scorne I used to him; for to write I had neither leysure, nor lyst to have my lines come to be scanned by any equivocating preists; though I forbare to tell her messenger so much, who I knew wold have made all worse than nought if I had spoken any free word unto him, in hope to get the dealings for the ward into his owne hands, as now he doth, specialy I having tould him so plainly at first that I could not beleeve his message.

How I came to be executor your Lordship will best perceive by the inclosed, which was sent me by Sir Thomas Grantham and Sir Tho[mas] Ellis, who for ought I know ar no more of kin to Sir Ed. Carre then myselfe, who will quitt my title of reversion to all his lands for 3 single halfe pence, and I am as ready to do the like for my executorship, now that I have discharged my duty to God and the dead father, as your Lordship will beare me wittnes I have, first by word of mouth, and after by writing.

But she hath made a witty tale of the wine fetched from the taverne. And did that make her forbeare prayers in her husband's house? Let my L. Hobert be judge. Againe, that Sir E. Carre had *scarce seen me 3 times*.[1] My behaviour then was more alluring as it seemes then all her conterseidg[ing] him was, that she could

God and herselfe best know this is scarce true.

[1] The words in italics are underlined in the MS.

preyvaile more to make me one of the executors then herselfe. Alas! she litle knowes how oft her husband and I mett in London, and what teares and complaints he depositated in my bosome, knowing my true affection to his and her good for her father and mother's sake, who both put me in trust for her. Had I had so much witt to have improved the opportunitie of my executorship and the wardship to have courted the widow, and left the dead to be buried by the dead, I had then shewed my selfe an honorable and a worthy gentleman, and a discreet and a kindly brother, and a true step-father to the children committed unto me indeed! I pray God her new ghostly fathers have not scholed her to equivocate with my deare Soverain Lord and Master; sure I am the divel hath taught her trucheman,[1] and he her to sclaunder me to your Lordship, that am not so harshly complexioned nor so currishly bred as to give any harsh language to a Lady whom I have called sister since she was 7 yeares old. But she is a woman, and must obey the old proverb: *Aut amat aut odit, nihil est tertium.* So with my many due thankes for your Lordship's so great care of me, and pardon craved for my teydiousnes, I humbly take leave, but will leave never to be

1618. Nov. 21.

Your Lordship's most devoted and bounden,

R. NAUNTON.

Whitehall, 21° 9bris, 1618.

Addressed: For his Majesties affayres. To the right honorable my singular good Lord my L. Marquis of Buckingham, at the Courte.

Whitehall, the 21th of November, at 2 in the afternoone. Hast, hast, post hast. R. Naunton.

London at 3 [?] in the afternoone. Waltham at 12 in nighte. Ware, 22m. past 2 in the morning. Royston at almost 6 in the morninge.

Indorsed: S. Naunton, La: Carre.

[1] Interpreter, *i.e.* the messenger who carried the messages between us.

No. XXXIX.

Sir Oliver St. John[1] to the Marquis of Buckingham.

[Autograph Signature.]

1618. Nov. 24. Most honorable. It pleased his Majestie to employ Sir James Balfoure hither for the examination of some articles exhibited unto his Majestie against Sir James Hamylton, with espetiall warraunt by his princely letters unto mee and some of the Councell here to receave such informations as his Majestie had committed to Sir James Balfoures trust, to be imparted unto us. In obedience of which, wee have with all care and secrecy proceeded therein, and given his Majestie a just accompt of what wee have found, wherewith I hope his Majestie hath receaved good satisfaction. And albeit my duty must ever tye mee to obey his Majestys royall commaundements before all other respects, yet I have suffered much in the opinion of noble and worthie personages as well in England as here, as if I had entred into a businesse unfitting the place of his Majestys deputy, who ought tenderly to preserve his Majestys subjects in peace and contentment, and not be an instrument of blemishing the reputations, or questioning the estates and fortunes of any man. The businesse of Sir James Hamylton is nowe brought to that estate as I hope, shall heare no more of yt; yet lest his Majestie may by information given unto him in the lyke nature bee drawen to employ my service againe in that kind of examination concerning the lyves and states of any of those who are by his Majestys princely favor committed to my charge and governement, I hope his Majestie wilbe gratiously pleased to joine to mine assistaunce his principall servaunts and counsellors of this kingdome, and that his warraunts and commissions may be open, and the proceedings in them faire and legall. Otherwise, if I shalbe commanded to handle them in a private manner, my selfe

[1] Lord Deputy of Ireland.

alone, or with some onely, whatsoever misfortune shall light upon any I shalbe reputed the causer of yt, and cast myselfe into a generall hatred, and be made unable to doe his Majestie that service in this kingdome which hee may expect from an officer employed in so weighty a charge. I humbly pray your Lordship to hearken to Sir Francys Blundell, whom I have entreated to wayt on your Lordship in this particular, and to vouchsafe unto mee your honorable care for my preservation, that I may in all mine actions make my selfe worthye of those greate favors I have continually receaved from your Lordship, and have the happinesse to be found still, as I shall infinitely desire, 1618. Nov. 24.

Your Lordship's devoted servaunt,

OL. ST. JOHN.

Dublin, 24 November, 1618.

Addressed: To the right honorable my singular good Lord the Lord Marquesse of Buckingham, Master of the Horse to his Majestie, and of his Majestes most Honble Privy Counsaile, dd.

Indorsed: Lo. Dep., Sir J. Hamilton.

No. XL.

SIR ROBERT NAUNTON TO THE MARQUIS OF BUCKINGHAM.

[Holograph.]

It may please your Lordship. Sir Lewis Stukelyes peticion was published yesterday;[1] the declaracion[2] is this day (upon the dispatch of this packet) to follow after. The printer hath sent me 2 copies of each for his Majestie and the Prince, and prayes pardon for some escapes committed in theyr haste, which was such as they were faine to watche 2 nights and sett 20 presses aworke at once. I have spoken to him for copies to send over to his Majesties ambassadors and agents abroad. Nov. 27.

[1] Reprinted in Harleian Miscellany, iii. 63.

[2] The Declaration of Raleigh's offences.

1618. Nov. 27. Mr. Balcanqual[1] is dispatched and gone. The Commissioners of the States[2] come not up hither before to day. I am tould Sir Nowel Caron went to them yesterday with purpose to accompany them up in his Majesties barge to day. Mr. Wake his' man came hither yesternight with lettres from his master to Sir Tho[mas] Lake and to Mr. Beecher, and told me that he made accompt his master wold be come to Paris by this time.[3] But I hope my last lettres (which directed him from his Majestie to goe to the Duke of Feria[4]) wold be with him before his setting out, and then (no doubt) he will attend that Duke first, unlesse his occasion to come hither be extraordinarily pressing and important.

I send your Lordship herewith a lettre come out of France to Mr. Beecher (which his man brought me to send away to him thither) because it may conteine some matter fit to be knowen to his Majestie. It holdes generaly that they speake there all they can to the disadvantage of our nation.

I have given order for the Committees for the water workes[5] and all the parties interessed to meet to morrow, which could be no sooner to have the buisines well done, in respect of Mr. Controllers[6] being forth of towne and Sir Ed. Coke's keeping in, and this day being a Starre Chamber day.

So I humbly take leave and remaine,

Your Lordship's most devoted and bounden
to serve you truly,
ROBERT NAUNTON.

Whitehall, 27° 9bris 1618.

My Lord of Doncaster and Mr. Chancellor of the Exchequer[7]

[1] This must mean to the Synod of Dort. If so, there is an error in Camden's Annals, who sends him off on the 27th of December.

[2] Come to treat on the disputes in the East Indies.

[3] On his return from his post at Turin.

[4] Governor of Milan.

[5] The New River.

[6] Sir Henry Carey.

[7] Sir Fulk Greville.

have bewrayed to me a willingnes to be Commissioners to treat 1618.
with them of the Low Countries. I have aunswered them, that his Nov. 27.
Majestie doth reserve the nominacion to himselfe, to fitt them to the qualitie of the Dutch. Sir F. Gr[eville] replied with some distaste at my coldnes that if he were Secretary he wold make me one. I retorned that I being Secretary wold gladly make myselfe none, unlesse I had time to study the buisines better. Your Lordship may do well to remember his Majestie of Sir Clement Edmunds and Mr. Dickenson to be imployed in the service, having both bene used in like imployments both to the States and into Germany. Sir G. Calvert will fall in of necessitie, because it will be his moneth to wait on the bord. Some civilians and some of the learned councel must likewise be used in the service.

Addressed: For his Majesties special service.

To the right honorable my singular good Lord my Lord Marquis of Buckingham at the Court.

Whitehall the 27 of November at past 10 in the forenoone.

Hast, hast, Post hast, for life, for life.

ROBERT NAUNTON.

Reseve at London at one at the aftarnone. Ware 27° at nyne in the nyht. Royston about one at midnight. Balram [1] past 7 in the morne.

[1] Perhaps the name of the postmaster at Newmarket, where the Court was.

No. XLI.

THE MARQUIS OF BUCKINGHAM TO LADY CARR.

[Draft.]

1618. Dec. 10.

Madame.[1] I leave to the testimonie of others how ready and carefull I have been to doe your Ladyship service in the business you recommended unto me, since your going from hence. Wherein if you receave not all that satisfaction which you desired and I have ever since laboured for, your Ladyship will excuse my freedome, and not hold it for a breach of that curtesie which a gentleman oweth to a ladie, if I tell you the true cause; especially when I have just reason to be grieved that I have dealt so earnestly for you upon so ill a ground. For Sir Thomas Grantham coming hither since, hath upon his creditt and word of a gentlemen assured me, and hath after upon his allegeance mayntayned unto his Majesty, that for that particular touching your refusing the Sacrament, which you alleaged to his Majesty upon the occasion of bringing the wyne from the taverne directly to the Communion table, he never heard speach of it, neither was there ever any notice taken of it in the cuntry, but that for the grossest points of Poperie you did not only maintayne them in profession, but defended them by your writing, and made your house a receptacle for Papists and priests in the tyme of your averseness from this religion, and that Sir Edward Carre was so farre from being satisfied of your returne to the religion wherein you were bred (though your Ladyship affirmed he had wonne you back again by those bookes he had given you to read), that on the contrary he often said your falling from the religion would be the cause of his death; and for confirmation that he was not satisfied in that point, he not only omitted to make you one of his executors by his will, but tooke expresse order therein that you should not have the education of your daughter who is

[1] See No. xxxviii.

now in your custodie, when she came to certain yeares specified in his will. 1618. Dec. 10.

Notwithstanding, such is his Majesties gracious care of you, who accounteth it never too late to receave those that returne to God and conforme themselves to that truth which he maintayneth through his kingdomes, that he hath been pleased upon my motion to graunt that you shall be joyned with the fower executors appointed by your husband for the bringing up of your children, and if at any tyme you finde just exception against any of those that are placed about your children, upon any advertisement therof to his Majestie he will take speedy order for your satisfaction therein, which I doubt not but you will take as a great measure of his Majesties grace toward you, and an assured testimony of my constancye to remayne ever

Your Ladyship's faithfull servant.

Indorsed : M. to the Ladie Carre, 1° Dec.

No. XLII.

Sir Robert Naunton to the Marquis of Buckingham.

[Holograph.]

It may please your Lordship. I have here retorned you the scribled minute your Lordship sent me, decyphered as neere as I could, whereby it is now apparent how his Majestie hath bene abused and myselfe vilely sclandered for giving no easier way to theyr mountebanqueries. I have encouraged Mr Hall the best I could to prosecute the service, who promised me to have made La Forest[1] drunke, and so to have taken a copie of all his lettres at Gravesend, but he tells me that La Forest's wife was there and could not be Dec. 11.

[1] The Government was at this time particularly on the alert with respect to French intrigues, after the discovery of the French agent's attempt to aid Ralcigh in escaping.

1618. Dec. 11. parted from him to give place to that project. This night he will see what he can do here. He hath detected that La Forest hath written allmost a quire of paper during this his abode at Gravesend, and that a French doctor, a silly man, hath undertaken to cary his lettres into France, upon Monday next, toward the evening. Now this doctor, having no other lettres to cary but La Forest's, if they shold be taken from him by a private man wold surely retorne backe and geve La Forest the alarme, and so he wold do the like both to Le Clerc[1] in France, and to Boote in Holland. We have therefore held it fitter to present to your Lordship's consideration our pore opinion, that the fittest course wold be to seize on this French doctor, at Dover, for a priest, and so to seize all his lettres and papers, and committ him safe and secretly to some corner in the Castle, where he may remaine unknowen, and La Forest never heare of his misadventure, and so his lettres may be retorned hither unopened, in which we may happily find just matter to lay up La Forest as close in another place, and so have it in our owne choise whither we will suffer any notice to go into France of his practise at all or not, or to make him write what we will, and intercept Le Clerk and the rest of his complices theyr aunswers they shall retorne him. I thinke it will not be amisse to awaken Sir D. Carleton's inquisicion upon Boote, to lay for his lettres, if he shall be scribling from thence into France; but I was doubtful to adventure upon either of thes courses, being different to your Lordship's first instructions (when you made accompt La Forest would have written by a post), without some approbacion from thence, though I cannot see how his lettres will otherwise be intercepted with that secrecie and safetie which was injoyned, but that La Forest will get and give knowledge of it, as I have said. I was therfore the forwarder to accept Mr Hall's offer to come down to your Lordship post to-morrow, and to returne with your aunswer on Sonday,

[1] The French agent, who had returned to France in consequence of the King's refusal to receive him, after his behaviour in connection with Raleigh's attempted escape.

which will be all in time to lay for our French Doctor (whom he hath undertaken to make him be forthcoming here tyll Monday night with his bundle of La Forest's lettres), then to hazard the bewraying of the whole buisines for want of such secreeie as will be necessarie to effect his Majesties desein, which in the first prey-scribed course will be hardly possible to observe. 1618. Dec. 11.

I send your Lordship our examinacion taken of Sir A. Gorges and Sir Lewis Stukeley,[1] whom we confronted, and committed Sir Artur to his owne house tyll his Majesties further pleasure shold be knowen. We cannot yet heare of Capt. Smith; but my Lord Chancellor and I have written our joinct lettres to Sir F. Gorges and to Sir Tho. Monke to stay his barque and himselfe, if he can be found in that country. I forbeare to troble your Lordship with a teydious accompt of our careful proceedings in the water workes, the Commissioners having layd it upon Mr. Comptroller[2] (one of our fellow Comittees) to informe his Majestie more particularly of the whole buisines, poinct by poinct, then could be done by lettre. And so I most humbly take leave, and am

Your Lordship's most devoted and bounden,
ROBERT NAUNTON.

Whitehall, the xj[th] of December 1618,
at 11 in the night.

Addressed: For his Majesties special service.
To the Right Honorable my singular good Lord my Lord Marquis of Buckingham at the Courte.

No. XLIII.

SIR ROBERT NAUNTON TO THE MARQUIS OF BUCKINGHAM.

[Autograph Signature.]

It may please your Lordship. Since my forenoones dispatch I have presented his Majestys lettres and the inclosed from the States Dec. 13.

[1] This must refer to some proceedings of the Plymouth Company for colonising what was then called the northern parts of Virginia.

[2] Sir Henry Carey.

1618. Dec. 13. and from his Excellency unto the Lords, who have thereupon given order to Sir Clement Edmonds[1] to offer an audience unto the States 4 Commissioners upon Twesday, in the forenoone, and if the Deputies[2] shall then offre to accompanie them of themselves uninvited, their Lordships will have formes prepaired to receive them in an inferior fashion to that of the Commissioners.

The cheife occasion of my sending away of this packet is to communicate the inclosed out of Fraunce, by which his Majestie will see how they begin to bethinke themselves there in part, and how this strangnes that is growen betwene this two States hath its operacion for the time to sweeten their proceedinges towardes them of the Religion. D'Agian, that was the contriver of M. d'Mayern[3] his disgrace, is now in disgrace himselfe, and the divisions and rentes which they plotted betwene the Protestantes doe now begin to gangren amonge themselves.

The minutes of the English lettre which was sent thither in censure of your Lordship and other honorable persons here, thoughe they be contemptible in themselves, yet could I not deteine them from your Lordship's knowledge. M[r] Beecher and my selfe betweene us will finde out the inditer of them er longe.

Stanly, the preist, shiftes from place to place here in towne, but I dowbt Father Patrick, the Scotishman, is hanging about the Court. My Lord Colvin saith his Majestie forgott to inquier at him of him, which I remember with the more care, because of an anxious apprehension I have of their mortall and hatefull mallice against his Majesties sacred person as the mall[er][4] and confounder of theyr batell, against whose mallignancie we cannot be too jelously watchfull. For my own part I must protest it in season and out

[1] Clerk of the Council.

[2] The mission was composed of Commissioners from the States General and Deputies from the Dutch East India Company.

[3] James's French physician.

[4] *i.e.* mauler, smiter as with a mall or hammer. The word is written with a contraction at the end, and looks like mall[o]. but there can be no doubt that it should be mall[r].

of season; *quicquid id est, timeo.* So I humbly take my leave, and rest 1618. Dec. 13.

Your Lordship's most devoted and bounden,

ROBERT NAUNTON.

Whitehall, the xiij[th] of December 1618,
at 8 in the eveninge.

Addressed: For your Lordship.

No. XLIV.

THE EARL OF SUFFOLK TO THE MARQUIS OF BUCKINGHAM.

[Holograph.]

My Honorable good Lord. I perceyve by my sonn my great oblygation to you, which, yf I be honest, I wyll labour to deserve by the fwe[1] meanes that are left me. Now, my Lord, I must fly to you as to my pryncipall advocate to medyate to hys Majestie for my coming to hys presence, for which I have humbly wrytten unto hym, and am bould to desyer your Lordship to delyver; at which tyme I desyer your Lordship may be a wytnes how I shall cary myselfe in seekyng to geve hys Majestie satesfaction in some things mysreported of me: and for other things that concerne me in pertyculer to your Lordship, I chuse rather to referr myselfe to my sonn's speach then to be tedyous by my to long letter; and, when I shalbe so happy as to wayte on you I doubt not but fully to satisfye you in whatsoever hath bene tould your Lordship; remayning more tyed then by bare professions to be 1618. Dec. ?

Your Lordships freand and cosen
to do you servyse,
T. SUFFOLKE.

[1] *i.e.* few.

No. XLV.

THE EARL OF SUFFOLK TO JAMES I.

[Holograph.]

1619. Jan.? May yt please your Majestie, Now to geve me leave most humbly to desyer you to call to mynd how I have with much grefe and affliction endured syx months[1] the want of my greatest comfort, your Majesties presence, whith some other heavy great mysfortune of my estate in having a myghty debt upon me, for which many of my frendes and servaunts stand engaged upon bounds forfeyted, besydes the interest that dayly eates upon me; but by this tyme I conceave your Majestie ys informed of all, and I doubt not that many are affyrmed as fowle in me that I showld omitt to set downe in that paper under my hand which I sent by my Lord of Lenox to your Majestie, which, yf yt please you to call me before your Majestie in the presence of my Lord of Buckyngham and my Lord of Lenox, I hope I shall well dyscharg my selfe of that imputation, and geve your Majestie further satisfaction in what hath bene objected agaynst me, and so I humbly submit my self at your feete, most humbly begging of your Majestie that I may be restored to your favour, and be aloued the meanes out of myne owne estate to pay all men the dwe debts I owe. For the estate of my lands are such as yf I showld dye before they were payed, my sonn ys not tyed to pay a shylling of them, for which my soule showld suffer; and I wyll ever pray for your Majesties long lyfe and happy estate as

Your Majesties faithfull subject and trwe servaunt,

T. SUFFOLKE.

Addressed: To the Kyngs most Excellent Majestie.

[1] Suffolk was dismissed from his office July 19, 1618 (Camden's Annals), which, if we suppose that he had not seen the King for some little time previously, would bring this letter to the first days of January or the end of December. From a letter of Sir E. Harwood to Carleton, written on the 20th of December (S. P. Dom. civ. 36), it appears that Suffolk's friends expected at that time that he would make his peace. On the 9th of January Chamberlain writes (S. P. Dom. cv. 7) that the King meant to bring Suffolk to trial. See, too, the following letter.

No. XLVI.

The Marquis of Buckingham to the Earl of Suffolk.

[Draft.]

1619. Jan. 11.

The care I have to acquitt myself according to the profession of my frendship toward your Lordship, makes me acquaint you at this tyme with some thing that fell out concerning you in the tyme of his Majestes last being at Whitehall. Some two dayes before his remove from thence, the Lords and other Commissioners for enquirye touching the mispending of his treasure repayred to his Majestie, and gave him an account of all their labours, and amongst the rest what they had found against your Lordship and your wife; and in conclusion did all upon their knees beseech his Majesty to be pleased that both your Lordship and your wife, togither with Sir John Bingley, might be called to the Starre Chamber, there to be sentenced for your misdemeanours in your office. The reasons for which they moved his Majestie to yield to this order were two; first, for his Majestes own honour, who could not otherwise be cleared except by such a publik and legall course in regard of his taking the staff from you; and for stopping the mouths of those that reported that your Lordship's office was taken from you, not upon just ground, but only by the partiallitie of a Court faction. The other reason was that by this legall and publik proceeding there might an example be made for securing his Majestie and his posteritie from being ill served by any that shall exercise that place hereafter. But though his Majestie (as himself told me soon after) disputed with them that it had been for his Majestes honour to grant you first a hearing upon all the points that you are to be charged with before a certain number of Lords before the tyme that you should be brought to any publick tryall, his Majestie alleaging that many things might appeare fowler to them then peradventure they would prove when you should be heard to answeare for your self; and that then upon your answeare his

1619. Jan. 11. Majestie might best discerne whether your offences were of so high a nature or not as to make you to be brought to a publik tryall; yet they all in one voyce insisted in their former suite, affirming that to give you first a more private hearing was against all custome in such cases, and that you could object no materiall thing against that that was to be layed to your charge, because you were accused of nothing that was not proved by oath of divers witnesses alltogither undeniable, so as though his M[ajesty], as every man knowes, be mercifull in his own nature, yet could he not resist this their sute, especially they adding to the former reasons that the burden would lye upon them as upon partiall surmisers and promoters, if the veritie of this cause were not once publikely cleared, leaving it then to his Majesties mercy to pardon and spare as should please him. I confesse, my Lord, I wish I could acquaint your Lordship with better news, but the sooner you be informed of the truth you may the better prepare you for it, and bethink you what you would have his Majestie moved in, and how farre assuring you that I shall ever faithfully represent to his Majesty what your Lordship will be pleased to employ me in. As to the expiring of their Commission, it is now expired for so much as may have reference to your Lordship, but in some other things which do very much import his Majesties service they do yet go on. This my privat advertisement to your Lordship I wish may be kept secret to your self, for I assure you upon myne honour never one of my fellow Counsellors knowes of this letter, nor of my acquainting your Lordship privatly any way of this purpose. And so I rest,

G. B.

Indorsed: My Lord to the E. of Suffolk,
11 January 1618.

No. XLVII.

Earl of Suffolk to King James I.

[Holograph.]

Most gratious Soveraygn. I have receyved from my noble frend my Lord of Buckingham that upon the importunytie of the Lords Commissioners about my late unfortunate offyce your Majestie was very gratious towards me in being unwyllingly drawen to yeald to a proceding in the Starr Chamber agaynst me, to which for the Commyssioners part I say no more but upon such mysfortune of thers God send them more tender harted Commissioners. For the great sums of money which I have hard ys layd to my charg to have deceyved your Majestie of, I mene not now nor heerafter to make any lardg contestations to, in what place soever I shalbe assyngned for my tryal, but to your Majestie I wyll aunser as to God in heaven, that having stryctly accounted with myself whether ever my hart consented to deceyve you in the least sum, I have found my zealous strong affection to your Majesties parson to be so great and honest to you for many yeares before I had the happynes to serve you as my Soverayn, as no thought of myne ever gave way knowingly to yeald to any base abuse of you in dysbursing of your Treasure, or any other way. I have heretofore confessed to your Majestie that some escapes might pass me, but how this fatall mysfortune of having so sore a course followed for my so great dysgrace, I know not by what evyll constellation yt is so sharply fallen upon me; but geve me leave, deare Soverayn, yet not to beleeve that your Majestie, who hath bene my earthly joy, wyll suffer me in my owld adge to goo to my grave with so much sorrow and afflyction; therfore my conclusion and resolution ys humbly to throwe my selfe at your Majesties feet, protesting upon all the dutyes I owe you, if I could conceyve what to do that might satesfye your 1619. Jan.

1619. Jan. pryncly displeasure conceyved agaynst me, I wold most wyllingly submitt myself to yt, and all the sequell of my lyfe after lyve

Your Majesties trwe subject and fathfull servaunt,

T. SUFFOLKE.

Addressed: To the Kyngs most Excellent Majestie, my gratious Soverayn.

No. XLVIII.

SIR THOMAS LAKE TO THE MARQUIS OF BUCKINGHAM.

[Holograph.]

Jan. 11. My ducty to your Lo[rdship] humbly remembred. After I had made up my other lettres concerning myne own busines, I receaved these enclosed from Mr. Cottington which are worth his Majesties reading; for thereby he shall see how thinges are like to stand between France and them.[1] One part of which he writeth I beseach your Lordship to procure his Majestys aunsweare unto, that it may be sent tymely to him, which is that if the King of Spain doe goe to Valentia to see his army[2] goe out, and to abide the successe of it, which may be a long tyme, whether his Majesties pleasure wilbe that he shall attend him. I make no doubt but his Majestie will thinke it fitt, for the King may perhaps abide there all the next sommer.

In an other lettre written two dayes after this about his own particuler busines he writeth this clause:—"His Majesties proceading with Sir Walter Ralegh hath given here so much satisfaction and contentment as I am not able to expresse it unto your honour, but all men doe much extolle his Majesties syncerity in it;" and in an other:—"It is even now told me that Diego de Sylva is come to this town, but as yet I have not seen him. His errant, as I conceave it, is to gett some order from the Conde de Gondemar about

[1] The Spaniards.

[2] The secret expedition against Algiers, which was causing so much consternation at this time.

the stuffe and goodes in the Low Cuntryes." So I most humbly take my leave. From Charing Crosse this 11 January, 1618. 1619. Jan. 11.
Your Lordship's, in all duety and service,

THO. LAKE.

No. XLIX.

SIR THOMAS LAKE TO THE MARQUIS OF BUCKINGHAM.

[Holograph.]

My duety to your Lordship humbly remembred. My Lords the Judges have this morning made me acquainted with a letter of his Majesties written to them upon a letter of my Lord and Lady of Excester's, wherin they are left at libertie to referr the matter of exceptions which my adversaryes may take to the byll against Luke Hatton to the Court, which is otherwise then his Majesties former direction that no such exceptions should be admitted without his Majesties privity and allowance, wherein I humbly beseach your Lordship that it may please his Majestie so farre to explane himselfe, as that his meaning is not for any formalities in the byll, or errors of clarkes in writing, the matter be overthrowen or delayed. For the Judges doe disceern that, howsoever shortnes [?] be pretended, the purpose is to avoyd the hearing of that matter of Luke Hatton, which is the first beginning and the introduction to the whole cause. My humble sute is that his Majestie wilbe pleased so farre to interprete himselfe that if it be found by the Court, or by the Judges, that the scope of the exceptions is to interrupt the order of hearing sett down by the Judges with his Majesties privity (and so that the matter of Luke Hatton should not be heard) that then the arguments of other side may be referred to be reported to his Majestie at his coming before the day of hearing; and he to judge of the worthines of them; to whose acute judgement I know that all sinester driftes will quickly appeare. I shalbe much bound to Jan. 23.

1619. Jan. 23. your L[ordship] for being mediator of this favor, and to his Majestie for granting it. And so rest your L[ordship's] in all duety and service,

THOMAS LAKE.

23 January, 1618.

No. L.

SIR EDWARD COKE TO THE MARQUIS OF BUCKINGHAM.

[Holograph.]

April 7. Most noble Lord. My peticion to his Majestie against the Lord Houghton beinge referred to the Lord Chamberlain, the Earle of Arundel, Mr. Secretarie Naunton, and the Master of the Rolles, they have made (upon an exacte examination of the cause) a certificat to his Majestie that I had just cause to complaine, so as there is good ground for an information against him in the Starre Chamber. The odiousnes of whose offence appeareth by the severitie of the punishment inflicted for the same by lawe, viz., imprisonment at his Majesties pleasure, and fine and ransome to his Majestie.

But besides his offence he hath committed a contempt with an high hand against his Majestie since the reference of my peticion, which is of so daungerous a consequence as he is to be comitted therfore.

This Lord Houghton hath bene twice alreadie sentenced in the Starre Chamber,[1] wherein in the service of my Soveraigne in the dutie of my place I had a speciall part; in unjust revenge wherof he had plotted my destruction, by raising and suborninge recusantes and others to accuse me of matters nothing concerning himselfe, whiles I was Justice of Assise; wherof I am innocent. All this good have you (noble Lord) effected for me in obteyning of the

[1] One of these sentences is well known from Bacon's charge against him and others when he was Sir John Holles. *Bacon's Letters and Life*, ed. Spedding, v. 213.

reference of my just peticion to these Lordes, for the which you have bound me eternallie to be a servant of your desires and comandementes, humblie prayeing your Lordship that you will crown your owne worke in obteyning a signification from his Majestie to the Lordes Committees that there certificat may be put in execution, which is just and honorable. And I shall ever remayne at your Lordship's comaundement and service, 1619. April 7.

EDW. COKE.

7 Aprilis, 1619.

No. LI.

[THE MARQUIS OF BUCKINGHAM] TO VISCOUNT DONCASTER.

[Draft.]

My noble Lord.[1] I have acquainted his Majestie with your Lordship's letter, who commaunded me to returne you this answeare to that point of the lettre of credence to the Duke of Lorrain, to whome he never wrote before, that it could be to no other end but to speake of a match, which would be a dishonor to his Majestie in the highest degree to enter into that businesse while the treatie between him and the King of Spayne is in hand, wherein the Count de Gondomar is shortly expected to bring some resolution. And, therefore, untill it be seen whither that match will breake of, it would be an odious thing for his Majestie to goe about another. Only he would have your Lordship, according to the directions he hath allready given you, to sound in privat discourse, and as of yourself, with those confident frendes you meet with, whither that ladie be free, and how such a matter would be affected in that State in case it should upon occasion be moved. July ?

[1] Doncaster's despatch sent by Killigrew, to which the latter part of this letter appears to be an answer, was written on the 9th of July, and is printed in *Relations between England and Germany*, series i. page 156. The question about the Duke of Lorraine must have been put in a separate letter to Buckingham.

1619. July ? As for the Kinge Ferdinand's[1] dilatorie answeare, his Majestie would not have your Lordship be discouraged therewith, especiallie since he had neither his own Counsell about him nor the Spanish Ambassador. And besides which the Spanish agent hath this morning assured him that the very same day that you sent your lettres by Killigrew the King his master sent a dispatch to the King Ferdinand, willing him to carry himself with honor to his Majestie in hearkening to a peace upon the motion of his Ambassador.

I hope the woefull newes your Lordship hath sent from hence touching the Bohemians wilbe followed with better, for now Sir Albertus Moreton is going with all speed, being fully instructed what assurances he shall give by word of mouth.

I had written this lettre inclosed to be sent by my Lady of Northumberland's man, who promised me her man should call for it, but he went away and left it behinde. I must desire your Lordship to excuse me that I am constrained to use another hand for this letter, being now going in hast to see his Majesties shipps, where I will wash away that offence with a health to your Lordship, and if there shall yet remayne any dregg of it, I will binde myself perpetually to be

Your Lordship's humble servant.

No. LII.

Statement by Sir Sebastian Harvey of his Treatment of Christopher Villiers' suit for his Daughter's hand.

[Autograph Signature.]

Oct. 2 ? Whereas the right honorable the Master of the Rolls[2] came unto me this daye and tolde me that his Majestie hath taken notice that

[1] King of Hungary, afterwards the Emperor Ferdinand II.

[2] Sir Julius Cæsar.

sithence the message delivered by the said Master of the Rolls unto me, Mr Christophere Villiers hath bene enterteyned very rudely and uncivilie both by me, my wife and daughter, cleane contrarie to that protestacion which by the Master of the Rolls I made unto his Majestie, I doe proteste (and many will witnes) that both my self and my wife did use Mr Villiers with all good respects wee coulde, and that my daughter (by my wife's leave) did spende an hour at leaste with him before dinner before my cominge home; soe that I am extreamely sorrowfull that his Majestie should receive anie contrarie informacion. And whereas the Master of the Rolls, aboute a monethe since, brought me thanks from his most excellente Majestie for my former good affection in this cause, and that I assured his Majestie by my promise that I would not match my daughter before I should make his Majestie privye thereunto, and that Mr Villiers should be welcome when he came, and withall to lett me knowe that his Majestie woulde (in respecte Mr Villiers is a younger brother) himself make him a fitt and competente match for my daughter, if I would tell him what I would demaunde. To whome I answered that she was not ready to talke of marriage with anie as yet, and I desired to be spared to speake of anie condicions in that cause with anie till such tyme as I might finde where she would sett her affection, and that alsoe before I woulde make anie demaunde in that suite I would consider of myne owne estate, and I was likewise to remember my wife, with whome I had received a good advancement, and that I thought his most excellent Majestie would herewith be pleased, viz', that I would not seeke to match her with anie before his Majestie were first acquainted therewithall, and that Mr Villiers shoulbe welcome, amongst others, to trie his fortune, and the rather for his Majesties recomendacion of him, wherewith I ame still contented, and more I cannot say in this matter.

1619. Oct. 2?

SEBASTIAN HARVEY.

October ii,[1] 1619.

[1] This is, I think, the right figure, but it may possibly be 11.

No. LIII.

Sir Sebastian Harvey to Mr. Robert Heath.[1]

[Autograph Signature].

1619. Oct.? Sir. I understande by your letter howe highlie his Majestie is offended with me, for which I cannot but be most hartilie sorrie, and for anie misbehaviour towards his Majestie at my beinge with him doe moste humblie crave his Highnes' pardon, which I hope I shall the rather obteyne if his Majestie be pleased to consider the infirmities of my age and sicknes at that tyme, for I proteste I newlye rose from my bed and was in greate extremytie of payne, havinge neither eate nor dranke that daie, besides I presumed uppon myne integritie and freenes from corrupcion in my proceedinges in the causes whereof complainte had beene made, or might be made againste me, which I nowe finde and acknowledge was but a presumption in me, seing *men's accions are subjecte to censure*[2] be theire hartes never soe upright, and the uprighteste may erre, and the wiseste have erred, and much more I, especiallie in such a place of governement, and amonge such a multitude of buisinesses as dependе thereuppon. And in that cause of Dartnall's, whereof complainte had then bene made, yt was not myne error alone, as you knowe, for yt was done in open Courte, and yt was our misfortune that you were then out of Courte whoe might have better advised us, yf yt were an error. For ourselves our breedinge hath not bene such but that wee may sometymes unwillinglie transgresse, which I hope his Highnes will gratiouslie consider and pardon.

For the matter of Mr. Villiers, I hope that when his Majestie

[1] Recorder of London.

[2] The words in italics are underlined in the MS.

shall trulie be informed of the proceedinge therein he will not conceive I have dealt otherwise then fairely in yt. Yt pleased his Majestie in the begynninge to move that match for my daughter, and that so gratiouslie as I thought it much for her good and myne honor *if likinge might growe on both partes, wherein my furtherance hath not bene wantinge;* and Mr. Villiers hath alwaies bene and *shalbe welcome unto me,* though yt hath pleased him to conceive otherwise. I onlie left it to my daughter to make her owne choice, as I doubte not but his Majesties gratious intencion is, and hath bene; and I never yet entertayned *anie other match since that was first moved, nor ever endeavoured to diverte my daughter's affections from Mr. Villiers, neither doe I thinke my wife hath done, or anie from us or by our meanes;* neither have wee anie cause to conceive that Mr. Villiers should whollie seeke my daughter for his preferrment onlie, when his Majestie hath propounded him soe fairelye; and I cannot distruste his Majesties gratious wordes on Mr. Villiers behalf, *and therefore I conceive yt shall not be needfull to enter into anie termes of treatye* in that kinde before yt be knowen whether Mr. Villiers and my daughter shall like each other or not. For my promise to his Majestie I entende (God willinge) with that integritie and respecte towardes his Highnes as shall become me therein. Oute of these I desier you (in the humblest manner that may be) on my behalf to make answere to those thinges whereof his Majestie was pleased to speake as you have written unto me. And likewise I desire you on my behalf to crave his Highnes' pardon, as well for anie offence paste, as also for my boldenes herein. And touchinge those complaintes whereof you write unto me, viz.: Dartnall's and the Constables', or anie other that may come againste me, I hope and humbly pray *that his Majestie wilbe soe gratious unto me as not to give waye that his sacred name be used* therein, but that those whoe complaine may be lefte to theire ordynarie remedy by accion to recover their amendes if they have had anie wronge, which, I pray, desire of his Majestie for me. Soe prayenge for his Majesties longe

Oct.? 1619.

1619. Oct. ? and prosperous raigne and gratious acceptance of these myne answeres and humble requestes, I committ you to God and reste

Your lovinge friende,

SEBASTIAN HARVYE.

Indorsed: S. Seb. Harvey to Mr. Recorder.

Addressed: To the right worshipfull my very good friend Mr. Robert Heath, Esq. Recorder of London, these.

No. LIV.

SIR ROBERT NAUNTON TO THE MARQUIS OF BUCKINGHAM.

[Holograph.]

Oct. 9. It may please your Lordship. I have at length gotten this aunswer inclosed from Sir Thos. Smith and the East Indian merchants, who complaine that they have bene much more wronged by the Spaniards and Portugals, and have gotten sentences for divers restitucions to be made them from theyr own judges in Spaine, but could never recover penie. Whereupon they have bene forced to sue for lettres of reprisal, and have obteined leave under the Great Seale to repaire theyr losses from the subjects of those nacions by whom they were formerly spoiled, with limitacion that they conteine themselves within the values and summes whereof they have formerly bene robbed, which they protest unto me that they have done.

Mris. Abington's peticion I have recommended in his Majesties name to my Lord Chief Baron [1] and the rest of the Judges in the Exchequer, from whom I have received promise of all lawfull favor that may be done her with justice at the hearing of her cause.

I have found out the cutter of the picture your Lordship sent me, one Thomas Coxton in Foster Lane, who tooke his invention

[1] Sir Laurence Tanfield.

out of an English pamphlet which he saith was printed by authoritie some six years since. I have recovered the plate it selfe which he cutt, and called in above a hundreth of the pictures, so many as I coulde heare of, some set in frames and limmed, and some in printed papers. 1619. Oct. 9.

I send your Lordship herewith Mr. Pie his accompt of Francis Heymarke the French prisoner that killed Giles the Deputie Customer. It seems by it. and the other articles that came with it, that Thomas Williams the Searcher there was partly a cause of this murder, and a very unfitt man to hold such a place, which in my pore opinion were fitter to be bestowed upon some honester man, as well for his Majesties service as for the releife of the pore widow and her nine orphans left her by her husband that was so fowly slaine. It may please your Lordship to let me know his Majesties further pleasure, what he will have done with the prisoner and with that Searcher's place. And so I humbly take leave and will persevere

Your Lordship's most devoted
and bounden to serve you truely,
ROBERT NAUNTON.

Whitehall, 9° Octobris, 1619.

Addressed: For his Majesties special service. To the right honorable my singular good Lord my Lord Marqnis of Buckingham Lord Highe Admiral of England &c. at the Court.

Whitehall 9th October at past 1 aftnoone. Hast hast post hast. London at allmost 3 in the aftarnone. Waltham att 6 in the afternoone.

No. LV.

Sir Fulke Greville to the Marquis of Buckingham.

[Autograph Signature.]

1619. Oct. 12. Right honorable my verie good Lord. Upon occasion of a late reference from his Majestie to me,[1] touching the change of one patentee for another, in a wayter's place at the Stilliard, I conceaving that office to have been long since discontinued, had conference with Sir William Garway in it, who assures me both that and the rest of the custome-house wayters, serchers, and other inferior officers of that kinde, are generallie a burthen and unnecessarie chardge, without use or service so long as the customes are continued in farme.[2] I did, in the last Lord Thresorer's[3] time, presume to deliver my opinion of them to the same effect, and am now confirmed in it by this man's experience ; so that, if it shall please his Majesty to approve me, I will call Sir Lyonel Cranfield with him unto me, and by their advice see what good may be donne in putting the present patentees to reasonable pension, for abating of that unnecessary chardg in the tyme to come. Good Sir, vouhsafe to retorne me answere herein with what convenyent speech you can, because this change may perchance prove a good president for diverse other of the like superfluous nature in other branches of his

[1] He was Chancellor of the Exchequer.

[2] This gives a good example of the abuses which were at this time being subjected to reform. The customs had been collected by the Crown in Elizabeth's reign. When they were, almost immediately upon James's accession, let to farmers, the interest in repressing smuggling was transferred from the Crown to the farmers who were now the only persons to be injured by it. But the old officials retained their places though they were now useless.

[3] The Earl of Suffolk.

Majesties revenues: and so, beseeching your Lordship's pardon of this boldnes with you in his Majesties service, I remayne 1619. Oct. 12.

Your Lordship's loving grandchilde
and humble servante,
FULKE GREVYLL.

Austinfriers, 12 October, 1619.

Addressed: To the Right Honoble my verie good Lord the Marquess of Buckingham, Lo. Admirall of England.

No. LVI.

SIR GEORGE CALVERT TO MR. JOHN PACKER.

[Holograph.]

Sir. I understand, by a letter which you sent of late to Mr. Secretary Naunton, that it is his Majesty's pleasure I should attend him presently after my Lord of Suffolkes day be past, which I shall most willingly obey yf it be his Majesty's pleasure, but I doubt his Majesty conceives that cause wilbe dispatched in one day, which assuredly it will not, nor in two, and therefore I pray yow send me word with all the speede you may whether his Majesty's meaning be that, howsoever the cause do not end on Wednesday next, that neverthelesse I shall wayte upon him immediately after that day, and you shall do a great courtesy. Oct. 17.

If his Majesty have not heard of it already, I pray yow lett him knowe, that by a letter I received yesterday from Naples, I understand certainely that instantly upon the newes of the Prince Palatine's election to the Crowne of Bohemia there were imbarked the 23. of the last moneth 9,000 men in 18 galleons from thence to Genoa, and so by the spediest and readiest passage they can fynd into Germany.

This letter inclosed is sent with some speed to my Lord of

1619. Oct. 17. Arundell; his servant brought it to me this night. I pray yow take care for the delivery of it. And so recommending me very kyndly unto yow, I rest

Your assured loving freind,
GEO. CALVERT.

St. Martin's Lane, 17 October, 1619.

No. LVII.

JULIAN SANCHEZ DE ULLOA TO [THE MARQUIS OF BUCKINGHAM.]

[Autograph Signature.]

Oct. 23. / Nov. 2. Most excelent Lord. I delivered unto his Magestie some dayes agoe in Tybolls a letter from the King my master, and I spoake unto him concerning the roberies and hostilitie which certaine Englishmen commit in the East India, requesting his Magestie to punish the delinquents, and commaund that which those of the Companie have taken be restored. For the facte being manifestly knowne, the King my master, out of the great confidence which he hath of his Magesties amitie and frendshipp towards him, doutes not but that he will graunt this his soe just a request; especially considering that the King my master hath soe exceeding a great care as he hath to observe al manner of good correspondence with his Magestie. And because the King my master hath commanded me presently to advertice him what his Magestie doth in the busines, I thought good to beseech your Excellencie he would doe me the favor to present this to his Magestie, because I must of force certifie the King my master of it in al haste; and I make no dout his Magestie will give all satisfaction to the King my master, especially in a thing soe just and approved as is the foresayd request.

Almighty God prosper your Excellencie with al increase of honor and dignity. Clarkenwel, the 2d of November, 1619. 1619. Oct. 23. / Nov. 2.

Your Excellencies most affectionated servitor,

JULIAN SANCHEZ DE ULLOA.[1]

No. LVIII.

JULIAN SANCHEZ DE ULLOA TO THE MARQUIS OF BUCKINGHAM.

Nov. 8/18.

Most excellent Lord Marques. Having understood of your Excellencie on Thursday last that his Magestie had remitted unto my Lord Dighby the answere of that which I proposed to his Magestie tuchinge the roberies which Englishmen have committed in the East Indies, I spoake unto the sayd Lord about the same, but I ame not satisfied with the answere he gave mee, for that I expected that his Magestie would command satisfaction to be made and justice to be done as is demanded in the King my master's behalfe in a thing soe cleare and manifest; as allsoe for that I ame assured that the answere given by my Lord Dighby will not satisfy them in Spaine; wherfore I ame constreined once againe to intreate your Excellencie he would doe me the favor to propose this to his Magestie; and if the Englishmen have anie complaint against the Portingales, let them demand justice in Spaine; and if the thing be found as certaine and manifest as that which the Englishmen have comitted, let them assure themselves that the King my master will command satisfaction to be given unto them. Thus desiring humble pardon of my bouldnes and your Excellencies prosperous increase, I conclude, ever remaineing

Your Excellencies most devoted servitor,

JULIAN SANCHEZ DE ULLOA.

November the 18th, 1619.

Indorsed: Sp. Secretary to my Lord.

---

[1] Agent to the King of Spain during Gondomar's absence. The letter is apparently a translation by a Spaniard

No. LIX.

Sir Robert Naunton to the Marquis of Buckingham.

[Holograph.]

1619. Nov. 11. My most honored Lord. I send your Lordship here inclosed a letter of the Agent for the Princes of the Union to Sir Edward Herbert, which he desireth that his Majestie might have a sight of it.[1] Though it import not much more then we knew before, yet it is the best peece of his last dispatche. With it I send for companie this weekes accompt of such as ar buryed and chistened here.

The peticioners touching the Mint buisines[2] gave no great satisfaction to the Lords, and were directed to bethinke themselves better of the matter, and to present theyr second thoughts with more deliberacion, as well what, as by what meanes they wold reforme that they tooke exception to.

The citizens and they of the out ports which cold be found in towne were warned and have promised to make ready theyr collections for the yeare paste of the contribucions to be imployed against the pyrates against the next moneth, which I shold have written yesternight, but I was not well, and am not yet in plight to troble your Lordship with any longer discourse. So I humbly take leave, and remaine

Your Lordship's most devoted
and bounden to serve you truely,
Robert Naunton.

Whitehall, this xi[th] of November, 1619.

Addressed: For his Majesties speciall service. To the right honorable my singular good Lord the Lord Marquis Buckingham Lord High Admirall of England &c. at the Court. Robert Naunton.

Whitehall the 11th of November at half an houre past vj in the evening. Resceved at Londone at 8 in the night.

---

[1] This letter from "M. Berstel" is referred to in Herbert's despatch of Nov. 4 as being "very considerable and worthy His Majesties sight." Add. MSS. 7082, fol. 68 *b*.

[2] The petition was against light gold. See a letter of Sir E. Villiers and the officers of the Mint to the Council, Nov. 1619. S. P. Dom. cxi. 51.

No. LX.

Sir Robert Naunton to the Marquis of Buckingham.

[Holograph.]

It may please your Lordship. I received all thes inclosed lettres and advertisements together, which, though they were written in 2 severall weekes, yet the contrarietie of the windes made them come together by the same passage. That indorsed to his Majestie came recommended from Venice to M. Burlimacchi, and is addressed from Girolamo Vecchietti, a Florentin. 1619. Nov. 27.

By thes his Majestie will see the proceedings in Bohemia, Hungarie, and Austria, the Venetians' disaccommodations with the Pope, the Earl of Argile's hopes in the Spanish Jesuites and in the Conde, and his designe in disposing his daughters, the project of the Spanish Armada upon the coasts of Flanders, now that the French have removed them from Graveling; which makes me wishe your Lordship wold advise well upon the ouverture which was presented you in Mr. Coke's lettres which I sent inclosed in one of my last dispatches to your Lordship. I am sorry to heare still that the contents of thos secret lettres shold still be thus communicated as they have been too to long. This occasion gives me the boldnes out of my devoted zeale to your Lordship's honor and service to let your Lordship know what I heare from out of the bosome of some of our practical Papists, who do not a litle please themselves in giving it out among theyr confidents by way of triumph that Mr. Lepton is now to be readmitted to his Majesties care, whom your Lordship's mediation hath wrought to commiserat him, in whom theyr hope is now growen rampaut as in a confident and active instrument to supplie theyr losse made in Sir Tho. Lake, which is not more acceptable to them then it is greevous to the best affected subjects, specialy in such a con-

1619. Nov. 27. juncture as that of thes times, wherein the Papists ar so desparately resolved and London doth so swarme with Jesuites and Preists.

Yesterday the proofes in Starre Chamber,[1] and the credit of the first wittnesses was much strengthened. The excepcion that was taken was at the late entring and antedating of the Order, which was held reasonable and just in the matter. Thes objections doe much satisfie the world and honor the Court, when such honorable and just resolucions and rules ar declared upon every such occasion.

The Lords have written a joinct lettre to the officers of the Mint, the Merchants Peticioners, and the Goldsmiths, to meet at the Mint and accord themselves if it may be; or els to set downe theyr several complaints, theyr differing opinions, with the reasons of both, and the best remedies they can for reforming what they find faultie, against Tuysday nexte. Sir Basil Brooke hath given in his Patent inhibiting importacion of steele, and praies a new Patent for the sole manufacture and exercise of his own new invention and some satisfaction from his Majestie for his charge he hath bene at, etc. For his first suite it was found reasonable, but the later we could geve no care unto. For that other matter of the pinnes, the learned councel are to attend upon Friday next with theyr opinions, whither that monopolie be against the treaties of commerce with them of the Low Countries. So for this time I humbly take leave, and am

Your Lordship's most devoted
and bounden to serve you truely,
ROBERT NAUNTON.

Whitehall, 27° 9bris, 1619.

I have yet received no directions how to aunswer Mr. Trumbull's[2] former, which remaine still with your Lordship.

[1] In the case of the merchant-strangers accused of exporting gold.
[2] The agent at Brussels.

LXI.

Sir George Goring to the Marquis of Buckingham.

[Holograph.]

My Lord,[1] I feare your Lordship eyther mistooke me, or I you, about the warrant that shoulde come for my Lord of Suffolk's liberty, which this last night I expected, in regarde your Lordship toulde me that you woulde wright presently after me. I beseeche you, my Lord, let it speedily be sent for my discharge, or else they will thinke that I have abused them; for I assured my Lord and Lady that it was his Majestyes pleasure, by your Lordship's meanes, that they should presently be inlarged. The rest that was committed to my chardge I have faythfully delivered, and shall as faythfully account for at my returne, which shalbe with all the expedition I possibly can; but my buisines will soe neerely presse me for three or fowre dayes as (without your Lordship's commands, whereunto all must subscribe,) I cannot stirr, my fortune and credit soe much depending upon it. One request more, my Lord, I must presume to make, and that is for my brother Bingly's[2] his remove, if not release to his owne howse, for whome there shalbe good security given that nothinge shall fall thereby to his Majestyes prejudice. The reason for this my petition is that he is suddenly fallen sick, and hath an eye muche endangered with the colde there taken. I beseeche your Lordship take these to your noble consideration, and honor me still with the beleefe that I am most 1619. Nov. 23.

Your Lordship's humblest faythfullest servant,

George Goring.

November 23th, 1619.

---

[1] Many other letters of this correspondence are in Harl. MSS. 1580, commencing at fol. 394.

[2] Sir John Bingley, imprisoned in the Fleet for participation in the misdemeanours of the Earl and Countess of Suffolk.

No. LXII.

Sir George Calvert to the Marquis of Buckingham.

[Holograph.]

1619. Nov. 29. My very honorable Lord. Amongst many of your favors whereby your Lordshipp hath for ever tyed me unto yow, I accompt it one of the greatest the noble care you have shewed in your last letter which your Lordshipp pleased to write unto me to preserve me in his Majestes gracious favor and opinion, by admonishing me of my duty in the carriage of this great busynesse wee have now in hand.[1] But I confesse unto your Lordshipp as I apprehend that with comfort and gladnesse, so do I some other words in your letter with some trouble and feare, as yf his Majesty should conceave some displeasure against me for not having that care which became me of his service in the late proceeding against my Lord Tresorer.[2] My Lord, I acknowledge with all humble thankfulnesse that besides the generall bond of duty which is common to me and all the rest of his Majestyes servants, as also the particular duty of my place, which requires a more speciall care from me of all things that may appertayne unto his Majesty then from many others, I have a streighter obligation then all these, which it is not possible I should so soone forgett, nor I hope shall never so long as breath is in me, and that is his Majestes infinite favor towards me in chusing me amongst so many of farre greater meritt to make me the subject of his power and of his goodnesse, by raysing me to that which I am. In which regard even for that goodnesse sake I humbly beseech his Majesty to beleive (which I protest before that God whom I serve is a truth) that yf I erred with those that preceeded me in that sentence, it was neither out of humor, nor popularity, nor for company, but was merely an error of my judgement, of which I

[1] The trial of the merchant-strangers for exporting gold.

[2] The Earl of Suffolk.

shalbe ready humbly to give his Majesty the best accompt I can, when I have the happynesse to wayte upon him. 1619. Nov. 29.

And for the busynesse now in hand,[1] though I must needes say unto your Lordshipp there have beene so many traverses in it at the entrance as I durst never write unto yow any thing by way of opinion untill it grew nearer an end. yet I dare boldly say for myne owne part, yf the proofes contynue as good still after the defence as they seemed to me on his Majestyes behalf upon Friday last, I shall make little doubt of the cause in my understanding. But untill the defendants have answered, your Lordshipp knowes a man cannot judge whether proofes will be avoyded or no. Alwayes I shall promise for my self, that his Majesty's service in this, nor in anything else that may be expected of me, shall want that dutifull care which becometh me, which I doubt not but shall withall sort with his Majestes contentment. And so againe with my humblest thankes to your Lordshipp for this great favor, I rest your Lordshipp's humbly and faithfully to serve you,

GEO. CALVERT.

I have sent a privy seale for as much as was allowed for the last yeares maske, with a blanke for the name of him to whom your Lordshipp will appoint the moneys to be delivered unto. They were the last yeare to Mr. Leach, the Lord Chamberlanes Secretary, who had the yssuing of them.

This other paper is an extract of a letter I receaved this day out of Italy.

St. Martin's Lane, 29 November, 1619.

---

[1] Of the merchant-strangers.

LXIII.

The Bishop of Llandaff[1] to the Marquis of Buckingham.

[Autograph Signature.]

1619. Nov. 7 Right Honorable. My ever acknowledged and (next to God and the King,) most adored best patron. I have presumed to write to the King my master in the behalfe of my poore lamentably ruined church of Landaffe,[2] whose révennewes (being the very sinnewes of any sea) are shranke from a thowsand pounds a yeare to seaven-skore pounds. No part of that which is lost can be recovered without a commission, and that which is left is in danger of loosing without a new charter.[3] Pittifully complayning of pillage, and making hue and crye after strong theifes, mighty robbers, our poore church, next to the King's, flyes to your honorable patronage and protection. To reskue and relieve her will be a deede of mercy and justice, of singular piety and charity, consequently of high honor and never dying fame; wherein your Lordship may have a great share, by lending an eye of pitty, a hand of helpe and furtherance, even one good and gracious word, towardes the obtayning of these two reasonable requests. Having not bin sufficiently thankefull for many former noble favours, I am much ashamed to beg a new. Necessity hath no law. Untill your Lordship be pleased to enable mee to render more then bare thankes (which your Honor easily may by shooting one arrow after another,) I beseech you accept of these. That beggar is not unthankfull who, having receaved an almes, ceaseth not to pray to the great Giver of all good things for a recompense to his benefactor; and He is a most bountifull rewarder,

[1] Theophilus Field.

[2] The restitution of the temporalities is dated Oct. 30, 1619, *Patent Rolls*, 17 James I. part 14.

[3] I do not find any charter or commission on the *Patent Rolls* during this or the following year.

who gives full oft Heaven for a penny. Amongst those many of my coate, whom his Majesties munificence and [your Lordship's bounti]full[1] favour hath preferred, I dare say (I may trewly, and therefore without arrogancy or hypocrysy,) there is not a better beadsman, more frequent, more fervent for your Lordship's health and hapines then your Lordship's most bounden in all faithfull duty and service 1619. Nov. ?

THEOPHILUS LANDAVENSIS.

Indorsed: Bp Landaff to my Lord.
Commission and charter.

Addressed: To the right honorable my very good Lord the Lord Marqness Buckingham Lord High Admirall of England, one of his Majesties most hon^ble^ Privy Council.

No. LXIV.

LADY HOWARD DE WALDEN TO THE MARQUIS OF BUCKINGHAM.

[Holograph.]

My Lord. I am extremly greefed to se the misfortune that is fallen on my Lord of Suffolke, because in the end it must reflect one me, especially if my Lord my husband[2] should not be reconsiled unto your Lordship, for I am fully perswayded that many ill offises have bene done betwext you contrary to his dessart if the truth ware knowen, and this I speake out of some good ressons, which I can tell your Lordship when I see you; if he should suffer any prejuduce, of necessety it must fall one me, being now his wife, and your Lordship so much my frend, as the world takes notice you are; therfor, as your Lordship respects my good and quiet, I beseech you lett me be the means to reconsile you together, that the King Nov. ?

[1] The words in brackets are very indistinct from the effect of damp.
[2] Lord Howard de Walden, the Earl of Suffolk's eldest son.

1619. Nov. ? for my sake would favour him as in former times, or other wayes he may well thinke that I have bene rather a means of his ill fortune then of any good by matching with me. I beseech your Lordship to returne me an answer, that I may accordingly make use of it; otherways I am like to be a missarable woman, which I know your Lordship would be loth to se one who will never aprove myself other then

Your Lordship's affectionated frend,
ELIZABETH HOWARD.

Addressed: To the right hon^ble and nobell Lord the Marquies of Buckinghame, these.

No. LXV.

SIR ROBERT NAUNTON TO THE MARQUIS OF BUCKINGHAM.

[Holograph.]

Dec. 1. It may please your Lordship. This day Trask's[1] submission was read in the Starrechamber, and their Lordships promised to interced for him unto his Majesty. Then the rest of the proofes against the buyers and transporters of coine were heard to the good satisfaction of the Lords and the auditorie. Their Lordships resolved to sit *de die in diem* tyll the cause should be sentenced, notwithstanding that the counccl for the defendants moved for one day's respit to have conferred among themselves, being so many defendants as they ar.

Having signified the contents of your Lordship's last touching the coine (as your Lordship directed me), their Lordships have resolved to write an accompt to his Majestie of theyr whole proceedings in that buisines, which they meane to signe to-morrow. This morning I received your Lordship's by Sir George Goring, by whom I perceived that Sir John Bingly spends the day at his

[1] John Traske was accused of Judaizing. Fuller's *Ch. Hist.* v. 459.

owne house, but he thinkes he goes to the Fleet every night. I sent Dr. Atkins and Dr. Roe to see his eye, who tell me that his eye was inflamed on Sonday, but the rheume is now fallen into one of the almonds under his chinne, and so his eye is much amended and out of danger, so that I have forborne to troble the Lords any further about him. I have sent twice for the Wardens of the Fleet to resolve me whither he lodge in the Fleet or not, because I conceive by your Lordship's lettres that his Majesty supposeth him to remaine continualy in prison. I am promised the Warden will be here before I shall have finished this despatch. 1619. Dec. 1.

The 2 despatches inclosed from Sir Dudley Carleton I received together, and have committed Brewer[1] to a messenger to be fairely used, tyll his Majesties good pleasure shall be further knowen, how he will have him proceeded with and by whom.

I received this inclosed discourse and inventorie of the peeces concerning his Majesties debts from the States and Townes under the Archdukes, from Mr. Trumbull, which he desires I shold shew them to his Majesty and then to his learned councel.[2]

It may please his Majestie to direct me whether I shall shew them to his councel at the common law, or at the civil law, or both, that they may consider whether they will be sufficient to cary the cause, or advise of such supplie as they shall find necessarie. His dispatche had no other advertisement worth the encreasing of this packet, saving that in the close of his lettre he added a postscript of an extraordinary currier newly there arrived from Madrid, who besides bills of exchange for 300,000 crowns for the Emperor brought them newes that the King of Spaine is so dangerously

[1] He was sent over from Holland for examination for having employed on the printing of books, held to be seditious, a certain William Brewster, a Brownist, no doubt the elder of the Leyden Church, who afterwards emigrated to New England. See Carleton's Letters, 389–437, *passim*.

[2] In his despatch of November 26, S. P. Flanders, Trumbull states that his advocate had made a discourse to prove the justice of His Majesty's pretensions upon the States General of these provinces for the sum of well near 100,000*l*. upon obligations given to Queen Elizabeth.

1619. Dec. 1. sicke, as he had received extreme unction, without likelehood of recoverie.[1] The Scotish gentleman that comes under the name of George Douglas is arrived at length from Mr. Trumbull, and will be with me to morrow in the evening, is curious to be knowen to none but his Majesty and my selfe, wherewith I beseech your Lordship to acquaint his Majestie, that I may receive his directions how he will have him proceeded with.

Thes other from my Lord Archb. of Spalata and to Sir Steven Lesieurs contein something not unfit for his Majesty to know, as that of the Polonian, and their purpose to question the election of Ferdinand to be King of Romans.

My Lord of Doncaster being held out so long beyond expectacion is likely to be short of mony. It may please your Lordship to move his Majestie that I may move the Commissioners of the Treasury as from his Majestie for his present supplie of some £200 more, which I presume will fall within the proporcion of his daily allowance and his extraordinarie charges and cariages. The Lords Commissioners have spoke with Sir L. Cranfeld about the currants and the tobaccho, and are promised a full aunswer to morrow upon further conference with the persons that ar interessed. They have given order to Mr. Attorney to treat with my Lord of Suffolk and Sir Jo. Bingley, and with Cortin, Burlimacchi, and Stampeel for their fines set upon them in the Starre Chamber.

So craving pardon for this very teydious scribbling, being nothing well, I pray God for your Lordship's most honor and happines, and remaine

Your Lordship's most devoted

and bounden to serve you truely,

ROBERT NAUNTON.

The Warden of the Fleet tells me that Sir Jo Bingly weares a scarfe before his right eye, but complained very much of it; that a day or two after my Lord of Suffolk's committment he had order

[1] Philip III. did not die till March 21/31, 1621.

from my Lord Chancellor to let him go abroad with a keeper to follow his buisines for 14 days, wherof x. are now spent; that he is to lodge in the Fleet. 1619. Dec. 1.

Whitehall, 1° Decembris, 1619.

No. LXVI.

Sir Robert Naunton to the Marquis of Buckingham.

[Holograph].

It may please your Lordship. I send you here the Lords' accompt to his Majestie of theyr proceedinges touching the peticion for the coyne.[1] It was drawen by Sir Clement Edmunds, but cast in a new mould by my Lord Chancellor. Thes from Sir Dudley Carleton, with the 2 copies of the Prince Palatine's to the States, I received this evening. The King of Denmarke's attempt upon Stoad[2] will alarme thos partes, and divert theyr succors from the Bohemians and the common cause. Dec. 2.

I have this evening spoken with George Douglas, (your Lordship knowes his true name,)[3] who presented me the inclosed from Mr. Trumbull. He is not forward to enter into the particularities of his errand tyll he shall receive his Majesties directions, whether he will hold it fitt and safe for him to attend him selfe in person, without danger of detection. He is well knowen to Mac Nauton, to James Haig and divers others, who if they shold see him about the Court, it would make him uncapable to do the service he pretends he can from Rome and other partes, where he is yet accepted as a confident.

His Majestie will perceive by the inclosed from Sir Jo. Fenwicke, how ductifuly he takes his being nominated by his Majesties owne free choice to the sherifwicke of that shire.[4]

[1] See note at p. 94.

[2] Stade.

[3] William Gordon, see p. 108.

[4] Northumberland.

1619. Dec. 2. This whole forenoone was spent in Starr Chamber in the defences of Peter Van Lore and of Sir Thos. Cooteals and his sonne. To morrow will be imployed for Robert de Lean and some few other of the new defendants. On Saterday his Majesties learned councel is to replie. So as we make accompt the sentance will not be given before Monday, there being twenty and one to give theyr censure in the cause, if theyr healthes do all hold out, so many having attended the hearing thoroughout. So I most humbly take leave and remaine

Your Lordship's most devoted and
bounden to serve you truely,
ROBERT NAUNTON.

Whitehall, 2° Decembris, 1619.

No. LXVII.

SIR ROBERT NAUNTON TO THE MARQUIS OF BUCKINGHAM.

[Autograph Signature].

Dec. 6.

It may please your Lordship. I am sory Sir Dudley Carleton's proceedings with Brewer have beene no more aggreable to his Majesties good pleasure: indeed he hath intermingled the instructions which wee directed him for the States with other heterogeneal counseils. This error of his must make me more wary and curious to crave particular directions for my course with him, having received nothing from your Lordship to that effect. He remaineth still with one of the messengers, unquestioned till his Majestie shalbe pleased to prescribe how and by whom he will have him examined. In my pore opinion Sir John Bennet and Sir Henry Martin will do it well this vacation time, and may use

Mr. Bill's his Majesties printer's attendance to informe them of the books he hath beene privy to, and of the characters with which they were printed.[1] 1619. Dec. 6.

I have commended the papers sent by Mr. Trumbull[2] to the Maister of the Rolls and Sir Henry Martin, and delivered him the authentical copies of all the bondes and evidences in the Threasury copied out under the seale of the Exchequer and ten several publique notaries' handes. I sent to the King of Spaines and to the Archduke's Agents to pray them to signe them upon inspection of the originalls as the notaries had done; but they both forbare to put to their handes, alleaging that they had no such commission from their maisters. Thes inclosed I received together from Quester this afternoone from France, Savoy, and Spaine.

The Dutch cause[3] continues still, and will hold us till Wednesday at the least, though we sit it out most dayes till neere one afternoone. It is a buisines of much intricasie, and receiveth everyday new variacion in the number of the defendantes, which ar every day reduced to be fewer and fewer in respect of the daily new exceptions which ar offred, in so much as my Lord Chauncellor himselfe hath tould it in mine eare, that if [he] had beene attornie and had had the following of the matter, he wold not have had so many blots in his tables. The rest of the learned councell seeme abashed at it, and professe they ar all strangers to the proceedings that have beene used. It is much muttered at, that so many ar discharged (yea and some of the greatest offendors) under hand; some by want of formalitie, as being unduely examined, as Demetrey the brewer (whose howse is deposed to have beene the rendervous of the transporters), and divers others by mistaking of the officers, and of Sir Henry Bretan and of I know not whom. I pray God send this cause a good ending. The Lords seeme to be wearie of it. I beseech your Lordship let me receive directions how his Majestie

[1] See p. 103, note [1]. [2] See p. 103, note [2].
[3] The case of the exporters of coin.

1619. Dec. 6. will have William Gordon proceeded with, of whose arrivall and attendance here I advertised your Lordship by the name of George Douglas.

So I humbly take leave and am

Your Lordship's most devoted
and bounden to serve you truely,
ROBERT NAUNTON.

Whitehall, this 6th of December, 1619.

No. LXVIII.

MR. PATRICK YOUNG[1] TO MR. JOHN PACKER.

[Holograph.]

Dec. 7. Mr. Packer. So soone as I came to toune I delivered the booke[2] and his Majesties letter unto my Lord of Winchester,[3] which was on Fryday, about foure of the clock in the afternoone. Since that tyme my Lord hath bene ever bussied about it, and layed all things else asyde. Yesternight, after supper, my Lord did returne it unto me sealed, and his letter unto his Majestie within enclosed; which presentlie I carried, according to your direction in both your letters, unto Secretarie Calwart, to be sent away poast with all speede, and before this I hoape yow have receaved it. I have sent unto yow here enclosed a paper, wherin you may see all these things yow desyred me to search out sett doune, safe onlie that place of Suetonius, which as yett I have not fallen upon; but in Julius Capitolinus and Ælius Spartianus I find verie pregnant places to that purpose This paper, if yow thinke fitt and worthie of his Majesties sight, yow may showe it to his Majestie, and learne of his Majestie what the title of the booke must be; and when yow

[1] Keeper of the King's libraries.

[2] This must be the King's book, A Meditation on the Lord's Prayer.

[3] Bishop Andrewes.

send the booke back againe for the presse, or shall have anie other occasion to wrytte unto me touching this bussines, direct your letters to Mr. Bill's[1] shoppe in Paules Church Yaird. Thus leaving of to length your trouble, I take my leave and remaines ever 1619. Dec. 7.

Your loving frend readie at command,

PA. YOUNG.

From my chamber at one Mr. Finch a crosse-bowmaker's house at the upper end of St. Martin's Lane.

December the 7, 1619.

Indorsed: Pa. Young. The King's Book.

Addressed: To the worshipfull and his verie worthie frend Mr. Packer secretarie unto my Lord Marquis of Buckingham give these at Courte.

No. LXIX.

SIGNOR GABALEON TO THE MARQUIS OF BUCKINGHAM.

[Autograph Signature.] Dec. 19/29.

Monsieur. Je croye que le chatiment que fust ordonné contre ceux qui mal traitterent les serviteurs de Monsr l'Ambassadeur de France eusse servy d'exemple à ce peuple d'estre un peu moins rigoreux aux estrangiers et plus doux envers les Ambassadeurs, mais à mon regret je voye au contraire.

Hier au soir sur le tard mon Aumosnier s'en revenant au lougis, proche à l'ordinaire des Italiens il fust rencontré par quattre Anglois, les queles luy occupants le chemin il contraignirent de passer au milieu d'eux, l'un des queles ayant traversé une de ses jambes entre les siennes et l'autre heurté, il gettaient presq' à terre. Le peuvre homme se voyant mal traitté il se mit en devoir de se defendre, mais en un istant tous quattres ils luy sauterent dessus et il battirent cruelement.

[1] The King's printer.

1619. Dec. 13/23. Au mesme temps le Conestable arriva, le quel cria la pais en langue Angloise. Le peuvre homme n'entendit point et tust, grandement estonné de se voyre en mesme instant, au lieu d'aydé, plus cruelement que par les autres battu par le dict Conestable, le quel cria au peuple de le prendre et de le conduire prisonnier.

A ce bruits courut très grand nombre de peuple et entre les autres le maistre de l'ordinaire Italien avec sa femme et un courier flamand, les quels ne manquere point de faire tous bons offices et de tesmoigner comment le peuvre patient estoit mon domestique et mon Aumosnier, ce que ne servit de rien; au contraire le dict Conestable, et l'on nommé Jan Sutten, l'ayant reconnu pretre, il mal traitterent d'avantage avec bastements le trainant par les rues tout ensi comme s'il fust esté le plus grand traistre du monde.

De cest assassinement je fu incontinent adverty. Je envoye pour le soccourrir. En chemin les miens rencontrerent un des Cirifz,[1] le quel par pitié il osta es mains du peuple et conduict au lougis du Milord Mer[2], le quel ayant entendu qu'il estoit un de mes serviteurs promit de s'en faire justice, et se contenta qu'il fust conduict à la maison, ou il est au present plus proche de la mort que de la vie.

Le desplaisir que je sent d'un si mal traittement est si grand que je ne le puis pas expliquer. Je voye le desordre tellement avancer que d'horesenavant les Ambassadeurs ils ne seront nullement assecurez en ceste Ville. C'est pourquoye je vous supplie, Monsieur, par l'amour que vous avez tousjours tesmoigné à l'androit de son Altesse mon Seigneur de faire scavoir à Sa Majesté tout ce qu'est icy passé, à celle fin que luy plaise de commander que les malfaiteurs soyent chatiez, et de m'excuser si trop je abuse de vostre courtoisie, et de croyre que je suis,

Monsieur,

Vostre tres humble serviteur,

GABALEON, Ambr de Savoye.[3]

Londres, ce 20 Decre, 1619.

Indorsed: Sr Gabaleone.

[1] Sheriffs. [2] Lord Mayor. [3] See the next letter.

No. LXX.

Sir Robert Naunton to the Marquis of Buckingham.

[Holograph.]

It may please your Lordship. Soone after I received your Lordship's last I had thes inclosed brought me from Sir Edward Harbard,[1] which will resolve his Majestie that I forgat not his instructions concerning the Prince of Condé, though the rough wether that hath bene at seas hath much hindred all passages to and fro, as your Lordship will better be informed by pore Sir Albert Morton's tedious and dangerous journey.[2] I must not forget one particular which Sir Edward Herbert wrote to my selfe a part, as making accompt it was proper to my place to proporcion his allowances, which I take it so to be for his transportacions and journies; but now that he tells me that the master of the ceremonies hath foretould him it wilbe expected that he shold put himself into an extraordinarie equipage at the time of the great ceremonie that is to be performed betweene the 2 Crownes at that King's renewing of his oath,[3] and he requires an allowance of £1000 or 1000 markes at the least, I dare not of my selfe take upon me to cutt so large thonges without his Majesties gracious pleasure first knowen, for which I shall humbly pray your Lordship that I may receive it backe with what convenient speed you may, that I may retorne him a speedy aunswer and neither discorage him nor goe beyond my warrand. 1619. Dec. 11.

These from Sir D. Carleton I received by Sir Albert Morton. I beseech you to send me what aunswer I shall retorne him concerning Boote. The other I received from the Archbishop of Spalato.

[1] Sir E. Herbert.

[2] He had returned from his post with the Queen of Bohemia, upon being made Clerk of the Council.

[3] At the renewal of the treaty of commerce between England and France.

1619. Dec. 11. I have yet no order what his Majestie wold have done concerning Brewer's examinacion. I moved that Sir Jo. Bennet and Sir H. Martin might have the examining of him, but received no approbacion of that course, nor prescription of any other from your Lordship.

Thes inclosed from Gabaleone.[1] I suppose they contein some complaint about a preist of his, who being extremely disguised and disordered in drinke, and abusing the constable, was by him put into the stockes, being unknowen what he was, as Mr. Burlimacchi tould me.

Theyr Lordships have sent out warrants to bring up divers gonfounders and officers of the port of Lewis for transporting of ordenance. Among others there is great complaint made against one George Bindles, Vice Admiral of Sussex, whom I caused to be forborne, though he hath bene sent for heretofore and could not be found, wherewith I thought it my part to acquaint your Lordship that your Lordship might proceed with him your selfe, being properly subject to your place.

So I most humble take leave, and will persevere

Your Lordship's most devoted

and bounden to serve you truly,

ROBERT NAUNTON.

Whitehall, 11° Decembris, 1619.

No. LXXI.

THE EARL OF NOTTINGHAM TO THE MARQUIS OF BUCKINGHAM.

[Autograph Signature.]

Dec. 23. My most honorable Lord and Sonne. Upon the receipte of your Lordship's letters I well hoped my nephew Charles (according to his duty and promise and as the truth of the cause required, as I

[1] See No. lxix.

have formerly related more at large in my letters to your Lordship, which I desired his Majestie should understand) would comformably have submitted himselfe and brought in those grauntes and pattents touching the offices of Windsor which he hath so unjustly procured and misinformed his Majestie therein, his Majestie having formerly passed them to Mr. Barker the officer there, who hath had his dwelling there and beene his Majesty's auncient servant and Queen Elizabeth's allso long before. But I find that he neither regardeth to lay upon me that I should enforme his Majestie otherwise then truth, nor yet to leave my yeeres and care of him altogether unsatisfied in so just and honest a course for doing justice in my place as Constable of his Majestes Castle and Honor of Windsor, which I recommend to your Lordship's honorable care and zeale in generall to justice, in particular to this my suffring and his obstinate ingratitude, praying your noble Lordship by some few lynes to my Lord Chauncellor to signifie his Majestes pleasure for calling in the said pattents and determining the matter for the security of Mr. Barker the officer there according to justice. So being bound to your Lordship for all your honorable favours shewen unto me, leaving you to the protection of the Allmightie to blesse you with all happines and honnor, I rest 1619. Dec. 23.

Your Lordship's most bownd ever to dow you sarvis,

NOTTINGHAM.

Reigate, this 23 of December, 1619.

Indorsed: E. of Nottingham to my Lord Mr. Ch. Howard.

Addressed: To the right honorable and my especiall good Lord and soune the Marquis of Buckingham Lord High Admyrall of England.

No. LXXII.

Sir Robert Naunton to the Marquis of Buckingham.

[Holograph.]

1620. Jan. 13.

It may please your Lordship. My Lord of Doncaster, my Lord Digbie, and I have met, and upon conference and comparing of the dispatches that passed betwene his Majestie and my Lord of Doncaster have cleared the synceritie of his Majesties intentions[1] and the integritie of his instructions, and my Lord of Doncaster's faithfull and punctual observacion of them all, which we did before Sir Walter Asheton,[2] who is to receive extracts of the material poincts, that he may liquidat all scruples when he shall come to the Spanish Court, and my Lord Digbie may do the like with theyr agents here.

Thes inclosed from Sir Isaac Wake and Bilderbeck and Le Monti I have received since his Majesties departure. The first will deserve his Majesties perusal, the later discover a spie a Benedictin Monke that by writing against the Pope's authoritie for deposing Princes hath gotten a toleration here, and abuseth it to hold correspondence with the Pope's Nuncios at Brussells and at Paris. He names him after the fashion of Italy, by his Christian name, Tomaso, by which it will be hard to find him; it may be his Majestie knows his surname, without whose direction I will follow him no further.

I have delivered his Majesties message and the copie of the Act of Councell touching Donato to the Venetian Ambassador, who seemes no more then satisfied with it, but protesteth to do all the best offices to make his superiors understand his Majesties signal favor hereby demonstrated and intended them in this conjuncture. Donato is lesse contented at it, and saith it is against the dignitie

[1] From all suspicion of having been concerned in Frederick's election to the Crown of Bohemia.

[2] Sir W. Aston was about to start on his embassy to Madrid.

and the libertie of this great kingdom. I conceave his Majestie hath taken the right and straight way, in the middest betweene the 2 extrems, without inclining too farre to either of them both. 1620. Jan. 13.

This inclosed peticion of the Earl of Ormond's was almost given way unto. But I remembered their Lordships that he stood out prisoner in contempt against his Majesties decree made[1] by his own royal person, and moved that his Majestie might be acquainted herewith and declare his pleasur before they gave any order herein.

Thes examinacions of William Carre I received yesterday from Durham. It may please his Majesty to direct what he will have further inquired and done concerning him by my Lord of Durham or myselfe.

Mr. Villarnown, that brought the news of the yong Prince's birth at Prague, attends his Majesties lettres, which he tould him he wold addresse them with his own hand, and humbly praies his Majesties signature to this safe conduct here inclosed.

So with my humble duetie and service, and daily prayers for your Lordship's most honor and happines, I take leave and am

Your Lordship's most devoted

and bounden to serve you truely,

ROBERT NAUNTON.

Whitehall, 13° Januarii, 1619

As I was sealing up this dispatch I received thes advertisements of Bohemia from Mr. Burlimacchi.

No. LXXIII.

SIR ROBERT NAUNTON TO THE MARQUIS OF BUCKINGHAM.
[Holograph.]

It may please your Lordship. Wee lose no time in his Majesties buisinesses recommended to the Bord and to his Commissioners for Jan. 20.

[1] In the dispute between the Earl of Ormond and Lord Dingwall.

1620. Jan. 20. the Thr[es]earie, which takes my time so wholy up, that it must excuse my seldome writing, and my forbearance to advertise the particularities of our proceedings, tyll we shall have ripened them to some profe.

Thes inclosed from the Baron Donah ar the cheife cause of this dispatch, which he hath importuned me to send to his Majestie, as persuading himselfe to give great satisfaction by them. He prayed me to tell your Lordship from him that he had receaved the Spanyards objections of Secretarie Calvert,[1] and that he makes no doubt to give full aunswere unto them to his Majesties full contentment when he shall have the honor to attend him at Newmarket.

I wrote unto your Lordship soone after his Majestie removed from hence, which I thinke were delivered in your Lordship's absence from the Courte. It may please your Lordship that Mr. Packer may retorne the lettres when his Majestie and your Lordship shall have done with them, that I may hold up intelligence with my correspondents abroad, and particularly let me know his Majesties pleasure touching the Earl of Ormond's peticion, which I sent inclosed in that dispatch, for which I suffer envie, having turned the resolucion of the table by putting them and myselfe in minde of our ducties and respects to his Majestie, in disobedience and contempt of whose own sentence given in his royal person that Earle stands out, and is in effect his own prisoner.

My Lady of Buckingham hath willed me to let your Lordship know that Sir Sebastian[2] and his lady and the yong gentlewoman ar all joinct suitors, that whereas Cortines debts[3] ar extended by

[1] "Ha la Mtà sua havuto da Doncaster una scrittura consignata a questo Imperatore, nella quale si espresimono le ragioni di esso Ferdinando. Ha po havuto un altra sopra l'istesse da questo Agente di Spagna, il quale se maneggia molto accortamente a tutto poter suo. L'una et l'altera ha mandate per Secretarie Calvert all'Ambasciator Dona, acciocbe responda ad alcune di quelle ragioni."—Lando to the Doge, January 20/30, 1620. Relations between England and Germany, Series II. 147.

[2] Sir S. Harvey, whose daughter and heiress was being sought in vain as a wife for Christopher Villiers.

[3] For his fine for exporting coin.

Mr. Attorny to the value of some £7000, he may be used with the like favor that others ar in giving good securitie to pay what his Majestie shall be pleased to set upon him and his credit preserved (which Mr. Attourney's[1] course of proceeding with him would shake) whiche they all three professe they will take for a signal favour, and she saith they beginne to shew themselves more kind and plyant then heretofore. She desires your Lordship wold procure his Majesties lettres to the Commissioners for the Thr[es]carie to give order that, upon good securitie given to the effect above mencioned, his debts may be no further questioned by Mr. Attorny. 1620. Jan. 20.

So with my daily prayers to God for your Lordship's most honour and true happines I remaine

Your Lordship's most devoted

and bounden to serve you truely,

ROBERT NAUNTON.

Whitehall, 20 Januarii, 1619.

No. LXXIV.

SIR ROBERT NAUNTON TO THE MARQUIS OF BUCKINGHAM.

[Holograph.]

It may please your Lordship. The occasion of this dispatch is the speedy conveyance of thes inclosed from my Lord Digbie, Sir Isaac Wake, and Mr. Cottington, which being so manye and so long I must not in conscience add to your Lordship's troble by writing at this time any more then needs I must. Jan. 23.

Tomorrow my Lords are to meet, and every bird to bring a fether to the eagle's nest. I pray God blesse our day's worke; divers of them wold willingly have put it over, as if all meanes had bene studied that the witt of man could compasse, &c. But my Lord Chancellor and my selfe pressed his Majesties instructions *iterato.* What the effect will be, Secretarie Calvert will better advertise by word of mouth then can conveniently be done by writing.

[1] Yelverton.

1620. Jan. 23. I will not then faile to call daily upon them to whom his Majestie hath referred the several businesses of my Lord of Suffolk's last submission, of Sir H. Breton's peticion, of the late graunt to the City, of Nicholson's patent, the diminishing his Majesties charge in unnecessary officers, and the rest. So for this time I humbly take leave, and will persevere

Your Lordship's most devoted
and bounden to serve you truely,
ROBERT NAUNTON.

Whitehall, 23º Januarii, 1619.

No. LXXV.

THE MARQUIS OF BUCKINGHAM TO THE LORD CHANCELLOR VERULAM.

[Copy.]

Jan. ? After my very hartie commendacions: His Majestie hath commanded me to write unto you that you know very well how earnest he hath been to make a match betweene my brother Christopher Villiers and Sir Sebastian Harveyes[1] daughter, wherein Courteen doth offer his travell and paynes to bring it to effect, so that he may be eased of the extent which is upon him by giving securitie unto his Majestie for the payment of the fine imposed upon him.[2] Herein his Majestie desireth you to be carefull that this be not a pretext used cunningly by Courteen to defraud him of his money, which is no small matter (being, as you knowe, two and twentie thousand pounds); but yf you find his intention be sincere, his Majestie is well pleased for incouraging him to use his endeavor in that businesse, to free him from the extent upon his goods, putting in good security for the payment of his Majestes money, but by no other way.

Indorsed: M[inute] to Lord Chancelor altered and signed by his Majestie.

[1] See Nos. LII. LIII. and LXXIII.

[2] For exporting treasure.

No. LXXVI.

Sir Robert Naunton to the Marquis of Buckingham.

[Holograph.]

It may please your Lordship. I have once more made bould to addresse this other dispatche of Sir Ed. Herbert's[1] to your Lordship, because I conceive your Lordship favors him, and you will see by the close of his lettre to my selfe that he promiseth himself your Lordship's assistance to his Majestie in that which he so much affecteth. I have received that King's oath,[2] signed and sealed and attested by all the four Secretaries. I cannot omitt to acquaint your Lordship with the comfort and joy which I conceive to heare how all the best sort of his Majesties people applaud and honor your noble forwardnes and furtherance in graceing the Bohemian Ambassador[3] with your visits, and introducing him to conferences and audiences with his Majestie. I make no doubt but God will stand for his own truth; and will in his good time inspire his Majestie to declare him selfe for it effectualy, after he shall be satisfied and resolved of the right. So with my daily prayers to God to direct his Majestie and your Lordship, so as shall be most for his owne glory and your highest honor, I humbly take leave, and will persevere 1620. Feb. 3.

Your Lordship's most devoted
and bounden to serve you truely,
Robert Naunton.

Whitehall, 3° Febr. 1619.

---

[1] Ambassador in France. [2] See p. 111.
[3] Baron Aetatins Dohna.

No. LXXVII.

Signor Gabaleon to the Marquis of Buckingham.

[Autograph Signature.]

1620. Feb. 3/13. Monsieur. La lettre où il nous pleut de m'escrire ces jours passées non seulement je l'envoya à son Altesse, afin qu'il voiast la faveur que Sa Majesté luy fit de publier en plaine assemblée de sa Court que les deux de la religion reformée executez desiniermeut en Piedmont estoyent deux meschants garniments, qui avoyent esté condamnés pour leurs crimes, mais encore je n'en donna plusieurs copies à de mes amis pour le publier en ceste ville, afin que le peuple, entendu la verité du faict, s'en ostat la croyance qu'il n'avoit au contraire. Neantemoins quelque mauvaisesprit par ignorance o par malice a fait imprimer en Anglois la lettre qu'un ministre du Marquisat de Salusses escrivit à Genève et eux mandé icy, la quels estant plaine de menteries et fauceté, il n'y a nul doubte qu'elle confirmera le dit peuple en la mauvaise croyance qu'il n'avoit desja conceue. C'est pourquoy, Monsieur, je vous supplie s'il se peult de faire en sorte que par ordonance de Sa Majesté les dittes lettres imprimées soyent retirées et bruslées en public comme fauces et plaines de sedition, qu'outre vous vous obligerez Son Altesse, vous donnerez sujet à moy d'adjuster ceste faveur à une infinité d'autres que vous m'avez reparty, et de me dire à jamais comme je suis,

Monsieur,

Vostre très affectionné serviteur,

Gabaleon, Ambassadeur de Savoye.

Londres, ce 13 Fevrier, 1620.

No. LXXVIII.

Mr. Anthony Warton to Mr. John Packer.

[Holograph.]

Quanquam te sciam, vir ornatissime, jamdudum certiorem esse factum me accepisse gratuitum et amplissimum illud donum tuum (odorem quidem, ut Apostolus ait, bonæ fragrantiæ, sacrificium Deo acceptum et gratum,) quod ad me per D. Boultonum transmiseras, tamen existimavi ad officium meum pertinere, ut grati animi aliquam apud te significationem prestarem. Ago igitur tibi gratias quas possum maximas, vir pluribus nominibus colendissime, et precor Deum per Jesum Christum, ut tuam multiplicem erga ministros et precones verbi Divini benevolentiam nunquam deleri sinat, sed cum fœnore tibi abundantissime rependat in hoc seculo, et misericordiam etiam exhibeat in illo die gloriosæ apparitionis Jesu Christi. Norim quidem, et gaudeo sane Evangelii causa quod profiteris, quantum tua ubique in pauperes prædicetur munificentia. Est hic cultus sane Christo acceptissimus: quatenus enim id fecistis uni ex istis fratribus meis minimis, mihi fecistis, inquit Servator. Sed tamen si comparationem instituere liceat inter munia tam sua natura prestantia et tam Deo grata, enimvero tum tua pace dixerim, hanc tuam quam ministris imo ecclesiis Christi præstas beneficentiam ex duobus, hoc tempore et ævo nostro, esse magis necessariam. Nam qui fame corporis premuntur, et victum sibi suo labore deficientibus viribus comparare non possunt, suas necessitates aliis exponent et petent cibum unde haberi potest. At, proh dolor! quibus non est fames habendi panis nec sitis aquarum sed audiendi verbum Jehovæ (ut prophetæ verbis utar) ii omnino non sentiunt hanc miseriam suam, nec conantur remedium aliquod contra illam adhibere sed voluntario pereunt in ignorantia et cæcitate sua. Utinam ergo ii, quibus divitiæ et opes hujus mundi abundanter suppetunt, talium misererentur. Utinam illorum opera prædicatione verbi frui possent. Certe qui-

1620. Feb. 24.

1620. Feb. 24. bus facultas est et desiderium præstandi bona opera, hoc, si quod aliud, offert se ut præstantissimum opus. Nam ubi alia bona opera corpori prosunt, hoc promovet æternam animarum salutem. Pergas ergo, ornatissime vir, obsecro te in nomine Christi communis Servatoris et Domini nostri, cujus ego minister indignissmus sum, ministerium verbi ejus, quantum potes opibus, authoritate, quin et gratia, qua plurimum apud regem nostrum serenissimum vales, sustentare. Cogites tecum quæso quam misera sit ecclesiæ nostræ facies iis in locis ubi subtrahuntur proventus annui, et desunt stipendia unde pastores alantur. Proh dolor! ibi exulat scientia, regnat ignorantia, et inde quidem superstitio alicubi, alicubi vero licentiosa et profana morum corruptela, ubique autem religionis syncerœ et veri timoris Dei defectus obtinet. Lachrymabilis fuit ea Israelitarum conditio, quando propter peccata sua dediti et venundati fuere a Domino in manus Ammonitarum, Philisteorum, et aliorum hostium qui rapinis et deprædationibus expilarunt et servitute eos presserunt miserrima. Ecce hic ipsissimus status est ecclesiarum appropriatarum nostrarum ut vulgo vocantur. Traduntur et venundantur in eorum manus qui vellera amant, et oves deglubunt, et animas sibi concreditas omnino non curant, sed lupos pro pastoribus agunt. Utinam, ô utinam rex noster religiosissimus remedium aliquod huic malo afferret. Utinam sicut ministros ecclesiarum Scoticarum preclare nuper in libertatem asseruit et a pauperie vindicavit; sic onus illud gravissimum a cervicibus nostris authoritate regia sua depelleret, quod illis jam diu (heu nimis diu) incubuit. Iniquissimum fuit in Pharaone, quod summam laterum ab Israelitis exigeret, nec tamen stramen illis, ut temporibus anteactis, suppeditaret, sed adigeret palabundos per totam terram Egypti stipulam pro stramine colligere. Perinde quidem nobiscum agunt appropriatores nostri, vel ii potius multis in locis, qui appropriationes istas ab illis tenent. Curam gregis Dominicæ nobis curionibus committunt; at ipsi stramen, quin et frumentum, et totum commeatum antiquitus ministerio destinatum sibi reservant, et cogunt nos vel aliunde conquirere, vel cum miserrima paupertate conflictari. Dabis mihi veniam spero, spectatissime et integerrime vir, si in hac justa quærela mea paulo vehementior fuerim. Ego enim, si quis alius, per longam et miseram experientiam, iniquitatem sensi horum aprorum silvestrium (si fas sit ita loqui) qui vineam Domini vastarunt. Vitam meam mihi acerbam fecerunt, dum libris studiorum fomentis privarunt, et in pauperiem summam conjecerunt. Qua propter non possum non loqui. Et tamen non hæc tam mei causa loquor (cui Deus pro misericordia sua, nonnullos dudum amicos excitavit, qui in spem meliorem animum meum erexerunt.) quam ecclesiarum Christi vicem miserabilem condolens quæ sub malis istis curatoribus degunt. Harum causam dolendam tibi commendat, vir ornatissime, qui te tuosque omnes in precibus suis quotidie Deo commendat, beneficentia tua ad hoc devinctus, 1620. Feb. 24.

ANTONIUS WARTON.

Wokingh[am,] 6 cal. Martii 1619.

Indorsed: Mr Warton to me.

Addressed: To the right worshipfull Master John Packer Esquier Secretarie to the right honorable the Lord Marquis of Buckinghame be this delivered.

No. LXXIX.

FREDERICK KING OF BOHEMIA TO MR. PACKER.

[Autograph Signature.]

Monsieur Packer. Encor que je n'aye jamais douté de vostre bonne affection, en mon endroit, si est ce que j'en ay receu des tesmoignages si signalez par l'advis que m'en a donné le Baron de Dona mon Ambassadeur, que je n'ay voulu laisser passer cette commodité sans vous en remercier, comme je fais, vous asseurant que la Reine ma treschere compagne et moy n' oublierons point l'assistance que vous et autres gens de bien font pour cette bonne cause, esperant que par vostre exemple plusieurs autres seront induits a le suivre, et moy je sera bien aise de rencontrer des occasions pour le recog- April $\frac{8}{18}$.

1620. April 7/17. noistre; priant Dieu de vous tenir en sa garde. De mon chasteau Royal de Prague ce 7/17 Avril 1620.

Vostre affectioné amy
FRIDERIC.

Addressed: A monsieur, Monsieur Packer,
Secretᵉ du Roy de la Gr. Bretagne.

No. LXXX.

THE BISHOP OF CARLISLE TO THE MARQUIS OF BUCKINGHAM.

[Autograph Signature.]

April 27. Right Noble Lord. I have represented unto my self your eminent place of service and most honorable imploymentes in the highest affaires of State, and thereupon now for a long time forborne to trouble your honor with any letters, though I have beene sundrie times importunately occasioned thereunto. But now (if I be not deceived) I have an errand to his Majestie soe contentfull that your honor will (I hope) be well pleased to recommend the same to his Highnes most gratious consideracon. The matter is a late accord wherein my poore endeavours have beene prospered with good successe. The shedding of innocent blood is a crying sinne, and that most enormous cryme hath beene committed well neare at the gate of his Highnes City of Carlile: the murtherers are some of them in prison; a more full declaracon of the matter is articulately expressed in the note of advertisements herewith sent unto your honor, wherein I have spared many pointes of circumstance, whereby the untoward proceedinges of Sir William Hutton might be displayed, by whose ridiculous pollicies soe good services for the honor of his Majestie and good of the Cuntrie might have beene interverted, if I had not beene well acquainted with his former complotments for his owne turne. Yet to avoid disparagement to himself bycause he had done nothing, he fell to another stratagem by dealing with the prisoners to confesse nothing to any other but to himself, whereat I smyled, saying that, as in the Apostles time some preached

Christ upon envye, soe in our time some will doe justice not upon zeale of justice, but upon envie. But all is well, if Christ be preached, and justice be done, both the one way and the other, and now we have a happie opportunitie for the common good of this cuntrie to his Highnes' great honor and glory of God, if the service which hitherto hath soe happily succeeded shall as perfectly be consummated and concluded by his Highnes' deniall of pardon to any of the bloody murtherers upon the suite of any that shall move his Majesty thereunto. My very Honorable good Lord, I first admired you for the excellencies of your person, nature and comportment, but now I tenne times more honor yow for your vertues and religion testified and recommended to the world by the most judicious and most renowned Monarch that ever sweyed the scepter of Great Brytaine. And as Mordochee said of Ester? Who knoweth whether thow hast beene advaunced for such a tyme as this: soe say I of your honor. This time hath need of vertuous and religious courtiers, and who knoweth whether you have beene advanced for such time as this? The purport of this tedious letter is this, that your honor would be pleased to move his Majesty that the foresaid crying sinne may be severely punished for the relief of the cuntrie by a terror to all future malefactors in that kinde. And if your honor shalbe pleased to signify his Highnes' gratious good pleasure herein to the most Honorable Earle of Arundell, I shall have speedy notice thereof from him, and be thereby yet more bound to love and honor you and to pray continually for your happines, and to rest

1620. April 27.

Your Honor's ever to doe you service,

Ro. Carliolen.[1]

Rose Castle, Aprilis 27° 1620.

Indorsed: Bp of Carlile.

Addressed: To the most Honorable George Lord Marquesse of Buckingham his very good Lord. At the Court.

[1] Robert Snowden.

No. LXXXI.

Sir Robert Naunton to James I.

[Autograph Signature.]

1620. May 8. It may please your Majestie. We have treated with the Spanish Ambassador according to your Majesties instructions from poinct to poinct, whom we found as yet somewhat distempered in his health, but more in mind; and that not so much for the importance of what Captn. North can do[1] (though he affirmeth that there ar 3 other ships attending them on theyr way, that set out before the ship and pinnace with which he went himselfe,) as for the unsoundnes of the intelligence which will be descanted upon this occasion to be betwene thes two Crownes, for all the treatie that hath bene so long on foot; specialy when it shall be advertised into those parts that any subject of your Majesties shall dare to thrust himselfe upon such an attempt contrary to your owne expresse commandement and pleasure signified by the Lord Admiral and by a Secretary of State; and that all the rather because he is thought to have presumed herein so much the more upon your Majesties douceur and facilitie, by reason of the under hand abetting and joyning in the adventure of some of your great Lords and Councel,[2] the like whereof he sayd no Grandee in Spain could have passed over without some signal exemplarie demonstracion of theyr King's high displeasure and indignacion in such an ouverture.

When we had tould him how much your Majesty was trobled with it, how you had expostulated it with your Lords that were adventurers, and how theyr Lordships had disavowed the fact and theyr being any wayes privy to it; what meanes and diligence you had

[1] He sailed to the Amazon in spite of the King's prohibition.

[2] The agreement (Harl. MSS. 1583, fol. 81) is signed by the Duke of Lennox, the Earls of Arundel, Dorset, Warwick, and Clanrickard, Lord North, Captain Roger North, Sir George Hay, Sir Edward Cecil, Sir John Danvers, Sir W. Hervey, Sir Thomas Cheeke, and Sir Nathaniel Rich.

directed to be used for his stay, revocacion, disablement and surprize by sea or land, either here or in Ireland, and that your Majesty assumed it to your selfe to take it upon you both in honor and conscience to discharge and free his Lordship in Spaine, and therfore required him to contribute his owne best advise and opinion what course he shold thinke fittest to be taken further for the redress and ratificing of this foule fault, and for the preventing any future inconvenience that might insue upon it in point of State or reputacion to either of your Majesties or unto his owne person, that had lately written as confidently into Spaine to secure them of Captain North as formerly he had done for Sir Walter Raighly; his aunswer was that he most humbly thanked your Majestie for your gratious and princely care of him, but sayd withall that both your Majestie and himself wold lye subject to he knew not what construction in Spaine, upon this third[1] mischance and traverse which had bene objected since the beginning of this treaty for the mariage, of all which three he esteemed this last to be the greatest and the most unseasonable: whereupon his last motion to us was, that we wold earnestly intreat your Majesty, as from him, that you wold be pleased to graunt him audience at Theobalds at your first convenience, where he wold offer up his true conceipt of all the buisines to the uttermost of his understanding and jugement to your Majesties princely consideration and wisdome, with that ingenuite and freedome which shold both content your Majesty, and befitt his owne place and person. 1620. May 8.

Sir Clement Edmonds hath received the patent[2] from my Lord of Warwicke, which I have taken into mine owne keeping. His Lordship, not finding it in his owne house, directed him to the Clerke of the Companie, where it was, and sent one of his owne servants to procure him the speedy delivery of it.

[1] The two former were, I suppose, the expedition of Raleigh and the robbery of an East India ship.

[2] It is not to be found upon the Patent Rolls, being forfeited before it was enrolled.

1620. May 8. So with my daily prayers to God for your Majesties most prosperitie and happines I most humbly take leave.

Your Majesties most obedient and devoted subject and servant,

ROBERT NAUNTON.

Whitehall 8 May 1620.

Addressed: To the King's most excellent Majestie.

No. LXXXII.

DR. JOHN BOWLE TO THE MARQUIS OF BUCKINGHAM.

[Holograph.]

May 18. Ryht Honorable, my humble duty præmised. I could not by any level taken frome my poore indeavors have measured the favor which your Honor graced mee withall in your Lordship's late letters; and scince itt pleaseth your Honor to ranke mee in the number of your orators whome you please to respect, I shall preserve that testimony to survive my buriall that my labors were accepted of the most honorable and judicious of the Court. My good Lord, the content and incouragement I received I cannot express, but scince nowe itt hath pleased God to take the Bishop of Norwich to his mercy, these lines do humbly intreat your Honor to lodge mee in that number whome your Honor will advaunce by this alteration. The Deanery of Westminster, wher I went to schoole, or some such place, is the uttmost of my desire,[1] wher I myght serve my God, and dayly praye for his Majesty and your Honor.

Your Honor's devoted,

by what man can bee obliged,

JOHN BOWLE.

Bradfeild, May 18.

Addressed: To the most Honorable the Lord Marques Buckingham, Lord High Admirall of England.

---

[1] Williams was made Dean of Westminster, and Bowle became Dean of Salisbury.

LXXXIII.

Frederick, King of Bohemia, to Mr. Packer.

[Autograph Signature.]

Monsieur. Outre les bons offices que je sçay que vous avez rendus pour le bien de mes affaires, vous m'avez de plus voulu tesmoigner de vostre main la bonne affection que portez à l'advancement d'icelles. Je vous en remercie presentement, attendant les occasions qui me donneront le moyen de vous faire sentir les effects de ma bonne volonté envers vous et les vostres; et vous prie cependant d'en prendre asseurance et de mon amitié, et me vouloir continuer voz bons offices en ce qui pourra concerner l'advancement de mes affaires par de la, ainsy que je me le promets. Sur ce je prie Dieu qu'il vous ait en sa sainte protection. 1620. July 6/16.

Vostre affectioné amy,

Frideric.

De Pragne le 6/16 Juillet A° 1620.

Indorsed: K. of Bohemia to me. 2.

Addressed: A monsieur, Monsieur Packer, Secretaire de Sa Ma^te de la Grande Bretagne.

No. LXXXIV.

Sir Robert Naunton to the Marquis of Buckingham.

[Autograph Signature.]

It may please your Lordship. Yesterday the Lords set into the buisinesses recommended by his Majestie. I began first with that of the registring the shippes, etc., which was digested into heades, and so sent to the Commissioners for the Navie to perfit up and retorne to the Lords, that an Act of Counsel may be passed upon it according to his Majesties directions at Theobalds. July 21

Then we entred into consideracion of Sir Thomas Dutton's suite for the inland forts in Ireland. In that Counsel's lettres and certificate we find they would not undertake to give us any advice for the fee ferming of them, though that were the maine point wherein

1620. July 21. we required their direct advise; neither do they give us any particuler survey of the lands lyeing to every fort, but leave them so *in confuso*, as the Lords found no reason to undertake to determine of that which is yet so unknowen unto them. The lettre inclosed will give his Majestie a general accompt. The particulers are committed to Secretary Calvert to relate by word of mouth at his coming.

The Tobacco fermers and the Virginian and Bermudas Companies were heard after, and order given to Mr. Solicitor to prepare the patent, and a commission to accord theyr articles, and a license for those Companies to import a porcion of tobacco, notwithstanding the last proclamation for sole importacion to the fermors.

After thes Sir Francis Blundel was heard touching the plantacion of Letrim and the lettres from Ireland read. And theyr Lordshipps, upon consideracion of the many imperfections and defectes and want of execution in the 3 former plantacions of Ulster, Wexford, and Longford, fell all upon a joinct resolucion to move his Majestie that those 3 former plantacions might be exactly surveyed and reviewed, and reformed, before they should setle that of Letrim, for persiting wherof the season of the yeare would be now overpast, before they could well set into the worke.

My Lord Chancellor, my Lord of Arundel, and my selfe, have corrected the Proclamacion for tenant rights, and sent it away to be ingrossed.

The Marchant Adventurors were heard this morning touching their proposicion of removing their staple, but because the Secretary of Middleburgh was absent (who we ar tould that he doth attend there at the Court), and the Marchants themselves desired the conclusion of that busines might be respited for a time, the Lords could not proceed any further in it as yet.

The complaint of the Counsel of Scotland of the want of silver was likewise appointed to have been heard this day. But because Mr. James Douglas, who was to have attended that buisines, is gone away with the Court, we sent to Sir William Alexander to have informed us what he could thereof, but he retorned us aunswer that he was utterly unacquainted with that complaint, and could say nothing at all of it, so as we could not settle any jugement what to do in that matter till we should receive more particuler informacions. 1620. July 21.

Maxwell[1] and Alured[2] are to be before the Lords this afternoone, and Mr. Solicitor hath theyr pamphlets to charge them with theyr several misdemeanors; whereupon we expect theyr recognicion[3] to make a way for the Ambassador's mediacion for them.

Tomorrow morning wee have appointed for Powles,[4] and the afternoone to dispatch the new bargaine of the Coales, if we can not end it this afternoone without Sir Lionel Cranfeld, who is not yet retorned from Court. Sir Nowell Caron[5] is to pay this day into the Exchequer £7,105 od money, and had paid in £5,000 more for de la Barre, besides the £1,600 which hath been seised into the Exchequer of his goodes all ready had he not been sequestred; for whom now my Lord Digby is to accompt, and Sir Nowell Caron to be discharged of de la Barr's part of the £60,000. Moses Tryon's pardon is past the Signet by me, but I must pray your Lordship that I may be discharged of the £5,000, which he hath given assurance to pay it unto others, it being a part of the £60,000 contracted for betwene Sir Nowell Caron and me. I must adde one worde more about the Baronetship of Sir Thomas Bishop, for whom Mr. Read tould me his Majestie shold have £6,000,[6] and I from him informed his Majestie as much. But now Mr. Read tells me the King must have but £500, and that £100 must go another way. And of that £500 he saith further, that he hath a lettre of

[1] On the 27th of November James Maxwell made his submission to the Council for publishing an opinion that the kingdom of Bohemia was not elective, and that the deposition of Ferdinand and the election of Frederick were unlawful. S.P. Dom. cxvii. 89.

[2] Author of a letter against the Spanish marriage.

[3] See Bacon to Buckingham, July 23, 1620, *Works*, ed. Montagu, xiii. 22.

[4] For the repair of St. Paul's.

[5] On behalf of Dutch merchants fined for exporting gold.

[6] So in MS. apparently by mistake for £600.

1620. July 21. Attorny to pay £200 to a Creditor of Mr. Gordon's in London, whereas his Majesties intencion was that this mony shold be all made over to Mr. Gordon to pay a debt of his Majesties in Polone which comes to £500, and had ordered that the Commissioners of the Thresory should have paid him £700 more (besydes the £300 he had with him) for the discharge of that debt and the interest of it; which I made accompt it should have been all saved by this Baronet, and so I tould his Majestie. Upon this new reckoning I have stayd the sealing of the bylls for that Baronetship, till I may know his Majesties pleasure whither the money shall be paid into the Excheqner for the true use it is intended for, or not; which I have held my selfe tyed in ductie and honestie to insist upon for mine owne due discharge of the trust reposed in me.

So craving pardon for my so long lettres, I humbly take leave, and will persevere

Your Lordship's most devoted,

and bounden to serve you truely,

ROBERT NAUNTON.

Whitehall, 21° July 1620.

Addressed: To the Right Honorable my singular good Lord my Lord Marquis Buckingham Lord Highe Admiral of England &c. at the Court.

No. LXXXV.

J. H. MARYE TO MARQUIS OF BUCKINGHAM.

[Autograph Signature.]

Aug. 5. Right honorable. The hope I have reposed in your Lordship's favour hath emboldened me to offer my service to your Lordship, whose resplendent virtues have like a cleare sonne given light to my sowle, enflamed my desires, and stirred me up to seeke so great a happiness; wherupon I sollicited Monsier LeGrand, Master of the

French King's Horss, who hath written to your Lordship in my favour, as also Madame the Marquis of Verneil to my L. the Duke of Lenox, to move your Lordship in my behalfe. I also composed a panagirick of the immortality of glorie, one for his Majestie, an other for the Prince, and the third for your Lordship. Moreover I have remayned fiveteene monthes in England, passed over once into France since, and spent in the meane while above three hundred pownds to no other end but to attayne the happiness to be retayned in your Lordship's service, the which I most humbly desire may be without putting your Honor to any charge. 1620. Aug. 5.

Your Lordship's most humble Servant,

J. H. MARYE.

This 5 of August 1620.

Indorsed: Marie Fr. 100cr[owns].

Addressed: To the right Honorable his very good Lord the Lord Marquis of Buckingham.

No. LXXXVI.

SIR OLIVER ST. JOHN TO THE MARQUIS OF BUCKINGHAM.

Most honourable. The many crosse accidents happening unto me in the place I hould make me fly unto your Lordship's favour as the surest anchour of my fortunes. There is a yong Man lately sworne a Counsellor amongst us, Sir Roger Jones, sonne of the late Chauncellor, who, with much insolency, in the presence of a greate nomber of the Noblemen, Bishops, and others at the Councell board, publiquely interrupted and reprehended mee, contrary to his dutie to his Majestie and the place he held. The manner whereof I have in this enclosed wryting laid downe. I should rather have chosen to have passed it by if I might have found any disposition in him to acknowledge his error, then to have troubled his Majestie and your Lordship with yt. But that I find him animated to repaire into England, as I suppose to countenance himselfe against mee. And therefore I have presumed humbly to make my greife Aug. 17.

1620. Aug. 17. knowen to his Majestie, and also to beseech your Lordship to second yt, and to honour me so much as to preserve me from so publique an affront. I have found of late a strong combination against mee even among the members of this Councell, such as seeke all occasions, by themselves, and their wrytinges, to blemishe mee in the good opinion of his Majestie, your Lordship, and the greate personages of that State, among whom this yong man is contented to beare a part. But if I may be so much bound to his Majestie and your Lordship that this man Sir Roger Jones may find that his Majestie is displeased with his undutifull behaviour, and be sente backe againe with admonition to carry himselfe better hereafter, I shall receave much contentment by yt, his Majestie wilbe better served, and others by his example be made to conforme themselves with more obedience and respect then hitherunto some of them have done. Otherwise I shalbe altogether disabled and discouraged to doe his Majestie service, and I shall rather wishe to retyre my selfe to a private lyfe, and spend my tyme in prayers for his Majestie and my good friends, then to see my selfe contemned and wronged by those that ought to be commaunded by me, his Majesties service prejudiced by mine unworthinesse and your Lordship dishonoured, who have hitherto so nobly valued and supported me. I most humbly pray your Lordship to afford me in this particular your best favor, who have faithfully honoured and served you, as a businesse in the consequence thereof so neerly concerning mee. And so with prayers to God for your Lordship's happie preservation I remaine

Your Lordship's devoted servaunt,

OL: ST. JOHN.

Dublin, 17 August 1620.

Indorsed: L. Dep. to my Lord. Sr Rog. Jones.

Addressed: To the right honourable my speciall good Lord the Lord Marquesse of Buckingham, Lord High Admirall of England. To be kept till called for.

No. LXXXVII.

Sir Lionel Cranfield to the Marquis of Buckingham.

[Holograph.]

Right Honorable my verry good Lord. I received yesterdaye this inclosed from Sir Nicholas Fortescue, one of my fellow Commissioners of the Navye. He desires, in the name of the rest of the Commissioners, my direction, which I dare not give, nor any opynion to your Lordship, but have thowght fitt to send the papers themselves, humbly referring the consideration of them to your wisdom, and attend your pleasure. 1620. Aug. 22.

For the buissines of the coales I do assure my self your Lordship hath hard what hath past at lardg and verry particulerly by Mr. Secretary Naunton and Mr. Pye. Eight thowsand pounds of the fyne is paid to Mr. Pye to clere my Lady Bedford, and £3000 to Sir Robert Maunsfeild by waye of imprest for the Kinges service. The remaynder of the mony remaynes in the Contractors hand to be disposed for his Majesties service upon the passing of their grant, which the King will have need of at his returne; for all the rest of his Highnes' revenue untill our Lady Daye next is anticipated.

In this byssines I have don your Lordship the best service I coulde, which I rather referr to the report of others then mention my selfe. And as in this, so in all other thinges that shall concerne your Lordship either in saffety, honnor, or proffitt, I shalbe as ready, as carefull, and as faithfull as any servant you keepe, wherof desiring your Lordship to bee assured, I humbly tack leave and will ever rest

Your Lordship's faithfullest servant,

Lionell Cranfeilde.

Chelsey, the 22th August 1620.

Indorsed: Sir L. Cranfield to my L. 22 Aug. Coales.

Addressed: To the Right Honorable my singuler good Lord the Lord Marques Buckingham Lord High Admirall of England, etc. At Courte.

No. LXXXVIII.

Sir Dudley Carleton to Marquis of Buckingham.

1620. Sept. 1. My most honorable Lord. By my wife's report since she went into England I have receaved the comfort that your Lordship is pleased to give eare to her sute for the amendment of my poore condition, whereof I take the boldnes to represent the true estate to your Lordship, to the end you may not be unfurnished of argument to his Majesty when you shall finde your owne best time to move him in my favour. It draweth now uppon five yeares since I came into this service, after having ended two Ambassages of as long continuance in Italy, one ordinarie with the state of Venice, an other extcrordinarie with the Duke of Savoy. This State I fownd governed by a contrarie faction both to God's service and his Majesties, which was supp[orted] by two extraordinarie Ambassag[es] of France, besides particular gentlemen sent from time to time, at no small cost of that crowne, for the same purpose, and a Resident Ambassador, who yet here remaines. These, without any one pennie of extraordinarie charge to his Majestie, I have incountered from time to time with such happie successe that the true religion is onely here publiquely professed, all novelties suppressed, and no Prince or State looked uppon with an eye of goode affection from hence in comparison of his Majesty and his kingdomes. This required as extcrordinarie diligences, so more then ordinarie expences, by relieving many poore but sufficient and serviceable men kept under in want and povertie by those who had all power in the state, and giving entertainment to the better sort, which, according to the fashion of this place, is onely tasted at table. My predecessor, Sir Ralph Winwood, having no such extcrordinarie occasion of expence, but many of benefit, which have not occurred in my time, had notwithstanding, being then but Agent, a liberal *Ayuda de Costa* owt of the Exchequer, and his meanes augmented towards the end of his time after he was Ambassador, besides the advancement he arrived unto at last for recompence of his service. All of my condition who have bin employed in my time, and some who went into service since me, have had both rewards and advancements ether in possession or revertion, besides that theyr allowance is greater in places lesse chargeable, mine remaining still at the auntient institution to which it was reduced by Sir Raph Winwood, when he came to be Secretarie, which withall hath bin ever so ill payed that I have bin continually exposed to the burden of interests and exchanges, and what shifts I have bin putt unto to supplie my wants to the end his Majesties service might not suffer it is not fitt for me to relate, though they have bin all honest and to no man's hurt but my owne, who therby am growne deeply indebted both here on this side the seas and in England, a heavie burden to an ingenious minde, which taking contentment in my publi[que] charge (as I must confesse I doe [that] all hath sorted so happily to his Majesties service) I may the better pleade in that regard for some favorable consideracion of my privat fortune, which I will humbly beseech your Lordship to continue to take into your care and myself into your favour, as one that will ever remaine

1620. Sept. 1.

Your Lordship's most humble
and most thanckfull servant,
DUDLEY CARLETON.

Hagh, this first of Sept. 1620.

Indorsed: Sr D. Carleton to my Lord.
Reasons for his sute.

Addressed: To my most honorable Lord the Lord Marquis of Buckingham Lord High Admiral of England. Court.

No. LXXXIX.

Elizabeth Queen of Bohemia to Marquis of Buckingham.

[Holograph.]

1620. Sept. 15/25. My Lord. I dout not but you have alreadie heard how Spinola hath taken three townes of the King's in the Lower Palatinat; two of them are my jointur: he will, if he can, take all that countree. This makes me write to you at this time (because I am most confident of your affection) that you will move his Majestie now to shew himself a loving father to us, and not suffer his children's inheritance to be taken away. You see how little they regard his Ambassadours and what they say. I ernestlie intreat you to use your best meanes with the King that he would now assist us, for he hath ever professed that he would not suffer the Palatinat to be taken from us. I doe most confidentlie relie uppon your affection to me, and you can shew it in nothing more then in this matter, which I ernestlie recommend to you, and rest ever

Your most affectionat frend,

Elizabeth.

I pray tell the King that the enemie will more regard his blowes then his wordes, and commend my love to your worthy ladie.

Prague, this 15/25 of September.

Addressed: To the Marquis of Buckingham.

XC.

The Marquis of Buckingham to the Earl of Suffolk.

[Copy.]

Sept. 21. My noble Lord. His Majestie was pleased upon mine undertaking for your Lordship, according to your promise to mee, that you would have the money readie to paie whensoever it should please his Majestie to call for it, to bestowe it upon my Lord Haddington; who being now come over, and having present occasion to use it, his Majestie hath commanded mee to write to your Lordship to deliver him, or to whomsoever he shall appoint to receave it, that [summ]e[1] of five thousand pounds which is the remaynder of the seaven thousand your Lordship was to paie,[2] and so I rest 1620. Sept. 21.

Your Lordship's.

21 September 1620.

Indorsed: Coppie to E. of Suffolk. L. Haddington.

No. XCI.

Sir Robert Naunton to the Marquis of Buckingham.

[Holograph.]

It may please your Lordship. In your Lordship's absence from Court, I wrote to Secretary Calvert to move his Majestie for some answer to the Venetian Ambassador's last lettres to your Lordship, for which he was a little importunate with me, as doubting that his Superiors wold hold him to be in small esteeme here if he could procure no aunswer at all to those lettres, which mocion I am bould to renew to your Lordship, having heard of your retorne to the Court, the rather because I am partly doubtfull that my former to Secretary Calvert may be retorned me unopened, since I heare he was upon coming hither at the very time when mine were to come thither. Thes inclosed to his Majestie contein the Commissioners of the Threa[su]rie theyr general aunswer to his Majesties commandement for payement of the forein pensions. Theyr Lordships had given direction to write a particular remonstrance of all the pressing payements lyeng upon them for his Majesties own im- Oct. 26.

[1] The paper is torn here.

[2] As the unremitted part of his Star Chamber fine.

1620. Oct. 26. mediate services at home, and of the arreares they ar in for them, which was signed by Mr. Chancellor, but the rest of the Commissioners thought it wold be too sad a spectacle to send unto his Majestie, and have held it more aggreable with theyr dueties to represent thos particulars unto his Majestie by word of mouth at theyr next wayting upon him.

So with my daily prayers for his Majesties and your Lordship's most happines I humbly take leave.

Your Lordship's most devoted
and obliged to serve you truely,

ROBERT NAUNTON.

Whitehall, 26° Octobris 1620.

No. XCII.

THE EARL OF HERTFORD TO JAMES I.

[Holograph.]

Nov. 2. Most religious King and peerlesse Prince. May it pleaze your excellent Majesty it is now above 7 yeares past sinse it pleazed your Highnesse to give me leave to wryte to your Majestie. But before I wryte I must by these my tedious lynes crave your pardon for my not attending your Majesties person according to my dewty and place at Salisbury.

Your Majesty knoweth men's purposes are disposed of by God by whom it pleazed Him through a fawll from my nag to be absent, and thearupon most humbly to excuse my self by my poore nephew Beauchamp, your Majestes most humble servant.

Not long after yt pleazed your Majesty out of your gratious care of me to send my Cousin Rytch [1] Captayn of your guard and Sir George Goring to coumfort me, which they did easely perceave and I hope delivered to your Majesty. I have sent my keaper of my

[1] Sir Henry Rich, afterwards Earl of Holland.

red deare parke to your Majesty, whose service if it pleaze your Majesty I beseach you keape, having none of myne but such as I bring up for your H[ighness'] service. I hope your Majesty's worthy Secretary Sir George Calvert hath acquainted your Majesty with my arredinesse to serve your Majesties most vertuous young daughter the Queen of Bohemia, whom I hope (as old as I am) to see an Empresse, and your Majesties self to be the overthrow of the Antichristian Pope and whosoever favor him against your Majesty, whom God preserve with all your most noble issue to the comfort of all good Christians. From my poore howse at Letley this Thursday the 2d of November 1620. 1620. Nov. 2.

Your Majestyes most humble subject
and faythfull servant
HERTFORD.

Indorsed: E. of Hertford to his M[ty].

Addressed: To my most gratious Souverain the Kinges most excellent Majesty.

No. XCIII.

ADOLPH STEINGEN TO THE MARQUIS OF BUCKINGHAM.

[Autograph Signature.]

Monseigneur. C'estoit le bonheur que Dieu me donna, lorsque j'eu l'honneur à Tibbolts d'estre congedié très gracieusement et honnoré de la Chevallerie par sa Majesté, que par vostre presence cet acte fust rendu tant plus illustre, ayant par mesme occasion trouvé sujet de vous presenter la bonne affection de Monseigneur l'Electeur[1] envers vostre personne, et quand et quand recommander l'equité de ses demandes faictes par moy à Sa Majesté, à quoy vous vous avez, Monseigneur, offert quasi d'aussy grande promptitude et sincerité de cœur, comme Sa Majesté avoit desja faict auparavant, Nov. 18.

[1] The Elector of Brandenburg.

1620. Nov. 18. de sorte que ne doubte nullement que Son Altesse Electorale en resentira à son temps des bons effects, et vous en aura eternelle obligacion et digne recognoissance, et de mon costé suis obligé d'en faire honnorable rapport. Il ne reste à present autre que vous supplier bien humblement qu'il vous plaise obliger tant plus et plus mon Maistre et moy, et commander que les joinctes soyent tres humblement presentées à Sa Majesté pour estre authorisées par sa subscription: et veu qu'il a pleu à Sa Majesté m'avoir (en regard de cette Ambassade) honnoré d'un present de huict cent onces en vaisselles d'argent doré, lequel je suis en œuvre de convertir en une chaine d'or avec le pourtraict de Sa Majesté enrichy de pierreries pour une perpetuelle memoire et obligation que moy et ma posterité aura à Sa Majesté en recognoissance de sa liberalité Royalle et ensemble de l'honneur de la Chevallerie receu de ses graces. Mais pour l'accomplissement du dit pourtraict me manquant encores quelque pierrerie pretieuse, j'ay prins la hardiesse, Monseigneur, de vous en faire cette ouverture, me soubmettant du tout à vostre bon plaisir, si me voulez faire l'honneur de remantevoir à Sa Majesté que l'An 1609 estant en Ambassade aupres d'icelle, et ayant pour lors faict la publicque congratulation à Sa Majesté en la présence de la Reine et des Enfants Royaulx de la reception de la Couronne de la Grande Bretagne, dont ma patente de la Chevalerie fait aussy mention, que pour lors ne sçay par quelle faute ou soudain depart nul present fut donné, ains promis, sans toutefois que jamais il me fust livré, si à cett heure plaisoit à Sa Majesté en dispenser graticusement pour l'employer à tant plus grand enrichissement dudit pourtraict Royal, vous asseurant y n'avoir nul autre interest particulier, ains seulement que ce n'est qu'un vertueux desir de gloire decoulante de la fontaine des graces et honneurs d'un si grand et incomparable Roy. Et pourtant vous supplie, Monseigneur, y contribuer l'entremise de vostre bon credit, quoy faisant obligerez infiniment un de vos plus humbles serviteurs, qui vous souhaite de tout son cœur l'establissement de vos honnorables et tres illustres charges et Estats, auxquels le bon Dieu vous a colloqué pour servir à l'advancement de la gloire de son sainct nom, du bien publicq, et au contentement de Sa Majesté; me consecrant à tout jamais, comme, 1620. Nov. 28.

Monseigneur,

Vostre très humble serviteur

ADOLPH STEINGEN.

De Londres, ce 18 de Novembre 1620.

Addressed: À Monseigneur, Monseigneur le Marquis de Bucquingham Grand Admiral d'Angleterre. En Court.

Indorsed: Brandeb[urg] Ambr to my Lord.

No. XCIV.

SIR GEORGE CALVERT TO THE MARQUIS OF BUCKINGHAM.

[Holograph.]

May it please your Lordshipp. The only occasion that I have now to trouble yow is to excuse my self for not attending on his Majesty all this while. Besides diverse other busynesses of Councell heere (at which perhaps I might have beene spared well enough) I have another in hand, which is the discovery of that seditious book called *Vox populi*, whereof I have a hope to fynd out the author,[1] and am now busy about it, having upon search of a suspitious person fownd out another pamphlett in his chamber of the like nature intituled Sir Walter Raleighes ghost, or a conference betweene Gondomar the Frier Confessor and Father Baldwin the Jesuite at Elye howse in Holborne. I assure your Lordshipp it is as seditious a booke as the other, yf not much worse, but not yet printed. The author is a poore Captaine about London one Gainsford, whom I have committed to prison, and shall upon this see yf I can worke out the other, yf his Majesty thinke fitt that I stay heere for that purpose, and shall send his Majesty the booke it self after I have taken one or two examinations. In the meane tyme I Nov. 28.

[1] Thomas Scot.

1620. Nov. 18. humbly beseech your Lordshipp I may understand his Majesties pleasure from Mr. Packer, either for my stay here or attendance there, and I shall willingly obey what I shalbe directed, and am ever

Your Lordshipp's with all devotion
faithfully to serve yow,
GEO. CALVERT.

St. Martin's Lane, 28 November, 1620.

Because his Majesty perhaps will be desirous to see this other booke, I have upon better consideration thought it my duty to send it now presently unto his Majesty, which I beseech your Lordshipp, when his Majesty hath done with it, may be returned unto me againe.

No. XCV.

SIR GEORGE CALVERT TO THE MARQUIS OF BUCKINGHAM.

[Holograph.]

Dec. 4. May it please your Lordshipp. I did yesterday receive your letter, by which I understand his Majesties pleasure for my attendance, which I will dutifully obey, and intend to be at Newmarket (God willing) some tyme this weeke. In the meane tyme, yf your Lordshipp have not heard it from any other hand already, it may please yow to understand from me, that in sequence to these libellous pamphletts and pasquills that are every where spread abroad and, as they say, factious sermons preached in many pulpitts about London more then heretofore, there is now at last an alarme given to the Spanish Embassador[1] from diverse hands of an assault upon his person and family, which was sayd to have bene plotted for execution yesterday in the morning being Advent Sunday (for so it was noted in a letter first sent to Sir Lewys Lewkenor by an unknowne

[1] The excitement against Gondomar was a result of the news of the battle of Prague.

person) and afterwards seconded by a discovery made to the Embassador himself by one who professed himself to be a Protestant, and was moved to be of the conspiracy. Hereupon by order from my Lord Chancellor and Mr. Secretary Naunton there was a strong watch appointed in Holborne neare unto the Embassador's howse early on Sonday morning and so contynued untill 12 at noone, and, his feare contynuing still, the like watch was sett all this last night, the Embassador and his whole family being up and armed the whole night both Saturday night and the last. I know not for my part what to think of it, it may be but a devise of purpose to putt the Spanish Embassador into a deffence of his owne safety, which may serve well enough to some ends, as your Lordshipp can well judge, and the rather I thinke it probable enough, because I heare the Embassador of Savoye hath done his best to encrease the other's feares by his earnest advises and warnings to looke to himself. But if it should prove earnest indeede (as God forbidd) his Majesty is so much interested in it, as there cannot be too much caution to prevent the worst. I humbly leave it to his Majesty's great wisedome to direct such order in it by my Lord Digby as he shall please, my self being likely enough to be come from hence before any order can come to me. In the meane tyme my Lordes that are heere acquainted with it wilbe as carefull as they can. And so humbly kissing your Lordshipp's hands, I rest

1620. Dec. 4.

Your Lordshipp's faithfully
and affectionately to serve yow,
GEO. CALVERT.

St. Martin's Lane, 4 December, 1620.

No. XCVI.

——— TO THE MARQUIS OF BUCKINGHAM.

My Lord. I humblie beseeche your Lordship to vouchsafe to reade this paper and to censure yt, though it bee to the fyer. Dec. ?

1620. Dec.? Theire lye at this tyme encumbrances upon my estate to the vallue of eight or nine thowsand poundes; for the redeeming of my selfe from these, I have no other remedie within my power but the sale of lande, which yf I now make, by reason that the market is so lowe and the skarcitie of money so great, I shall loose much in the vallue and abate much of my present meanes.

I have (besydes my Essex landes) in Hampshire and Barkshire three Mannors that are now woorthe sixteene thowsand poundes and wilbee woorthe twentie and more; they are antient land of inheritance, free from any question of tytle, entayle, or anie encumbrance whatsoever.

I humblie desyer leave (having no children, nor kindred of my name living,) to assuer by good conveyance these three mannors upon your Lordship and your heires yf I have no heires males, and that your Lordship would bee pleased to procure the making of an English Baron, and bestowe it upon mee yf I can finde a gentleman in birthe quallitie and relligion fitt for yt, and this allso upon condition that yf I ever have heires males, these landes bee made lyable to the repayment of so much.

This I knowe beeing effected in your Lordship's name, will neither beguett wonder nor envye, and maye easilie by your Lordship's directions bee privatelie and securelie desposed of to this use.

If I knewe anie other suit, so free from question, prejudice or uncertaintie as this, I would not present this, and in this let mee have the priviledg of a servant to bee denyed without scruple and commanded without limitation, and let your Lordship's beliefe conclude that my desyers ende where your deslyke beginns, so as this paper beeing burnt they vannish with the smoake of it, for theire is no creature privie to this devyce which is but a dreame of mine yf your Lordship give yt no beeing. If your Lordship's noble favour to mee and the conveniencie of these tymes (wherein theire is a reporte of the making of some Barons before the Parliament) maye encourage your Lordship to this noble rescue, I shall acknowledge the support of my fortunes from your Lordship, and my acknowledg-ment shalbee as full as my fortunes can fill up. Your Lordship's commanding of John Waterhowse to sende for mee shalbee sufficient intelligence of yt to mee; yf hee sende mee no such message, all thoughts of this shall dye with mee and your Lordship's trouble conclude before yt beguinns. 1620. Dec.?

But, good my Lord, pardon this presumtion, which ariseth more out of the affection and desyer that I have that these landes of mine and more (yf I have no heires males) should fall entyer to your Lordship's desposall then out of the necessitous occasions of my fortunes which I cann remedie by the sale of parte of them (though with some pregiudice), and reserve the remaynder to serve your Lordship withall, for theire is no man whose heart is larger in devotion, or lyfe and fortunes more entyerlie consecrated to your Lordship's service, then mine is and ever shalbee.

No. XCVII.

The Marquis of Buckingham to Elizabeth, Titular Queen of Bohemia.

[Copy.]

Madame. I should be most unworthy of those infinite favors which I have received from the King my Master, yf I should be wanting in any duty or respect towards your Majestie his only daughter, and therfore as I have hitherto endeavored to advance all things that I thought might tend unto your Majestie's service, so I conceave I cannot now give you a greater testimony of my fidelity, then by humbly perswading you to be a meanes to induce the King your husband wholly to rely upon his Majestie's councell and advice which he hath now sent by my brother Sir Edward Villiers as his full resolution, having formerly debated and consulted it in the presence of the Prince, my Lord Duke of Lenox, Marques Hamilton, the Lord Chamberleyn, the Lord of Arundell, the Lord of Kelly, Viscount Doncaster, the Lord Digbye, the two Secretaryes, Dec.?

1620. Dec.? the Chancellor of the Exchequer, and my self, who all with one joynt consent approved what his Majestie now adviseth, as most honorable and most safe for him to councell, and for the King your Husband to followe. Thus much I presume to make knowne unto your Majestie, referring other particulars to the bearer, who thinketh himselfe happye in this occasion, as I shall do in having many whereby I may be imployed in your Majestie's service. So wishing your Majesty all increase of happyness and content, I remayne——

No. XCVIII.

The Marquis of Buckingham to Lord Chancellor Lord Verulam.

[Draft.]

1620? My honorable Lord. Though I had resolved not to write to your Lordship in anie matter betweene partie and partie, yet at the earnest request of my noble friend the Lord Norreis, to whome I account myselfe much beholden, I could not but recommend unto your Lordship's favor a speciall friend of his, Sir Thomas Monck, who hath a suitt before your Lordship in the chancerie with Sir Robert Bassett, which upon the reporte made unto me thereof seemeth so reasonable that I doubt not but the cause it selfe will move your Lordship to favor him, yf upon the hearing thereof it shall appeare the same unto your Lordship as at the first sight it doth unto mee. I therefore desire your Lordship to shew in this particular what favor you lawfully may for my sake, who will account it as donne unto my selfe. And will ever rest

Your Lordship's——

Indorsed: M. to L. Chancellor. Monck at L. Norreis sute.

No. XCIX.

THE MARQUIS OF BUCKINGHAM TO LORD CHANCELLOR LORD VERULAM.[1]

[Copy.]

My honorable Lord. I know that to a man of so much noblenes nothing will be so acceptable as sinceritie and plainess. And therefore before I move his Majestie in your sute I will take the libertie of a frend to deliver unto you myne opinion of it. And to begin with that which is within the compasse of myne own knowledg, the example you alleage of Sir William Candish[2] is no more but the prevention of that honour which no man knoweth how soone it may by his own right fall upon him,[3] and only stretched a little higher at the sute of my Lord Chamberlayne and my Lord of Arundell. That to my Lord of Doncaster was at his Majesties going into Scotland and upon a consideration whereby he was no gayner, being for buying of hangings to furnish the houses. If Secretarie Winwood obtayned a Baron, it was, as I can assure your Lordship, the only gift his Majesty gave him in reward of long service, and in a tyme when it was not a matter of such difficultie to gett as now it is, when to my knowledg his Majesty cannot endure to heare of making any for his own benefitt, notwithstanding the 1620. Dec. ?

[1] The suit would hardly have been made after Bacon's own advancement in the peerage, and, even if it had, Buckingham would probably have referred to his having received sufficient favour already. If this is the case, the date of the letter is fixed between November 3, 1620, and January 27, 1621, the dates of the creation of Viscount Mansfield and of Bacon's own creation as Viscount St. Alban's.

[2] Sir W. Cavendish, nephew of the first Earl of Devonshire, created Lord Ogle and Viscount Mansfield, Nov. 3, 1620.

[3] His mother, Catherine, widow of Sir Charles Cavendish, was the younger of two sisters, daughters and co-heirs of Lord Ogle. The barony was in abeyance, but the elder sister Joan, though married to Edward Talbot, was without children. At her death, Lady Cavendish was declared Baroness Ogle by letters patent.

1620. Dec. ? great necessities wherein he is. What the custome hath been for rewarding Chancellors after the Parlament I never heard, but it seemes by your letter, the last claymed it not. Whatsoever the use hath been after the end of the Parlament I assure my self your Lordship will hold it very unseasonable to be done before, and likely to doe more hurt then good to his Majesty's service (whereof his Majesty hath found no man more carefull then your Lordship) if, while he is asking with one hand, he should be giving with the other. Having thus freely delivered to your Lordship my opinion, I now leave it to your self whither I shall move his Majesty in your sute or no, wherein I will be ready so to carry myself as I shall be further directed by your Lordship, and as it becometh

Your Lordship's faithfull frend and servant

G. BUCKINGHAM.

Indorsed: Coppie to my L. Chanc. from my Lord. His sute.

No. C.

SIR GEORGE CALVERT TO THE MARQUIS OF BUCKINGHAM.

[Holograph.]

1621. Feb. 7. May it please your Lordshipp. I acquainted his Majesty a little before his departure from hence with a dispatch sent to Mr. Secretary Naunton from Sir Isaac Wake, and brought by this bearer Mr. Jacob, who his Majesty was pleased should attend him this afternoone at Theobaldes, having somewhat to say unto his Majesty for his further information touching the matters contayned in the pacquett.

There are many baites offered his Majesty by the Duke of Savoye; how farre it is fitt for him to accept of them, his great wisedome can best judge.

I humbly beseech your Lordshipp to give me leave by this to convey a letter unto his Majesty to be signed unto the East India

Company, for which he gave order, and that Mr. Packer may send it me againe because it is for the service of his Majesty and the kingdome, and requires haste. 1621. Feb. 7.

Wee are yet busy in Parlement about elections and returne of our Members. Sir Henry Brittaine and Sir John Holles are cast out this morning as unduly returned, and Sir Thomas Beaumont's election for Leicestershire will not hold. Sir Thomas Wentworth's for Yorkshire is also questioned. These are the greatest busynesses wee yet have had.

I shall give his Majesty an accompt of something more materiall by the next, whose health and happynesse I beseech God long to contynue, and so kissing your Lordshipp's hands I rest

Your Lordshipp's humbly and
faithfully to serve you,
GEO. CALVERT.

Whitehall, 7 February, 1620.

No. CI.

SEC. GEORGE CALVERT TO THE MARQUIS OF BUCKINGHAM.

[Holograph.]

May it please your Lordshipp. I presume to trouble yow with this letter enclosed from his Majesty to Sir Dudley Carleton, because I know not whether his Majesty would have any else acquainted with it. He gave me order for it yesterday, and it is for the stay of his daughter the Queen of Bohemia from comming into England. Your Lordshipp may please to procure his Majesty to signe it, and to returne it me inclosed in some other cover by this bearer. Having nothing else now to trouble your Lordshipp withall I humbly kisse your hands and rest March 13.

Your Lordshipp's much obliged
to do you service
GEO. CALVERT.

St. Martin's Lane, 13 March 1620.

No. CII.

1621. March 26. SIR EDWARD HERBERT TO THE MARQUIS OF BUCKINGHAM.

[Autograph Signature.]

Right honorable and most worthy my Lord Marques. With my last I sent your Lordship a copie of a Declaration[1] said to be made in his Majesties name by your Lordship unto the Spanish Ambassador in England; which I then stayed from printing. Since when an other printer, without my knowledge, hath set it forth in somewhat a larger manner, whereof I have complained, as thinking it not fit to be published, without your Lordship's leave first obteyned. And now (my Lord) I must humbly againe desire your Lordship's good answer to my former of 26 Febr. since it concernes mee so much, and to keep still in your Lordship's good favour.

Your Lordship's most humble and most
thankfull servant
E. HERBERT.

Paris, 26 March 1621. St° Ang°.

Indorsed: S^r Ed. Herbert to my Lord, this lre printed.

No. CIII.

SIR WALTER ASTON TO THE MARQUIS OF BUCKINGHAM.

[Holograph.]

June 13. My most honord Lord. By my last of the 23. of May I acquainted your Lordship how carefull I had beene to stope such rumors as had here beene raysed laying many scandalls (without cawse) upon the proceedings of Sir Robert Manssell with his Majesties Fleete: since when, upon new informations, itt seems that the King and his ministers have taken some distast, as your Lordship will more att larg see by the copie of a letter here inclosed which was lately sent me from the Secretarie Çiriça. Your Lordship will alsoe therin finde the obligation put upon me to present itt unto his

[1] A declaration that Gondomar had never promised that his master would not invade the Palatinate.

Majestie. By the copie of my letter to the Secretarie you will perceave how little reason they had (att least as I conceave itt) to give creditt to so improbable an adverticement: but itt beeing there desire, I shall intreate your Lordship to acquaint his Majestie with what I here send you, and to be a means that I may retourn them from his Majestie such an answeare as he in his wisdome shall thinke fitting, since they will here expect as much from me. 1621. June 13.

I have not receaved any letter from Sir Robert Manssell since his last departure from this coast, but by a letter from Malaga I am adverticed that there put into that port a barke the 3. of June, that left him in Mayorque on the last of May *stilo veteri*, and that he had not in this voyage as then beene before Argirrs.

By the first oportunitie I intend to give Sir Robert Manssell notice of this complaint that is come against him, and as soon as I understand from him the trewth and ground (if there be any) of this errowre, I shall not omitt to represent unto this Kinge and his ministers the relation which he shall give me, wherby I dowte not but they will finde in this that they have too easily given creditt to so fowle an aspersion.

Ther is only left me further att this time to intreat your Lordship that you wilbe a means that such monnys as you releevd me withall last winter may be payd you out of my allowances, and the overplus that is dew to me to assist my present occations in his Majesties service, and that I may no more come so neere such a misery as your Lordship's care redeemd me from, lett mee humbly intreate your Lordship to procure that his Majestie's allowances may be assighned me in some sure place, that I may not be so unhappy to importune his Majestie in this kind, nor forced to exceed all good maners with your Lordship, to whom wishing all increace of hapiness I rest

Your most bound servant,

WA. ASTON.

Madrid, 13 June 1621. St. vet.
My Lord Admirall.

No. CIV.

Sir George Calvert to the Marquis of Buckingham.

[Holograph.]

1621. July 6. May it please your Lordshipp. I must desire your pardon yf in so much hast I send you an yll favored piece of paper and a scribling hand. At this instant I received a letter from Mr. Trumbull which advertiseth the Archduke's death at Brussells, for which there is great lamentation there, as appeareth both by his letter and by the messenger's report that brings it. If it had pleased God it had beene to have beene wished that he might have lived longer, being so respective as he was to his Majesty, and so willing to do all good offices. There will not be any great change there yet awhile I believe untill matters be well advised of in Spayne. The bearer tells me that they all believe at Brussells that the Infanta will retire herself into her Monastery, and that, for a while, the government wilbe committed to Marquis Spinola. For condoleance his Majesty will consider of that tyme enough, and of such instructions as he will be pleased to give Mr. Trumbull, agaynst his returne on Monday to London, or as his Majesty in his wisedome shall thinke fitt. In the meane tyme I humbly kisse your Lordshipp's hands and rest

Your Lordshipp's faithfully to serve you,

Geo. Calvert.

Whitehall, 6 July 1621.

No. CV.

Sir George Calvert to the Marquis of Buckingham.

[Holograph.]

July 19. May it please your Lordshipp. Though you have given me the liberty to use the hand of one of my servants, yet so long as a little more paynes and care will serve the turne, I had rather use my owne, yf this will serve. His Majesty will perceive by this letter which I send of Mr. Trumbull's that there is a beginning of some change in the Emperor's affaires, both in Hungary and Bohemia. So long as the Prince Palatine shall keepe himself disengaged from medling in them, I hope it will be to the advantage of his service and facilitate the present negotiation. That great Captaine the Count Bucquoy is certainely dead. 1621. July 19

The Lords have this morning given my Lord of Oxford order to attend his Majesty, and a coppie of his examination I send your Lordshipp before hand, that you may see how farre he is faulty by his owne confession. And so I rest

Your Lordshipp's very humbly
to serve you,
GEO. CALVERT.

St. Martin's Lane, 19 July 1621.

Your Lordshipp may please to move the King, or else yourselfe in his name, to lay a charge upon my Lord of Oxford that he do not out of jealousy question any person whomsoever for having upon examination testifyed anything against him, nor any way to touch them in their good name and reputation, though the particuler persons neede not be knowne unto him.

No. CVI.

ATTORNEY-GENERAL SIR THOMAS COVENTRY TO THE MARQUIS OF BUCKINGHAM.

[Autograph signature.]

Most honorable Lord. This afternoone came unto me the Lord Ambassador of Spayne and entered into speech with me concerning some recusantes that were extraordinarily vexed by informers and promooters, and mencioned two, whereof one as he sayd was prosecuted by five informers, and the other, being an aged gentlewoman, was sued by fower. I made him answere that, if I might have par- July 23.

1621. July 23. ticuler advertisement of the names of the persons, and of the courses that were held against them, I should do my best that the prosecucion against them for breach of the lawes of the realme might be carried with a fitting moderacion, and without vexacious pressure or extremity. His Lordshipp went no further to the particulers, but att his departure left a gentleman in my chamber that tooke on him to informe me of the old gentlewoman's cause; and he rested not att the complaynt against the informers, but told me that the gentlewoman being prosecuted and indicted of recusancy was like in short tyme to be convicted, and desired her conviction might be stayed by some direction from me. Now because this course of indictment is the ordinary proceeding against recusantes which I have not yet observed, either by his Majesties charge to his Judges, or otherwise, was meant to be stayed, I do make bold to advertise your Lordshipp and humbly pray yow att some convenient opportunity to acquainte his Majestie therewith. For if my Lord Ambassador, in suying to his Majestie to ease them from the vexacions of informers and other unjust pressures or strayned extremities, should involve therein the ordinary prosecucion used against recusantes by waye of indictment to cause them pay the twenty pounds a moneth, it is more then I dare give way unto, without his Majesties further direction: but the vexacions of informers and other new devised straynes I shall endeavour to represse. This being the first busines of this nature that my Lord Ambassador hath recommended to me, lett me be so much bound to your noble favour that, by your meanes, I may receive such a direction from his Majestie as may best sort with his gracious and honourable ends, and may be a guyde to me in this particuler and all other of like nature. And in the meane tyme I shall in some fayre course respite myne answere to this particuler. And so with my most humble duty and service I remayn

Att your Lordshipp's comand,

THOMAS COVENTRYE.

Inner Temple, 23 July 1621.

No. CVII.

PETITION TO THE MARQUIS OF BUCKINGHAM.

Your Lordship procured for Sir Thomas Gerrard and others the Corporation for the Tobaccopipe makers, uppon which there is 4000 li layde out and loste. 1621. July ?

His Majestie hath recalled the grant, and therefore in equity ought in grace to geve recompence.

Wee present to his Majestie one without exception to be made a Barron whoe will geve 10,000 li.

Humbly craving out of this, such a somme as his Majestie shalbe pleased to grant in lieue of the 4000 li loste, besids the long services of the sutors and the overthrowe of Sir Thos. Gerrard's estate, being bownd for his father for 7000 li, which if his Majestie vouchsafe not to releeve, his lands wilbe all seased uppon and utterly lost, to the undoing of him, his wife, children, and famyly.

No. CVIII.

DR. JOHN DONNE TO THE MARQUIS OF BUCKINGHAM.

[Holograph.]

May it please your Lordship. Ever since I had your Lordship's letter, I have esteemed myselfe in possession of Salisbury,[1] and more then Salisbury, of a place in your service; for I tooke Salisbury as a seale of ytt I hear that my Lord Keeper finds reason to continue in Westminster, and I know that neyther your Lordship nor he knowes how narrow and penurious a fortune I wrestle with Aug. 8.

[1] *i.e.* the Deanery which would be vacant if Bowle (see the next letter) succeeded Williams in the Deanery of Westminster. Bowle, however, remained at Salisbury, the Westminster Deanery being retained by Williams in commendam, and on the 27th of November Donne was elected to the Deanery of St. Paul's.

1621. Aug. 8. in thys world. But I ame so far from dependinge upon the assistance of any but your Lordship, as that I do not assist myselfe so far as with a wishe that my Lord Keeper would have left a hole for so poore a worme as I ame to have crept in at. All that I meane in usinge thys boldnes, of puttinge myselfe into your Lordship's presence by thys ragge of paper, ys to tell your Lordship that I ly in a corner, as a clodd of clay, attendinge what kinde of vessell yt shall please you to make of

Your Lordship's
humblest and thankfullest and devotedst servant,
J. DONNE.

8° August 1621.

Addressed: To the Right Honorable my singular good L. the Marquis of Buckingham.

No. CIX.

LORD KEEPER WILLIAMS TO MR. JOHN PACKER.

[Holograph.]

Aug. 11. Sir, I doe send you the Royall assent to my election,[1] with the whiche the other buisines[2] (as yet dependinge and in your handes) is to be dispatched, if at all. I am the more encouraged, because I am assured by Jo. Bembo, that Mr. Dean of Sarum[3] doth most willingly give way to my retayninge thereof, for the which I am much obliged to him, howe ever I speede.

I praye you heartilye, to desire my Lord, (in my name) to pardon my importunitye for this one thinge: and to ymagin it is the necessitye of supportinge this great place (without drawinge of ayne summes out of the Kinges purse) which makes me soe bold d daringe: the which his Lordshipp maye the rather conceive,

[1] As Bishop of Lincoln.

[2] The retaining in commendam of the Deanery of Westminster, which was granted him on the 14th of August. Patent Rolls, 19 James I. part 10.

[3] Dr. John Bowle, who continued Dean of Salisbury till 1629, when he became Bishop of Rochester.

because I never beg'd smaller or greater preferment in my life before this time. 1621. Aug. 11.

The Bushoppricke (the narrower I looke unto it) the more lamentable it proves: Howses, some demolished, others ruinous, the woods close shaven, and all like a See wherein I shall comm the fifte Bishopp in one fifteene yeares. But I love the last Bishopp[1] soe well that I saye not more of the Bushoppricke. My Keeper's place is a great deale more closely poul'd and very much dismembred; and yet am I soe much envied by most, as I knowe not where to complayne but in my Lord's bosom onelye.

I leave all to Him that must content us all, even to God's will and good pleasure; who beyond all expectation hath (to some purposes best knowne to himselfe) raised me from the dust to what I have, and hadd affoorded me long before such a portion of his blessinges, and soe much contentation therein, as I could well have lived upon lesse, and never desired more. To His protection I leave you, and rest ever

Your assured lovinge friend,
JO. LINC. EL. C.S.

Westminster College, this 11th of August 1621.

No. CX.

LORD KEEPER WILLIAMS TO MR. JOHN PACKER. Sept. 1.

[Holograph.]

Sir. I thank you very heartilye for your kynde remembraunce in all my buisinesses. I hadd some sudden occasion to send my man unto the Court, about matters concerninge myne owne office. I thinke it will fall upon you to send backe an awnswere, which desire you to doe with all speede. About the middle of the next weeke (or towards the end) I purpose to wayt upon my Lord agayne. Happie in the meane time (as I accompt my selfe) that I have soe lovinge and carefull a friend in my absence, which I will never

[1] George Montaigne, translated to London.

1621. Sept. 1. forgett nor burye (if opportunitye serve) in unthankefulnes. The Bishopp of Exeter's death is here befor your letter. Dr. Sharp importunes me for my letter, which I dare not write unto my Lord *bonâ fide* and seriously. I could wish my Lord of himself wold thinke upon Dr. Carey or Dr. Richardson. But I never presume to recommend but when I am asked. And soe I cease to trouble you, and commend you to God in my devotions, as resting ever

Your assured lovinge and true friend,

Jo. Lincoln. el. C.S.

Westminster College, this 1 of September.

Addressed: To the wor: my worthy good freynd Mr. John Packer Esqr. at Court.

No. CXI.

The Marquis of Buckingham to Sir George Calvert.

Sept. [Copy.]

His Majestie hath commanded me to write to your Honor to cause a lettre to be drawen from his Majestie to the Marquis Spinola to this effect. First to give him thanks for his freedome in advertising his Majestie of those points concerning his sonne in law and of the opinion he hath of his Majesties sinceritie in all his proceedings: who as farre as he may undertake for another man is perswaded allso that his sonne in law is free from anie imputation that may justly be laid upon him for the Count Mansfeild's courses,[1] and the rather his sonne in lawes own protestations and of his Majesties knowledg of Count Mansfeild's estate, who being in a desperate fortune, having sold his own meanes and driven to begg of other Princes, and seing no hope of being reconciled to the Emperor, followeth perhaps the fashion of the Banditi, setting up his rest to plaie his last prize. The truth whereof his Majestie doubteth not but my Lord Digbie will shortly cleare from Vienna where he now is and whence the certaintie of the whole matter is best knowen, and his Majestie hopeth shortly to be cleared therein from his sonne

[1] In the Upper Palatinate.

in law himself to whome he hath written to that purpose. But if his Majestie should finde that his sonne in law doth assist him either with money or councell or anie other waie, he professeth that he would quitt him and never meddle more in his businesse. In the meane tyme desireth him to be a good instrument of settling all thinges in a faire course, notwithstanding anie uncertaine report that may come to his eare. 1621. Sept.

His Majestie would likewise have your Honor cause a courteous lettre to be framed to the Infanta[1] in answeare of that which his Majestie lately receaved from her.

I have this daie read the Instructions for Sir Thomas Roe[2] to his Majestie, who liketh all but one point touching the mover, which he would have be thus changed:—"It was only his Majestes guift to the Ambassador," instead of, "for levying soldiers &c." I now send your Honor all your lettres again, saving the letter from Padre Maestro.[3]

No. CXII.

Lord Keeper Williams to Mr. John Packer.

[Autograph Signature.]

Good Mr. Packer. I did in my lettre to my Lord[4] like well of the proclamacion against the Scriveners,[5] but did desyre an exception of his Lordship, my Lord Treasurer, myselfe, and the judges, or rather all the Lords of the Counsaile, who ar as much excluded from presenting anything to the King as the Projector and the Scrivener. Oct. 17.

[1] The Infanta Isabella.

[2] In the instructions dated September 9, printed in *Sir T. Roe's Negotiations*, p. 2, the change has been made at the end of the first paragraph.

[3] Diego de la Fuente.

[4] Printed in Cabala, (ed. 1691) p. 262.

[5] The following is the form in which the proclamation (Patent Rolls, 19 James I. Part 14) was finally couched, so that no alteration appears to have been made:—"The King's most excellent Majestie observing the inordinate libertie that hath byn taken cheifelie of late tymes, in exhibiting to his Royall signatnre as well bills to passe his greate and privie seale and warrant for preparing such bills, as also letters and other instruments and writings of sundrie natures

1621. Oct. 17. Some things we must offer to the King's signature when the clarkes are not to bee found, and I hope his Majestie hath noe cause to mistrust any of us. I desyre therefore to know my Lord's meaning concerning this exception only. To this yow have not answeared.

Let the King resolve what his Majestie will concerning the Commissioners for irregularity,[1] I have acquaynted his Majestie with my conjecture of the event of the same.

The pardons are in part past and irrevocable by any power of myne. For those that are to come I will endure the envye to make some pawse upon them.

Yow know that to accommodate my Lord of Exeter[2] I was faine to remitte two benefices out of myne owne guift for his Majestie to make up a Commendam for him. Hee is in consideracion thereof

drawne by scrivenors and other like persons, and not by his Majestie's officers to whome the care thereof appertayneth, whereof ensueth a contynuall vexacion to his Majestie, and many tymes exceeding danger and prejudice both in his revenue and otherwise, is fully resolved to abolishe those abuses which have of late yeares crept into his service, and to reduce it to the auncient order and institucion; and therefore his Majestie doth hereby straightlie charge and commaund that no person or persons whatsoever (other than his Majestie's owne ordinary officers to whose places itt appertayneth) doe att any tyme hereafter presume to entermeddle with the drawing, writing, or preparing for his Majestie's signature of any bill, warrant, letter, or other instrument or writing whatsoever, uppon payne of his Majestie's indignacion and displeasure and such imprisonment and other punishment as may justlie be inflicted for their contempt. And that no person or persons, under the like paine, presume to preferre to his Majestie to be signed any such bill, warrant, lettre, or other instrument or writing not drawen or allowed by such his Majestie's ordinarie officers, and by them signed and docqueted, in cases where the like instrument have heretofore byn used to be signed and docqueted. And that none of his Majesties owne officers doe presume to drawe or prepare for his Highnes' signature any bill, warraut, lettre, or other instrument or writing untill they have received direccion to drawe the same either by some significacion of his Majestie's owne royall pleasure, or by warraut from such as have byn accustomed and allowed to give such warrant, uppon paine of his Majestie's displeasure and to be debarred from the exercise and execucion of their offices and places for such their default and abuse. Given at his Majestie's Courte at Royston the seaventh day of October.

"Per ipsum Regem."

[1] The irregularity incurred by ArchBishop Abbot in shooting Lord Zouch's gamekeeper.

[2] Bishop Carey.

willing to resigne up unto me the Prebendary of Stowe in the Church of Lincolne. It is a very poore thing, and under the clowde of an ould and a long lease before the statute. I presume his Majestie will not be displeased that I am a suitor for it, being originally myne owne (out of his Majesties grace and goodnes) and having parted (as I said before) with better things for the fitting of my Lord of Exeter. 1621. Oct. 17.

I recomend unto your love, for the same, the bearer hereof Mr. Clarke[1] a learned Bachelor of Divinity and an excellent good Preacher, now my chapleyne, but once my fellow chapleyne in my Lord Chancellor Elsmer's howse; whome I leave to the King's mercy and your favor for this poore prebend.

Thus with hearty comendacions unto you, with thankes for all your trowbles and paynes about myne owne and my freinds' affayres, I comend me unto yow, and yow to God's protection, and rest

Your assured true and loving freind,

Jo. LINCOLN. elect.

Custos Sigilli.

Westminster Colledge, 17 October 1621.

Addressed: To the right worshipfull his very loving freind Mr. John Packer Esq[r] at Court, deliver these.

Indorsed: L. Keeper to me 17 Octob.

No. CXIII.

LORD KEEPER WILLIAMS TO MR. JOHN PACKER.

[Holograph.]

Sir. I thanke you for Mr. Clarke, or rather for my selfe, whom upon all occasions you doe soe much engage unto you. But I beseech you, when I send any one to have a buisines dispatched doe not refuse your ordinarye fee, or els I will be more sparinge hereafter. Oct. 22.

Yeat I doe not heare of your opinion whether this newe pro-

[1] Robert Clarke, B.D. collated to the prebend August 12, 1622.

1621. Oct. 22. clamation[1] is to be sealed without those exceptions I sent unto you: to witt of the Privye Counsaile and the Judges, who must sometimes present thinges immediately to his Majesties signature, and wold be loath to encurr his Majesties highe displeasure by Proclamation.

I have written unto my Lord a long letter (as forced thereunto by many occasions), God send his Lordship the leysure and patience to reade it. I expect awnswer onely to one point, which is our newe Commission here, which troubles me infinitlye this terme time. I pray you call upon his Lordshipp for his awnswer to that. His Majesties going to Burleigh makes me suspect that I shall have noe quicke returne.

I am called awaye, not by the crie of the dogges, but by a more unpleasing noise, of the lawyers in Westminster Hall. And therfore I must abruptly take my leave and leave you in God's protection, restinge ever

Your assured faythfull and true freynd,

JO. LINCOLN. EL. C.S.

Westminster Colledge, this 22th of October 1621.

Addressed: To the right worshipfull his very loving Freind Mr. John Packer Esqr at Court, deliver these.

Indorsed: L. Keeper to me 22 Octob. 1621.

No. CXIV.

THE ARCHBISHOP OF CANTERBURY TO THE KING.

[Autograph Signature.]

Nov. 13. May it please your most excellent Majesty. I have received the letter sent from your Majesty concerning the consecration of the three Bishops of Salisbury, St. David's, and Exeter, to bee performed on Sonday next. Unto whiche my humble and true aunswere is that on Friday last in the presence of them all three I ordered that to bee done at the same time whiche your Majesty now requireth. And so, God willing, it shall bee accomplished; but not understanding

[1] See p. 161 note [5].

till the Wednesday before that the Lord Keeper had a purpose to bee consecrated on the Sunday folowing, it was impossible by the shortnesse of the time to have the instruments ready for all the Consecrations upon the Sunday after. Secondly, the Bishop of Exeter had not the certificate of his election, out of whiche the confirmation was to bee made, but hath now sent a post to Exeter for that purpose and doubteth not but it shall bee heere by the ende of the weeke, so that hee may go on then with the other two. Moreover the Churche of Westminster being an exempt and privileged place, and consequently out of the Archbishop's jurisdiction, I held it not unfit, since it could not bee performed on Sonday last, that it should bee done in the Bishop of London's Chappel, whiche is a place within my Province, and there where by mee eleven yeeres since the Archbishop of St Andrewes and the two other Bishops of Scotland were consecrated. And for the Commission to performe these things I gave order now foure dayes since, as also for all other matters appertaining thereunto: the intervening of eight dayes well permitting that the Certificate may bee brought from Exeter and all the instruments bee orderly drawne up without flawe or exception. So that there being no default in mee, to whome it was indifferent whither their consecration had bene on Sonday last or were to be on Sonday next, I hope your Majesty in your princely judgement will discharge mee of all blame. If care bee had for their restitution to their temporalties the next day after their consecration, they may very well bee present at the beginning of the Parliament. And so humbly thanking your Majesty for all your gracious favours towards mee, and namely for that speciall one at the day of your departure hence, with my prayers to the Almighty for your Majesties prosperity, I remaine

1621. Nov. 13.

Your Majesties most humble servant

and obliged Chaplein,

G CANT.[1]

Addressed: To the Kinges most excellent Majesty.
Indorsed: L. Cant. to his Mtie 13 Nov.

---

[1] George Abbot.

No. CXV.

Lord Keeper the Bishop of Lincoln to the Marquis of Buckingham.

[Autograph Signature.]

1621. Nov. 13. My most noble lord. I have bene much tormented with a flying report of your Lordship's crazynes and indisposicion, although your Lordship's late letter and another sithence that time from Mr. John Packer puts me in good hope that things are not so ill as they are reported.

My Lord of Southampton (who, coming to Towne in hope to kisse his Majestie's hand, stayd there untill this day,) is very willing to followe his Majestie's directions in that busynes your Lordship understands of. He only (as your Lordship may find by his lettres) desyres his Majestie's leave of absence, which is usuall and reasonable. But his Majestie may choose to graunt this leave immediately by his owne gracious lettres, or to give me power (under the signet, or by a lettre from your Lordship to that effect,) whereby I may be enhabled to dispence with the necessary absences of this Session. Men in my place have heretofore (as from the King) graunted these indulgences; although at this time (by reason of the Prince's præsence) I am of opinion this dispensing power were more fittly placed in his Highnes.

My Lord of S[outhampton] is touch'd with some feare of his two pencions, but relyes alltogeither upon his Majestie's mercy and your Lordship's good mediation; and I cannot yet but wish him all good successe in that perticular.

Mr. Packer moved his Majestie for the revercion of a poore place (under me) for one of my servants of good birth and qualitie, and returnes unto me his Majestie's denyall to graunt any revercions. I am sorry and somwhat discomforted that this resolution takes place against me only, but failes in all others whose revercions (even of places under my judicature) I use to seale dayly. My meanes are so short both for men and maister (nor will they grow better till wee grow worse) that, if his Majestie's bountie in this kinde be thus closed up towards mee, I shall have noe men of breeding or qualitie that will long continew in my service. 1621. Nov. 13.

I was by my Lord of London's hands (and your Lordship's speciall favor) put into a rochet this last Sunday, which occasions mee to remember (what I cannot forget) my innumerable respects and obligations unto your Lordship. Yow have advaunced me in the comon wealth to serve yow, in the Church to pray for yow, in both to honnor yow to the utmost of my power; and let me be soone weeded out of both, when I first declyne from persisting

Your Lordship's most faythfull servant and creature,

Jo. Lincoln. C.S.

Westminster College, 13 November 1621.

Addressed: To the right Honorable my most noble Lord, the Lord Admyrall at Court, deliver these.

Indorsed: L. Keeper to my Lord.

No. CXVI.

Lord Keeper the Bishop of Lincoln to Mr. John Packer.

[Autograph Signature.]

Sir. Sythence the writing of your last lettre his Majestie hath twice broken his resolucion for revercions. This seemes not straunge unto me, who ever was of opinion that the King was above his lawes. I remitte the wholle buisines (as I doe all my hopes and ambitions) to his Majestie's good will and pleasure, and the read-vauncing and suppressing of the same to your discrecion and future oportunity. Nov. 13.

The Rectory of Grafton was designed by my Lord to three severall men, Mr. Scott; a schoolefellow of Mr. Porter's; and, as

1621. Nov. 13. farre as I remember, afore either of these two, to Mr. Cade his Lordship's Schoolemaster. Upon your last lettre I have made a presentacion thereof unto this last man, which being allready sealed, yow shall doe well to send for, and I shall entreat yow to excuse me to my Lord for the other two.

I have conferred allso the Chauntership of Lincolne upon Doctor Berridge, according to the intencion of a lettre of my Lord's which he formerly wrote unto me by Sir Gregory Fennor. Also I have bestowed my prebend at Peterborrow upon one Mr. Swifte at the recommendacion of my Lord's mother, and my donative upon my Lord of Spalato by the King's commaundement. And soe this dole is ended.

It is now full time that Mr. Doctor Gwyn's bill for the poore Archdeaconry of Huntington be passed, and my thankes returned unto my Lord Admyrall and your selfe for the same. I have some litle blessing in store to mend this place for him, which otherwise doth not exceed £30 a yere, alle charges deducted. And so I commend you for this tyme to God's protection, and doe remayne as yow have well deserved

Your assured loving freind,

Jo. Lincoln, C.S.

Westminster College, 13° Novembris 1621.

Addressed: To the right worshipfull my very loving Freind Mr. John Packer, Esq. at Court, deliver these.

Indorsed: L. Keeper to me. Mr. Cade.

No. CXVII.

Lord Keeper the Bishop of Lincoln to Mr. John Packer.

[Autograph Signature.]

Nov. 16. Good Mr. Packer. I thanke yow for keeping mee still in the fruition of my ould freind the poore parsonage of Walgrave, wherewith I am not yet in any mynd to depart. The necessity of my attendance upon committees this present Parliament hath made me inquire of the Judges and others how I might be restor'd to my temporalties without doing my homage for the Bushopprick of Lincolne, my occasions not suffering me by any meanes to come downe in person to Newmarket. I am resolved that, as I might have done my homage when the King was here before my consecration (if I had bene so learned, and soe well read in the statute) soe I may be restor'd to my temporalties with a respite of homage (which the King grants every day to laymen) if his Majestie will be pleased to signe this restitution hereinclosed, differing nothing from the ordinary forme, but in one line onely, where his Majestie doth respite my homage untill Christmas eve. I could not all yesterday get the Clarke of the Signet to docquet the same, as being no where to be found, and therefore I have sent yow inclosed Mr. Attorney Generall's opinion which (by reason of this new addition of respite of homage) I held more satisfactory to his Majestie then the subscripcion of the Clarke of the Signet; besyds that the Clarke drawes these things upon my warrant usually.[1] 1621. Nov. 16.

For revercions that have passed in my tyme they are very many. Sir Raffe Freeman had a couple, of two Auditor's places of great consequence and importance. Mr. Mewtis had one or two revercions in my court, and without once asking my leave; which was never heard of in the memory of any man. My Lord Davers had one or two. One Mr. Shawe had another the last day, and I never open my seale but there passeth one or other. Poore Mostyn is the onely man that I heard of stopped, whom I must leave to your love and further oportunities; and so, with my thankes unto you for all

[1] A blank is left here in the MS.

1621. Nov. 16. your paynes in my busynes, I leave you for this time in God's protection, and rest ever

Your assured loving and faithfull freind,

Jo. Lincoln. C.S.

Westminster College, 16 November 1621.

Remember my humble respectes to my Lord and both the Ladyes: and knowe of his Majestie whether I shall deliver the donative for my Lord of Spalato, or reserve it untill his Majestye coms hither.

Addressed: To the right worshipfull my very loving Freind Mr. John Packer Esquier at Court deliver these.

Indorsed: L. Keeper to me. Respit o homage.

No. CXVIII.

Lord Keeper the Bishop of Lincoln to Mr. John Packer.

[Autograph Signature.]

Nov. 22. Sir. I thanke yow for your favor in making me a Baron of the Parliament,[1] which otherwise I had not bene before Christmas, and withall for your many other dayly and greater courtesyes, which I will by all occasions that ever shalbe offred endeavor to deserve in some proportion. Although the restitucion of my temporalties doth enable me to bestowe the poore Archdeaconry of Huntington upon Doctor Gwyn (for what was in the King of that Bushopprick upon Munday last, is now invested in me,) yeat I desyre you to passe it from the King as you have kindly beganne, because it wilbe a greater securitie and more honor unto the Doctor to have it after that maner. And so I cease to be further trowblesome at this time, and rest ever

Your assured loving freind,

Jo. Lincoln. C.S.

Westminster College, 22° November 1621.

Addressed: To the right worshipfull his very loving freind Mr. John Packer Esqre. at Court, deliver these.

Indorsed: 22 Nov. L. Keeper to me.

[1] Temporalities restored Nov. 20, see p. 169.

No. CXIX.

Sir Robert Heath to the Marquis of Buckingham.

Right Honorable my singuler good Lord. An unhappye accident is fallen out lately, which doth much concerne me in mine owne private, wherin I humbly beseech your Lordship to be mine honorable good Lord and a Mediator for me to his Majesty. It hath been my folly to be too deeply ingaged for Sir Thomas Watson's dettes. He is lately dead in the Kinges dett, and I am bound for him in some good sums for which I have security by landes. I am also bound for him in some other good sums borrowed lately to pay the King part of his dett for which I have noe security. My humble suite to his Majesty is but this, that he would be pleased to recommend his owne cause for his owne dett to my Lord Treasoror and Mr. Atturney, and that I may have the favor, as farre forth only as they two shall find to be just, to be relieved by his Majestyes means, his owne dett being first truly satisfied. The delays of the Ladye Watson, who is the sole executor to her husband, give me just occasion to suspect that ther is not soe just a course intended towards me as I knowe I have deserved at ther handes. I beseech your Lordship be pleased to move his Majesty for me with as much convenient speed as your greater affaires will give leave, that I be not prevented and his Majesty otherwise engaged. For your Lordship's services I only give this account for the present, that I goe on in the busines about the Straungers, and prepare the Bill for the fishing against a fitt opportunity. For other thinges I shall remitt them to my noble frend Sir Georg Goring, by whom I humbly intreat I may be bound unto you for an aunswer. 1621. Dec. 3.

Your Lordship's most bounden
and most devoted to doe you service,
Ro: Heath.

3 Dec. 1621.

Addressed: To the right Honble my singuler good Lord the Marquess Buckingham, Lord High Admirall of England.

Indorsed: Mr. Sollicitor to my Lord.

No. CXX.

The Marquis of Buckingham to Sir George Calvert.

[Draft.]

1621. Dec. Sir. His Majestie hath commanded me to write to you that you beware you have not given the House too great scope in giving them libertie to deale with any offences committed directly against the House or any member thereof in Sir Edward Coke's case, and that thereupon they touch upon the point of conspiracie, which if they doe, that whole businesse wilbe foyled and the blame will light upon you.

Besides his Majestie would have you advise with his learned Counsell, whither actions intended wilbe comprized within the generall pardon, and, if you finde they be not, his pleasure is you deale with the pursuers of the busines to put in presently a Bill into the Starchamber against Sir Edward Coke which his Majesty thinketh fitt, how ever it be.

Indorsed: My Lord's lettre to S. Calvert.
Sir Ed. Coke.

No. CXXI.

The Marquis of Buckingham to Sir Henry Wotton.

[Copy.]

1622. Jan. 2. My Lord. I have all this while respited my answeare in expectacion of the issue of a treatie I had in hand between my Lord Treasurer that now is [1] and the Master of the Rolls [2] touching an exchang of their places, whereupon my deseigne was to have left it to your choyce whither you would have taken a reversion of the Mastership of the Wards after Sir Julius Cæsar (which I doubted

[1] Lord Cranfield. [2] Sir Julius Cæsar.

not but his Majestie would have granted) or expected the avoydance of the other place[1] upon that clayme you have to it. But that busines being now broken of, and there being no other coarse left but to stick to the interest you have in his Majesties gratious promise for the Rolls, I thought it now time to send away your man after this long stay, with assurance that when the occasion serves you shall find me 1622. Jan. 2.

Your constant friend
and servant

2° Januar. 1621.

I thanke your Lordship for the bedd and pictures and other present you sent me, and for your good husbandrie in the other pictures you bought for me.[2]

Indorsed: My Lord to Sir H. Wotton.

No. CXXII.

Lord Keeper the Bishop of Lincoln to the Marquis of Buckingham.

[Autograph Signature.]

My most noble Lord. I have receav'd a lettre from his Majesty concerning the discharging and freeing of the Lord Hollys[3] from a suite in the Star-Chamber followed against him in the King's right; but by the sollicitacion of Sir Edw. Cooke I forbore (upon conference with his Majesty) to doe any thing herein, in the sitting of the last Parliament, for feare of styrring up that waspe which hath sythence so bestyrr'd himselfe. If his Majestie be still graciously disposed to have the Lord Hollys freed, I beseech your Lordship to Jan. 17.

[1] The Mastership of the Rolls.
[2] The postscript is written across the back of the sheet.
[3] A mistake for Lord Houghton (John Holles).

1622. Jan. 17. let Mr. Packer write a word unto me to that effect.[1] I cease to be further troublesome, and rest ever

Your Lordship's faythfull Servaunt
and creature,
Jo: Lincoln. C.S.

Westmr Coll. 17 Jan. 1621.
Addressed: To the Right Honorable My most noble Lord the Lord Admyrall at Court.
Indorsed: L. Keeper to my Lord L. Hollys.

No. CXXIII.

Sir George Calvert to the Marquis of Buckingham.

[Holograph.]

Jan. 17. May it please your Lordship. Understanding that the Archbishopp of Yorke is dead,[2] and that it may be the occasion of diverse removes in the Church, I beseech your Lordshipp give me leave to recommend unto your remembrance Mr. Doctor Wright, one for whom I have beene often a sollicitor heretofore, and who is now so well knowne unto your Lordshipp and his abilityes by commendation also from others, to whose judgement I presume your Lordshipp will attribute much, as I neede not speake more of his sufficiency and worth. If by your favorable meanes he may be advanced at this tyme, your Lordshipp shall much bynd him unto yow, and putt the like obligation upon my self, who am

Your Lordshipp's very humbly to serve you,
Geo. Calvert.

St. Martin's Lane, 17 January 1621.
Addressed: To the Right Honble my singular good Lord the Lo: Marquis of Buckingham Lo: Highe Admirall of England.
Indorsed: S. C. to my L. Dr. Wright.

---

[1] Marginal note, "A lettre written to that purpose, 19 Jan."

[2] This was the same rumour, said to have been designedly spread by the Archbishop himself, which induced Antonio de Dominis to make application for the vacant see.

No. CXXIV.

LORD CHIEF JUSTICE LEY TO THE MARQUIS OF BUCKINGHAM.

[Autograph Signature.]

My humble ducty and service to your Lordship remembred. It pleased the Lordes of the Councell to call my Lord Hobard and me before them about the assessing of the prices of wynes, at which tyme it was declared unto us, that because they were not willing to put us to a double labour, therefore they thought fitt to propound unto us, that we would let them know what Benevolence we would willingly bestow towardes the Palatinate. To whome we answered that, in the generall, we were very willing to give according to our abilities, and in the particuler we did humbly present the summe of an hundred poundes apeece, with this, that to declare our willingnes we would doe our best endevors to incourage all others of our vocation to doe the like, according to their proporcions, which free offer of ours the Lordes did accept with good approbacion and to our great comfort, which we must acknowledge to proceed from those worthie direccions which it pleased your Lordshipp by your letters to give us. It now followeth that your Lordshipp would vouchsaffe to give me leave to make a mocion for that which all or most of my predecessors and others have formerlie obtayned, towardes which, if your Lordshipp will be pleased to looke upon my age and late sicknes, I hope your Lordshipp will not thinke it unreasonable for me to be an humble suter to be allowed a circuit for my most ease and saffetie, which is in the Westerne partes. And if it shall please your Lordshipp to move his Majestie for the same and to procure a warrant to my Lord Keeper to that effect, with a *Non obstante* of my being that Countrey man, your Lordshipp shall doe therein (as alwaies you have done) an extraordinary favor unto me, whereof the short tyme for appointment of circuites doth require the more expedicion. And to take awaie all excepcion, Mr.

1622. Jan. 29.

1622. Jan. 29. Justice Hutton whoe goeth that circuit is as glad to exchaung for my circuit as I am for his. And soe wishing your Lordshipp all increase of honor and happines, I humbly take my leave,

Your Lordship's alwais faithfully to serve you,

JAMES LEY.

From Serjeants Inne, Fleet Street, the xxix[th] of January 1621.

Addressed: To the right hon[ble] his very good Lord, the Lord Marques Buckingham, Lord Admirall of England.

Indorsed: 29 Jan. 1621. L. Chief Justice to my L.

No. CXXV.

LORD FALKLAND TO THE MARQUIS OF BUCKINGHAM.

[Holograph.]

Feb. 1. My deare M[ris].[1] I lately receyved a letter from my Lady of Wallingford,[2] wherein she desired my mediation to your Lordship for the farther extention of the lyne of his Majestyes grace in my Lord and Lady Sommersett's liberty to one myle longer, because she hath an other howse called Niew Elme, the best and holsomest ayre for the Spring of all hir howses, whereunto she purposes to goe veary shortely, which would be then within the compass of their allowed circuict, being 4 miles from Grayes and farther from any of his Majestyes howses or resortes then any of the other: and this is desired by way of addition not of alteration, which is to my poore seemeing soe reasonable and moderate a request as I presume your generous and confident noblenes will never deney it. One word under his Majestyes hand or under your Lordshipes owen signifying his pleasure wilbe good and sufficient warrant for that matter. Your Hanns in the Kelder[3] is passing well, and like to make a francke

[1] Apparently Mistress, probably from some joke.

[2] Sister of the Countess of Somerset.

[3] A Dutch phrase for an unborn infant. Buckingham's first child Mary was born in the following April, and the Marchioness had, I suppose, been playing at the game of cards called gleek.

gamester, for all ready he loves gleeke with all his harte, and I with all my harte love and honnor my M^ris^ to whom I will ever be 1622. Feb. 1.

Your honest trew harted servant,

FALKLAND.

Whightehall, this first of February 1621.

Addressed: To excellent and singulerly most noble Lord, my Lord the Marquiss of Buckingham, Lord High Admyrall of England &c. Att Courte.

Indorsed: L. Falkland to my Lord. E. of Somersett.

No. CXXVI.

SIR JOHN SUCKLING TO THE MARQUIS OF BUCKINGHAM.

[Autograph Signature.]

My humble service to your Lordship remembred. I am bolde to addresse theis fewe to your Lordship touching the busines of steele which the interessed parties will begin this moneth to make. And because Mr. Doctor Fludd, to whom it was at first granted, hath not yett passed the great seale for the same, it being hetherto no further then the privie seale, I humbly pray your Lordship that his Majestie woulde vouchsafe to give order to the Master of Requests now attending at Court for his gratious pleasure to be signified to the Lord Keeper to send for the sayd Doctor Fludd to attend him, and withall to require him to passe it presently under the great seale, to remaine with his Lordship untill securitie be given for the true answering of the third parte to his Majestie's use of the profittes which shall therof arrise, as was agreed before the Lords of his Majestie's Privie Councell. My reasons for this are two, thone for that his Majestie is not interessed in the profittes of the sayd third part untill it be under the greate seale: thother that I cannot signifie his Majestie's good pleasure on the behalf of Mr. Christopher Villiers about the moietie of the sayd third part before it be under the greate seale, which it pleased him to bestow upon Mr. Villiers in my audience at Rufford in the moneth of August Feb. 8.

1622. Feb. 8. last. I have been twice at Lymehouse where the houses, furnaces, and watermill are buylt for the making and working of the sayd steele, it being a very faire busines and likely to proove very profitable, and against it no just exception can be taken. For his Majesty restrains not any person either from bringing it from beyond the seas nor from making of it within the land; and yett he is neverthelcs to have a third parte of the gaine by the voluntary offer of the contractors; and I did purposely hetherto forbeare to call upon the passing it under the great seale, in regard the housing and other necessaries were but lately finished, and not ready to make any steele till this present moneth. I humbly desire the contynuance of your noble favoure towards me, and beseech your Lordship to have this good opinion of me that no man can or shall serve you more honestlie justlie and faythfully then

Your Lordship's humbly devoted at commande,

Jo. Suckling.

8th February 1621.

Addressed: To the right Hoble the Lo. Marques of Buckingham, Lo: High Admirall of England.

Indorsed: 8 Febr. 1621. Sr Jo: Suckling to my Lord Steele.

No. CXXVII.

Lord Keeper the Bishop of Lincoln to Mr. John Packer.

[Holograph.]

Feb. 25. Sir. I pray you to deliver this letter unto my Lord, and desire his Lordshipp to reade it over, though it be somewhat long. It is my opinion about Mr. Murray's maner of proceding in the obteyning of this place:[1] for I speake nothing against the matter, as wishing the man all good, and remembring whose tutor he was. Comend me to Sir Sidney Montague, I pray you, with my thankes for his letter with the petition of that clamorous ladye the Lady Dacres.

[1] The Provostship of Eton. The letter referred to is printed in Cabala (ed. 1691) 264.

I have already acquaynted the King with what I did, and justified it in the Parliament, and shalbe able to doe soe still. But his letter was soe delivered unto me amongst a 100 petitions, with such slight and contempt, that it was never opened and presented unto me by my Secretarye untill within this halfe howre. I will eyther write or bring an awnswer within these 3 dayes, the time being nothing soe nere spending as is enformed. 1622. Feb. 25.

I beseech you if opportunity be offred put my Lord once more in mynde of Dr. Piers for Peterburgh. I forgot it when I spake with his Lordshipp.

Soe I cease (for this time) to be further troublesom, comending you to Godes protection, and rest ever

Your assured loving freynd

Jo. Lincoln. C.S.

Westminster College, this 25 of February, 1621.

If you hold it fit I pray you seale up the enclosed when you have read it.

Addressed: To the right worshipfull my assured loving Frend Mr. John Packer Esqre, at Court deliver these.

Indorsed: L. Keeper to me 25 Feb.

No. CXXVIII.

The Earl of Nottingham to the Marquis of Buckingham.

My most honorable Lord and Sonne. I can shew in writing of allmost three thousand deere red and fallow which I have forborne the taking of by my warrants since his Majestie came into this Realme, besides some parkes which I never sent to at all, but have forborne to preserve them for his Majestes pleasure, as St. Jeames, Greenewich, and the litle parke of Eltham, and never had any deere out of them. Now my humble suite is unto his Majestie that it would please him to geeve me 16 or 20 male deere out of the great parke of Nonsuch, which may very well spare them. I desire to have them to put into my parke at Reigate, which is alltogether March 28.

1622. March 28. decaied of male deere, that I may have now in my old yeeres, being not able to goe farr of to hunt, to have some sport theare now and then to kill a bucke with my beagle, which may peradventure prolong my life a yeere or two. Thus your Lordship sees how bold I am to trouble you; for, my good Lord, all my life and bringing up was in warr, hunting, or hawking ever since I was a man. If the abilitye of my body were as able as the willingnes of my hart I would attend oftener upon his Majestie with my service, but insteed of that I doe daylie and nightlie pray for his Majestie's long life and happie raigne, and your Lordship long to live to doe his Majestie and the Realme service.

So I allwaies rest

Your Lordship's most assured in all love
and affection to doe you service,

NOTTINGHAM.

Haling, this 28th March 1622.

Yet my Lord I must confesse trulie unto yow that I am this winter and now at this instant better in health and strength of body then I was ten yeere agoe.

No.

Addressed: To the right Honble and my very good Lord and Sonne, the Marquis of Buckingingham, Lord High Admirall of England. dd.
Indorsed: E. of Notingham to my L.

No. CXXIX.

THE BISHOP OF CHESTER TO JOHN PACKER.

[Autograph Signature.]

July 31. Salutem in Christo. I pray God blesse you and yours for that unusuall (and I think unmatchiable) blessing which you afford unto God's Church here in this country, which like a dry and barren soyl drinks in that heavenly water (which you have showred down upon them) with greedynes. Mr. Hyat hath ever since his coming emong us preached at a place caled Goosnargh, not farr from Preston in Lancashire. I hold that the most needful place for his labors though the most unfitting place for his living, for it cannot fitt him for a house to lodge in (as they promised he should have) though it afford him auditors, the church full. I purpose he shall divide his paynes emong diverse auditors, though he bestow most emong those with whom he shall dwell, unles you otherwise dispose (for at your disposall it must be, as is most reasonable seeing you pay him his wages) and if you please to signify to me at any tyme you will I shall order him acordingly in all things. The country blesses God for this great benefit and pray for you and yours heartely, and my prayres shall never be wanting for you that God will multiply this your goodnes by his graces dayly unto your bosome; he that suffereth not a cup of cold water to be bestowed upon one of his litle ones unrewarded will (no doubt) retribute (for this so great a work) much more to you and your posterity, seing so many of his litle ones are continuall fed with that spirituall food which you have sent them. 1622. July 31.

I wrote long since to my Lord Bishop of Litchfield[1] about the other preacher, to know his pleasure for the placeing of him here or in Staffordshire as you wrote, and I receaved his lettre in answere desireing me not to presse him for this country, but that he might labor you to plant him in his dioces: wherupon I forbare to write more to you about that busines, presumeing that my Lord himself hath long since written to you about it.

The God of Heaven continue and encrease these good desires in you, and work the like in others by your example, to the glory of his Son, the good of his Church, and your endles comfort in another world.

Your true and much bounden friud,

Jo: Cestren.[2]

Wigan Hall, Ultimo Julii 1622.

Addressed: To the right worshipful and Religious Gentleman John Packar, Chief Secretary to the Right Honble the Lord Marques of Buckingham.

Indorsed: B^p^ of Chester to me.

---

[1] Thomas Morton.

[2] John Bridgeman

No. CXXX.

Mr. William Fenner to Mr. John Packer.

[Holograph.]

1622. Aug. 20. Worthie Gentleman. What cause I have of thanckesgiveing both to God for you, and to you for your love, my heart tells me. You for your various good deedes may well be, like the Bishop of Alexandria, called Johannes Eleemosynarius, in regard as well of soule as bodie. What favour I have found with my Lord of Leichfield and Coventrie, that same *περιφανὴς ὁ ἀνὴρ καὶ πρόμαχος τῆς εὐσεβείας* as Theodoret stiles Gregory Nazianzen, for your sake, without ingratitude to you both I cannot conceale. I am bound to respect and honor his Lordship (besides that I heard of his worth before my comeing, which makes him fair and high renowned) as long as I live, his love is such toward me; I make no question but you will give him thanckes for his so great kindnesse. I have bene hitherto at his Lordship's and have preacht at his appointment where he seeth that there is need. Now I have a place, a set aboad assigned most according to your religious intent. It's fit indeed such a noble purpose should be carefully lookt unto. Greater liberality then which there can hardly be any. Not an ordinary commendation in this close-fisted world. Wherein many are not unlike the shipmen in Sigebertus his chronicle that being askt a piece of bread by a poore man answeared *Se nihil prœter lapides habere.* Forthwith the beggar cursed sayeing *Omnia ergo vertantur in lapides*, whose curse God heard so as all their food was no better then stones for their eating. But the spirits of the poore blesse your tender heart every where, and their blessings are effectuall with God and for this heroicall intendement of yours much more. This one thing heartens me, the confidence that God will prosper the proceeding in so much that its for so royall an end. For my part I am not onely to satisfie your desires herein, which are very bountifull and pious, but have respect to God himselfe by all sedulousnesse in the charge, who suggested it to your heart. I have and shall have my Lord of Leichfield and Coventrie[1] his directions in the performance (which I will folow in all things) meaning to use all meekenesse, humility, discretion, diligence, fidelity that I can therein, together with continuall thanckes unto your worthinesse for the same. *Quem cœpisti amare, porrò ama,* and you shall (God willing) never repent it. The Lord of Heaven keep you for much good. Thus with remembrance of my best respect unto you (I might adde without suspicion of insinuation, Patron) I rest 1622. Aug. 20.

Yours to command in all love,

WILLIAM FENNER.

From Ecclesall in Staffordshire, August 20, 1622.

Addressed: To the Worshipfull my very much respected friend Mr. Packer, Secretary to the Right Honourable and his very good Lord the Marquesse of Buckingham, these. At Mr. Packar's house, at the Cloister at Westminster.

No. CXXXI.

SIR FRANCIS ANNESLEY TO THE MARQUIS OF BUCKINGHAM.

[Autograph Signature.]

It may pleas your most honorable Lordship. I am told by Mr. Francis Cave that your Lordship was offended with me for signeing of a letter to the Lords with the Commissioners concerning the plantacons, wherein ther was indeed impertinent mention of Mr. Wrayes graunt of the natives' fines, which I knewe belonged to your Lordship. I will eaver acknowledg my self to be so highly bound to your Lordship for your manifold favors, as I wear the ingratefullest man liveing if my harte or hand should willingly consent to any thing that might geove your Lordship the least Sept. 20.

[1] Thomas Morton.

1622. Sept. 29. occasion of dislike; and as touching that lettre I did make open protestacion against the wholl contentes therof, and took particular exception to that claus of the natives' fines which I have eaver strongly argued to be rather increased then abated so long as they contynue their contempt against his Majestie's proclamacion, and I withstood the signeing of that letter till I was (somewhat unmannerly as I conceaved) asked by Sir William Jones wheather I thought myself wiser then all the Commissioners to oppose that which they had concluded upon, whereuntoe I made a more modest answere then his rude question deserved, that I neaver affected singularity of opinion either in myself or any other man, but desiered that my reasons might be heard with patience, and then I would submitt to better judgements, and when I had urged all I could against the impossibility of getting treable rents from the undertakers and against severall other pointes of the lettre, for which I am still constant in my opinion there was noe ground of reason, yet I was overruled by most voyces to subscribe therunto, eaven against my will, as by my letters to the Lord Treasurer of England I did then express, doubting that some of the Commissioners might informe his Lordship that I was opposite to the Kinges proffitt, which by Godes grace I will neaver be wher I can discern honorable waies for thaccomplishment therof, but I did and doe still conceave that the standing for treable rentes, to which the undertakers neaver did nor will I thinke consent, doth to his Majestie's great disproffitt tooe long protract the effecting of double rentes and geoveing of £30. upon every thousand acres by way of composicion for the graunte of the natives' fines, to which most of the undertakers assented; and butt that Sir Francis Blundell told me he would then write to your Lordship touchinge that letter and the cariadge of itt, as he still sayeth he did, I would have presumed to have addressed my letters to your Lordship, as I did to the Lord Treasurer. I will not further interrupt your Lordship's high imployments but doe most humbly beseech you to contynue mee in your good favour and proteccion as one that honors you, and studies to doe you service more then to any subjecte, and I wish that neither I nor myne may prosper longer then I am your most honorable Lordship's faithfull servaunte, 1622. Sept. 20.

FRA: ANNESLEY.

Dublin, this 20th of September, 1622.
Addressed: To the most honorable Lord the Lord Marquess Buckingham, Lord High Admirall of England.
Indorsed: Sir Fr. Annesley to my L. Apologie.

No. CXXXII.

THE EARL OF KELLY TO THE MARQUIS OF BUCKINGHAM.

[Autograph signature.]

It may please your Lordshipe. You warr soe busied att your beinge here in toun that I did not thinke it good manners to trowble yow with this busines of my Lady Purbeck's; I have done my best to have drawn the soume[1] to eight hundreth pounds, but could not prevale, soe that I muste humbly intreate your Lordshipe wilbe pleased to lett it be £1,000 as you did say to me. There restes nothinge but a howse, whareof I have putt hir oute of all hope that any can come from your Lordshipe: and I have of myselfe delt with hir mother, whoe sayes she hes no mynde to have hir doghter in hir company, least shee may incurr your displeasor, whiche I thinke a strange conceate in hir mother. In my opinion if your Lordship wilbe pleased to signifie soe much to me by two lynnes that yow will thinke it more convenient that shee be with hir mother then alone, then I hope to sattle that poynt with the rest, which I thinke shall give your Lordshipe a great dale of qwyetnes. Thus remittinge the rest to your Lordshipes directions, I will end this, but ever remane your Lordship's affectionat servaunt, Oct. 16.

KELLIE.

Cheringe croce, 16th October 1622.
Addressed: To the Right Honorable and my very good Lord My Lord Marqnes of Buckingham, Lord High Admirall of England &c.
Indorsed: E. of Kelly to my Lo.

[1] Lady Purbeck's alimony, her husband being insane.

No. CXXXIII.

Sir George Calvert to the Marquis of Buckingham.

[Holograph.]

1622. Oct. 21. May it please your Lordshipp. I am much bownd unto your favor, and so am I for your patience in that you are pleased to give me leave thus to trowble yow. I am sorry that your last letter, which was so full of noblenesse and courtesy, should stand neede of any replye. But for that I see that my Lord Tresorer takes no notice to me of any such matter as your Lordshipp writes of, nor of any conference betweene yow concerning me, notwithstanding that I have beene in his company diverse tymes synce your Lordshipp's departure hence, I shall humbly pray your Lordshipp to signify the King's pleasure unto the Clarke of the Signett attendant for drawing of a privy seale for the £2,000, without which I knowe he can pay no money, and then it will be some grownd for me to attend him; otherwise I have no coulor to offer it, and shall be in danger of a repulse, which I would not willingly have for twise so much money, my Lord Tresorer and I being now upon so good termes of understanding each other, as I do not doubt but he holds me for his servant, and I should be very unhappy if any new occasion should happen that might make me doubt him to be my friend. Your Lordshipp will pardon this freedome, and give that dispatch to my suite which may advantage me much though the thing in itself be small, and I shall humbly attend your answere by Mr. Packer, remayning ever,

Your Lordshipp's faithfull and true servant,

Geo. Calvert.

St. Martin's Lane, 21 October, 1622.

Addressed: To the Right Honorable my very good Lord the Lord Marquis of Buckingham Lord Highe Admirall of England.

Indorsed: S. Calvert to my L.

No. CXXXIV.

Lord Keeper the Bishop of Lincoln to Mr. John Packer.

[Holograph.]

Mr. Packer. I pray you present to my Lord these patents for Justices, and these enclosed letters of my Lord of Northampton and myne. Alsoe I pray you to acquaint my Lord that I have not yet received the Kinges reference concerning the juste difference betwene the Earles of Ormond and Desmond, but doe much suspect that one of the two Earles doth suppresse it; both of them afraide of us. But I have taken great paines in informing my self in the cause, whereof I will give his Lordshipp some accompt at Theobalds. I thought his Lordship would have directed you to write somewhat unto me concerning the Bushopprick of Bristowe.[1] But I referr that to his Lordshipp's pleasure and leasure. Onely I recommended to his thoughts, Dr. Wright, Dr. Collins, and Dr. Price nowe imployed in Ireland: but without any suite of myne, which I never did nor will make for any man in this kynde, unles mere necessitye shall put me in mynde of the Deane of Westminster[2] hereafter. And soe leave you for this time in God's protection, and rest 1622. Oct. 28.

Your assured lovinge freynd,

Jo. Lincoln. C.S.

Westminster College this 28 of Oct. 1622.

Addressed: To the Worshipfull my assured loving Freind Mr. John Packer esquier at Court, deliver these.

Indorsed: L. Keeper to me. Bp of Bristoll.

No. CXXXV.

James I. to Sir George Calvert.

[Imperfect fragment of draft.]

Right trusty &c. Wee cannot but wonder that those of our Counsell who were appointed to meet with the States have been so Nov.

[1] Bishop Searchfield died October 11, 1622, and was succeeded by Dr. Robert Wright, Warden of Wadham.

[2] *i.e.* of himself.

1622. Nov. negligent as to disappoint them. And therefore wee would have you acquaint our dearest sonne the Prince therewith that he may in our name command them all to meet with them as speedily as may be. And our pleasure is that your self goe to the States' Ambassadors and divert them from coming hither to take their leave,[1] but to desire them both in our owne and our sonne's name to be contented once againe to meet with our Counsell, whose negligence is inexcusable, being pittie that the busines should be hindered being so neere an end for want of their——

Indorsed: M. from his M. to S. Cal:

No. CXXXVI.

The English Commissioners for the East India Business to James I.

[Copy.]

Nov. 19. May it please your moste excellent Majestie. Wee have, according to your Majestie's commandement and direccions at Theobaldes, given divers meetinges to the States' Ambassadors, not omitting anie one day when your Majestie's other greate affaires woulde permit, and following therein the way your Majesty prescribed us. We began first with the charge of Bantam, which had bene so much disputed before your Majestie, and the better to prepare and ripen that question, the marchantes on both sydes were ordered to meet togeather, which they did accordingly, the English not failing except onely one time, when they were commanded to attende us your Majestie's Commissioners here about that businesse, which we are bolde to intimate to your Majesty, because the States complaine thereof to us as a neglect, and we gave them this answere, wherewith we hope they were satisfied. But for the matter it selfe of the account, your Majesty's

[1] The Dutch Commissioners for negotiating a settlement of the East India disputes threatened to take their leave, in consequence of the alleged neglect of the English Commissioners to attend the meetings. See the next letter.

marchants founde it so unreasonable and exorbitant as it [seemed] to them rather to be devised here then otherwise. From this point being put into the marchantes handes, we fel to other thr[ee] points which were before left incertaine, namely the discount of the pepper brought into Hollande, the restitution of the goodes at Lantor,[1] and the exchange of the reals of eight, in none of which coulde wee for the present obtaine any reasonable satisfaction from them. 1622. Nov. 19.

Neverthelesse, to shewe our earnest desire of an accommodation, and to omitt nothing that might conduce thereunto, we proceeded to the reiglement of trade, hoping that, if that had bene wel setled for the future, the rest woulde more easilie have followed; and whereas your marchants had presented unto them a draught of many particular demandes, with a preface which the States dislyked, we caused all that might be anie way distastefull to be put out, and of those thinges which remained in our conference with them we principally insisted upon three, which seemed of such necessity as our marchants being earnestly pressed by us in private to yeilde to the uttermoste they coulde, protested vehemently that without redresse in those thinges they coulde not maintaine that trade, nor draw adventurers to contribute thereunto. One of these was to have places assigned where your marchants might erect forts; touching which, though we conceive them to be at libertie for the Moluccas, Amboina, and Banda, there being now expired the tyme of three yeares which is limitted by the Treatie and more explained by an Act of Counsell by your Majestie's expresse commandement on the 24th of June 1619, yet the Ambassadors not onely denie it in those places without their consent, but also in any other places of the Indies:

Secondly we required that each Companie might have the governing, correcting, and imposing of taxes upon their owne nation; But hereto we coulde finde them no way inclining; For howsoever they avoyded the name of Souverainty (against which

[1] In the Banda Isles.

1622. Nov. 19. we ever earnestly protested,) yet they pressed the act and practise thereof. Lastly we desired to have the nomber of twentie ships, which semes certaine by the treatie, to be left indefinite in nomber, with a power to the Counsel of Defense there by common consent to appoint the nomber more or lesse, as the exigence of the affaires may require. For the English Companie protesteth that neither the trade as it hath bene hitherto caryed, can maintaine their proportion of ten, nor hath there bene anie necessitie of maintaining that nomber for defense of their trade ; and for offense it is not warranted by the treatie. And this question coming into dispute we holde the decision thereof to be left unto your Majestie and the States by the 30th Article of the aforesaide Treatie. All these points of reiglement having bene long debated yesterday amongst us, at laste it was the Ambassadors' desire that the Marchantes on both sydes shoulde withdraw themselves that we might speake privately together; we conceiving their purpose to have bene to accommodate the businesse betwene our selves as we have often done heretofore. But contrarie to our expectation, passing by all busines, they acquainted us with their resolucion to begin their journey this morning towardes Newmarket, wherein we finding them firme helde it our duties to give your Majestie this account, and withall that we thought it strange they should never acquaint us with this their intention til six of the clock yesternight, our caryage (we hope) having deserved wel at their handes, though we must confesse to your Majestie that yesterday the language both of the Ambassadors and their Marchants was in a higher straine of Souveraintie in the Indies then we expected. And humbly praying your Majestie to pardon this length, since the necessitie of the businesse enforceth it, we doe in all humilitie kisse your Majestie's royall handes and rest, &c.

Whytehall, the 19th of November, 1622.

Indorsed: Copie of the former letter touching this subject.

No. CXXXVII.

LORD SAY AND SELE TO THE MARQUIS OF BUCKINGHAM.

[Holograph.]

My Lord. I am very unwillinge to err in any circumstance whearby his Majestie's displeasure agaynst me might be farther occasioned, and thearfore although I stir not out of the house whear I lye,[1] yeat shall I not thearin rest secure, except I may understande the little stay I desyre uppon just occasion to make in this place may be pleasinge to him. I beseech your Lordship doe me the favour that I may in a word from you understande wheather his Majestie will be pleased to give me leave to stay in London for three weekes or a fortenight before I goe to myne owne house, both because I feare my bodye by soe longe a restraynt is become ill able uppon the sudden to indure the open Countrye ayre, fyndinge I have nead to use some healpe of physicke, as alsoe that in this time I may dispatch some businesses I have hear and provide thinges necessary thear. My Lord, these are the true causes why I desyre to stay; notwithstandinge, if your Lordship fynde this shall not stande with his Majestie's good likinge I will presently repayre to myne owne house though it should prove dangerous to my 1623. Feb. 13?

[1] He had been committed to the Fleet in June 1622, for dissuading persons from contributing to the benevolence. (Chamberlain to Carleton, June 8, 1622, S. P. Dom. cxxxi. 22.) There is a letter from him to Buckingham amongst the State Papers (S. P. Dom. cxxxviii. 5) explaining his conduct. Mrs. Green states, from the Council Register, that he was removed from the Fleet to his own house at Norton, February 4th. There must be some mistake in this, the date being perhaps that of the order for his removal, as he was evidently still in London on the 13th. See the next letter.

1623. Feb. 13? health and other wayse inconvenient. Your Lordship will please to excuse my boldnes, and accompt me

Your Lordship's humble servant,

W. SAY AND SEALE.

13 Feb. 1622.

Addressed: To the Right Honorable Lord George Lord Marques of Buckingham, Lord High Admirall of England.

Indorsed: Lo. Say to my Lord and copie of answeare.

No. CXXXVIII

THE MARQUIS OF BUCKINGHAM TO LORD SAY AND SELE.

[Copy on the fly leaf of No. XCVI.]

Feb. 13. My Lord. I have acquainted his Majestie with your desire to remayne in London a fortnight or three weekes, to take phisick and settle your businesse, which his Majestie is gratiously pleased to grant, and hath commanded me to signifie so much unto you.

Your Lordship's

13 Feb. 1622.

No. CXXXIX.

SIR ROBERT NAUNTON TO THE DUKE OF BUCKINGHAM.

[Holograph.[1]]

Oct. 6. My most noble Lord. Though my person be still under restraint[2] (my due obedience whereunto must be my best sacrifice,) yet my

[1] The handwriting is not the usual one, but is yet, I think, from Naunton's own pen, but written with great care and deliberation.

[2] Confined to his own house for entering into an unauthorised negociation with Cadenet, the French ambassador.

penne is so free, as that it can not hold from an intire congratulation of this happie and holy day,[1] the happiest that mine eyes have seene, since that of his Majesties moist joyful entrance into this his kingdome. No other words can so fully expresse my hart's Jubile for this happines, as those of that glorious Angel "GLORIE BE to GOD in the highest, on earth peace, good will towards men." The rest of it shall be made up by faithful Simeon, *Nunc dimittis servum tuum Domine secundum verbum tuum in pace.* And though I can not be yet so happy as was imported in that spiritual sence of his, yet will it be no small secondarie happines in a secondarie sence, upon this so longed for apparition of his Highnes and your Lordship's as the two good Angels of our Church and State, to be dismissed in so good an hower and made an ocular wittnes and a free behoulder with the rest, of both your own and the kingdomes happines in this your safe returne, which the same God that hath so graciously graunted it, blisse and prosper it to both yourselves and to all that truely zeale your truest prosperities, as doth 1623. Oct. 6.

Your Grace's most faithful

Beadsman ever obliged

ROBERT NAUNTON.

Charin Crosse, 6° Octobris, 1623.

Addressed: To the right honorable my singular good Lord my Lord Duke of Buckingham.

Indorsed: Sir Rob. Naunton to my Lord, 6 Octob. 1623.

No. CXL.

LORD KEEPER THE BISHOP OF LINCOLN TO MR. JOHN PACKER.

[Holograph.]

Mr. Packer, with my heartiest comendations unto you. If my Lord's Grace be there, I pray you to remember unto his Grace my 1624. Jan. 14.

[1] The day of the Prince's arrival in London on his return from Spain.

1624. Jan. 14. most humble dutye, and desier his Grace to present unto the Kinge this enclosed submission of my Lord Say, which (the meannesse of his offence, beinge but an omission in his office of a Justice of the peace, considered) his Majestye maye without any diminution of regalitye accepte. But herein I submitt my opinion unto his Grace. If my Lord Duke be not there, I pray you present it your selfe unto his Majestye, and returne unto me with all speede his royall direction.

You may saye unto his Majestye that if my Lord of Wynchester[1] cannot (because he preacheth the daye before) discharge the sermon of the first daye of the Parliament, I doe conceyve the Lord Bishop of Liechfield[2] or the Lord Bushop of Exeter[3] will very well discharge the place. The latter is the better preacher, the former better esteemed by the Lords and other Parliamentary men. Both are greate schollers. I will not further trouble you at this time, but doe comend you to God's best protection, and rest

Your very assured lovinge
and faithfull freynde,
JO. LINCOLN. C.S.

Westminster College, 14 January, 1623.

Addressed: To the Right Worshipfull my very loveing Frend, John Packer Esqr. at Court. In his absence to my Lord of Anan, or Mr. Heurie Gibb.

Indorsed: 14 Jan. 1623, Lo: Keeper to me.

No. CXLI.

LORD KEEPER THE BISHOP OF LINCOLN TO JAMES I.

[Autograph Signature.]

Jan. 15. May it please your most excellent Majestie. I præsent unto your Majesty here inclosed the humble submission of the Lord Saye.

[1] Launcelot Andrewes.
[2] Thomas Morton.
[3] Valentine Carey.

And, the boundles ocean of your Majesties sweetenes and mercye together with the nature of his offence (falling but within his office of a Justice of the Peace) being considered, I doe most humbly expect your Majesties pleasure for dissolving of his Lordshipp's confinement and his restitution to the Commission, wherein he hath at other tymes performed very great service unto your Majestie. 1624. Jan. 15.

I doe not doubte but his Lordshipp wilbe soe sensible of this gracious clemencye as to imploye his best abilities (which are more then ordinary) to doe your Majestie all acceptable service. God Allmightie blesse and præserve your most excellent Majestie.

The most obliged of all

Your Majesties vassals,

Jo. Lincoln. C.S.

15 January, 1623.

Addressed: To the Kinges most excellent Majestye.

Indorsed: Lo: Keeper to his Ma[ty] Lord Say.

No. CXLII.

Lord Kensington to the Duke of Buckingham.

[Holograph.]

My best and dearest Lord. I have acordinge unto your comendment returned you your letter intended unto Monsieur Le Grande by the bearer. I expect to rescive that other that your Grace purposes for him. The sooner you shall bee pleased to send it unto mee, my jurny will begine. Tomorrow in the morninge I must waight upon the Prince to acquaint him what comandments his Father the Kinge hath given mee, and likwise to reseive his, the which I hope will bee a litle more clear and particular, since it conserns him nearer. Jan. 22.

My Lord, though the favers and honers that I have reseived from you bee infinit, as is the goodnes of that hart from whence they

1624. Jan. 22. kame, yet is my will and desires as large as man's gratitude can bee to acknowledge them; but I confesse they can present no words unto mee suficiently fitte to cloth my thankfulnesse as becomes my unspeakable obligasions unto your Lordship, the which hath made all that I can saye and indeed the best of all my services in comparison of what is deserved by you, slight and weake returns; but this I will saye, and with a vow unto my God, untill I returne to that of which hee made mee, I will unchangably be

Your Grace's most devoted creature
and humblest servant,
KENSINGTON.

This 22 of January.

Addressed: For Your Grace.

Indorsed: Lo. Kensington to my Lo.

No. CXLIII.

SIR RICHARD KNIGHTLEY TO DUKE OF BUCKINGHAM.

[Holograph.]

May? May it please your Grace. My duty is to your honour all I knowe, your company is the best medicine against mischief here. I am sure we are almost fallen from that active word hope by your absence, though I am confident your good there will bringe us hoame to the best good, God being on your cause's side. The reasons of discomfort in men's mouthes (which will certainely hinder the subsedies till they be blowne over), the malignity of Spaine, that it should make any trouble with his Majestie, that he should heare such whose verie presence is a torment to good men that noe proclamacion is come forth, nor none heard of; that the Treasurour's busines should have such a delay, which is interpreted a gapp for an escape if any can be made either by mischeife or money. The disturbance in men's thoughts are, that soe much duty really showne should not produce a speedy dispatch, the time of the yeare require-inge noe dallyinge. You must excuse me, if I write not that which will please you, since I write it as my duty to you, thinkinge it fitt for you to knowe. Your goodness hath ever the best interpretations, my innocency shall cleare any thinge when I may really showe my self whose harty servant I am. 1624. May ?

Your Grace's in all obligacins,

RICHARD KNIGHTLEY.

Addressed: To the illustrious Prince George Duke of Buckingham these be dd.

No. CXLIV

ELIZABETH TITULAR QUEEN OF BOHEMIA TO THE DUKE OF BUCKINGHAM.

[Holograph.]

My Lord. Pringle must have this letter to you, who I assure you is much your servant. He hath brought me verie good horses from my deare brother. I am confident those you will send will be so too, for you never sent me other. I am glade to heere you beginn to recover your health againe, which I pray take care of. I assure you that none wisheth your weldoing more then doth June 13/23.

Your most affectionate frend

ELIZABETH.

The Hagh, this 13/23 of June.

Addressed: To the Duke of Buckingham.

Indorsed: Q. of Bohemia.

No. CXLV.

THE DUKE OF BUCKINGHAM TO LOUIS XIII.

[Draft, with autograph corrections and additions.[1]]

Sire. L'honneur des lettres de Votre Majesté surmonte toute possibilité de recognoissance. Mais sa bonté qui a precedé mes Aug. 16.

[1] The letter itself is in Packer's hand, but the portions in brackets are additions in Buckingham's own writing. We must not, therefore, take too literally the expres-

1624. Aug. 16.

mérites me contrainct de confesser que la grandeur de ses incomparables vertus en bonté et courtoisie, qui la rend recommandable entre tous autres Princes, a produict en moy de tels effects que je ne sçay bonnement à quoy me resoudre ou à la passer soubz silence, ce qui me feroit mourir d'impatience ou à tascher de l'exprimer par paroles qui sont trop foibles pour tesmoigner la passion dont je suis porté à l'admiration de voz vertus qui surpassent toute flaterie. Estant en ce combat d'esprit et ne sachant de quel costé me tourner pour rendre service à Vostre Majesté, je me suis addressé à Monsr. le Marquis d'Effiat son Ambassadeur Extraordinaire, lequel m'a donné une si vraye et vive impression de voz perfections en capacité, jugement, et meureté au gouvernement et conduicte des affaires que je ne me suis pas servi du chemin ordinaire des Ambassadeurs, quoy que mes privés et confidents amys, mais en la sincerité de mon ame prens l'asseurance de m'addresser à Vostre Majesté, pour luy remonstrer que le Roy mon maistre n'a rien plus à cœur que d'estreindre l'alliance des deux Couronnes et des personnes de Madame vostre sœur et son tres cher filz, tant pour le contentement qu'en recevroyent leurs incomparables personnes, que pour le bien de la Chrestienté, pour lequel conduire à heureuse fin le Roy mon maistre a resolu de consentir à tout ce qui luy sera possible, et se confiant que le reste des Articles sont accordés, a couché le dernier en termes contenus au papier cy-adjoinct. En quoy je prie très humblement Vostre Majesté de croire que c'est l'extremité [à que je le puis insiter, et en mon povre opiniou] tout ce que l'on scauroit desirer avec raison, car le Roy mon maistre ne peut abollier les loys, et par ce moyen ill joueront copieussement des effects de la bonté et clemense de Sa Majesté, et je ne suis neulement en doubte que Vostre Majesté ne vise princepalement à l'oneur et heureus estat du Roy mon maistre,

sion in a letter written a few days later by Effiat, in which he reported that Buckingham objected to write a French letter in his presence, as it was impossible for him to do so; "ne sçachant pas escrire en François, estant vray qu'il a grande peine a le parler, n'en sachant que bien peu de mots." Effiat to Ville aux Clercs, Aug. 25 / Sept. 4 1624. Harl. MSS. 4595. fol. 238 b.

preferrant la seureté et paisible governement de Sa Majesté aus efrené et immoderés desires de ses subjects Catholicks Romaines, qui ont bien de subject sur ceste occation si lon leur deprevoir a leur propre soulagement non seulement de sau contanter, et ains d'ampoyer tous leur creditt envers le Pape pour faciliter la dispensation, considerant l'extremité ausquell ills estoyt reduis despuis nageres, et la grand apparance quill seront en pire estat que jamais, si ce traité se venoyt à romper, et que par ce moyen ce Prince sera contrainct de se marier à une de nostre religion: mais je suis si certaine des bonnes intentions de vostre Majesté et de la sincere affection que vous portes tant au Roy mon maistre qu' à son fis unique, que je ne puis douter que vostre Majesté ne coupera la broche à toutes impediments pour doner un bone et heureuse fin à ce treté pour le bien non seulement de vostre Majesté et le Roy mon maistre ains ausie pour la bien et la pais de tout la Cretienté, ainsi [supplicant] Vostre Majesté de me faire l'oneur de [me fare] sçavoir sa resolution [par les Imbassadeurs de mon maistre] aupres de vous, le plus promptement que faire se pourra, afin de ne perdre plus de temps en un affaire de telle consequence et expedition, et de recevoir les assurances que luy donnera Monseigneur le Marquis d'Effiat de ma rondeur et integrité que j'estime le plus beau moyen de luy rendre preuve de mon zele à son service. 1624. Aug. 16.

Indorsed: 16 Aug. 1624. My Lo: to the French King.

No. CXLVI.

Capt. John Chudleigh to the Duke of Buckingham.

[Autograph Signature.]

May yt please your Grace to understand that, accordinge to your commaund, I have heare at Vlushinge landed Comte Mansfield this 13th of October, it beinge the seventh day after our departure from England. The reson of our soe tedious passage was calmes Oct. 13.

1624. Oct. 17. and cross windes, but noe detraction either of time or meanes which was to be used by me. I purpose heare to attend his retorne,[1] or untill I heare to the contrary from him. Thus havinge nothinge elles to informe your Grace of at this present, I rest

Your humble and devoted Servant,

Jo. Chudleigh.

From abord his Majestes Shipp the Speedwell at Vlishinge[2] the 13th of October, 1624.

Addressed: To his Grace of Buckingham, Lord High Admirall of England, these with speed.

Indorsed: Cap. Chudleigh to my Lo.

No. CXLVII.

Sir Thos. Chamberlain to the Duke of Buckingham.

[Original Letter with the signature torn off]

May it please your Grace. At my being at Hanwell, when I waited ther upon your Lordship, you were pleased to present me to the Kinges Majestie, who then made knowen unto me his Royall pleasure that I should be his Justice of Chester,[3] unto which I did most humblie submitt my selfe, and shalbe ever readie to doe what service his Majestie shall commaund me. I am now become an humble suter to your Grace neither for place nor profitt, but, as I was made a Judge by your gracious favoure, soe I desire to live and dye a Judge, assuring myselfe that his Majestie will rather grace then disgrace me in sending me downe about his Majesties service. I did understand this night after supper that ther is a writt

[1] On the return voyage, he was wrecked on November 1.

[2] Flushing.

[3] He had been a Justice of the King's Bench, and now returned to the office of Chief Justice of Chester which he had formerly held, making an exchange with Whitelocke. The reason for this was said (Chamberlain to Carleton, October 23, S. P. Dom. clxxiii. 82) to be a disagreement between Whitelocke and the Lord President of Wales, the Earl of Northampton.

made and to be scalled for my dischardge from being a Judge 1624.
(unles his Majestie shall speedilie signifie his royall pleasure to the Oct. 17.
contrarie); whereas I conceave, and the Judges are of opinion, that I may remayne a Judge, having a writt onlie of my dischardge for my attendaunce and execucion of the place in the Kinges Bench; but, if his Majesties pleasure be otherwise, I most humblie submitt myselfe thereunto. In Kinge Edward the Fourthes time Needam was Judge of the Common Pleas and Justice of Chester all at one tyme, and in Kinge Henrie the Seaventhes tyme Englefield was Judge of the Common Pleas and Justice of Chester at one tyme, and soe was Sylliard in Kinge Henrie the eighth's tyme, and in Queene Elizabethes tyme Corbett was Judge of the Kinges Bench and Justice of North Wales at one tyme, and Crooke Justice of South Wales and Judge of the Kinges Bench in his Majesties tyme, which is all one as Chester. I seeke after noe such matter, but onlie to honnor the Kinges service with the name of a Judge in my antiquitie and habitt, wherewith the Judges are all well pleased, and noe cause of offence to any; for otherwise men will conceave that I was rather in disgrace then in grace with Majestie. And on this daie senight, when I wayted upon your Grace in London, I did receave a most gracious aunswere from you therein. And soe, most humbly craving pardon for my presumption herein, resting onlie under the shadowe of your gracious winges, I shall ever be

Your most bounden Servant to comaund

London, 17 October, 1624.

Addressed: To the highe and mightie Prince George Duke of Buckingham, Lord Highe Admirall of England.

Indorsed: Sir Th. Chamberlayn to my Lo.

No. CXLVIII.

The Earl of Oxford to the Duke of Buckingham.

[Holograph.]

1624. Oct. 18. My Lord. I latelye wryte unto you by Sir Jhon Wentworth, wherin I intymated unto your Grace my request that if anny [were][1] to command as Colonell Generall over our Nation under Mansfilde, you wolde be pleased to honor me with your favour in the obtaining of that charge. When theis businesses weare first in agitation, I moved your Grace in generall termes concerning this point, and received a noble answer from you, which was seconded by performance as farr as the ocation presented, and as then I depended wholye uppon your Grace; for in this and all things els will I never devide my acknowledgments by using anny other means, but refer my selfe unto your disposing, unto whome I confess my thankes and servises due. Since Sir Jhon Wentworth's departure their has been no alteration hier,[2] nor annything attempted on either side; we have this daye finyshed our entrenchment at Walwike, from whence theis lines bring you my affectionate well wishes, as uppon all ocations I will, whatsoever I am master of, so aprove my selfe

Your Grace's most faithfull and humble servant,

H. Oxenford.

From Prince Hemyes quarter at Walwick, the ould 18 / new 28 of October, 1624.

Addressed: To His Grace the Duke of Buckingham, Lo: Hygh Admiral of England.

Indorsed: E. of Oxcford to my Lo.

---

[1] Paper torn away.

[2] At the siege of Breda.

No. CXLIX.

Lord Keeper the Bishop of Lincoln to Mr. John Packer.

[Holograph.]

Mr. Packer. As soone as ever I hadd remov'd Sir Thom. Chamberlayne[1] from his place in the King's Benche (with his full assent and likinge) a certayne qualme came over his stomacke to be of a Judge noe Judge, that you must tell my Lord Duke that if he wold have him live to goe downe into Wales, his Grace must move his Majestye to signe him this writt, whereby he may be a nominall Judge of the Common Pleas, with his place in Wales, he dis'clayminge from all fees and profitts of the place in the Common Pleas, which I have assured the rest of the Judges there. This his Majestie may well doe, and this is the onelye way to preserve him a Judge, which he most ambitiously affectes, the poore man beinge tormented with the stone, and allreadye up to the gyrdle in his grave,[2] but much offended at me (who ever did and doe heartilye love him) that this preservation of his honor was not thought of before, which with the helpe of all the Judges in Westminster Hall wee hadd much adoe to fynde out nowe. The effect (if the Kinge shold aske you) is this; to make him a supernumerarye Judge of the Common Pleas,[3] without fee or charge, that soe, havinge once beene a Judge, he might die a Judge, which otherwise by his place in Wales he shall not doe, but playne Sergeaunt Chamberlayne. 1624. Oct. 19.

This is the first letter (and that inclosed) I have written these

[1] See No. CLXVII.

[2] He lived till September 17, 1625.

[3] In the reign of Charles I. he actually sat upon the Bench of the Common Pleas. This letter gives an explanation of the fact which Mr. Foss (Lives of the Judges, vi. 276) had some difficulty in accounting for.

1624. Oct. 19. ten dayes, wherein I have been tormented with the newe sickenes,[1] but nowe (I thanke God for it) I have not been forced to goe to stoole these 17 or 18 howres and I hope it is at a stopp, althoughe I am still ready to sound at the very thought of any meate.

I rest ever your assured lovinge freynd

JO. LINCOLN. C.S.

Westminster College, 19 October, 1624.

Addressed: To my very lovinge freynd Mr. John Packer Esq. at Court deliver these in haste.

Indorsed: Lo: Keeper to me Sir Th. Chamberlayn.

No. CL.

LORD KEEPER THE BISHOP OF LINCOLN TO MR. JOHN PACKER.

[Holograph.]

Nov. 20. Mr. Packer. I doe send Dr. Wilson unto you, for your furtheraunce in his suyte, without all commendacions. For you knowe the man, his learninge, pietye, and discretion every waye. I will onelye say unto you, that he is well beneficed, and a good housekeeper nere unto Rippon in Yorkeshire, that he is prebendarye and sub-deane of that poore church. Nowe my earnest suyte unto you and humble petition unto my Lord is this, that this Deanerye of a hundred markes a yeare beinge nowe voide, you wold be pleas'd to doe your best endevoure, to take away this *Terminum diminuentem* of *sub* and make him playne Deane of Rippon. Soe worthy a man (I knowe) will not appeare in the competicion for soe unworthy and meane a remote northerne Deanerye. I beseech you doe the Dr. what favoure herein you maye, and remember my most humble

[1] According to Chamberlain, Oct. 23 (S. P. Dom. clxxiii. 82), three or four hundred persons were dying of the disease every week.

dutye and service to my Lord Duke. Soe I recommend you in my prayers to God's protection, and doe rest 1624. Nov. 20.

Your very assured loving freynd,

Jo. Lincoln. C.S.

Westminster College, 20 November, 1624.

Addressed: To my very worthy freynd Mr. John Packer esq. at Courte, these.

Indorsed: Lo: Keeper to me. Deane of Rippon.

No. CLI.

Sir Thomas Roe to the Duke of Buckingham.

[Autograph signature.]

My Lorde. I have long esteemed your Grace my protector and therefore presume now to find you my deliverer; I shall have finished my ovenant with the Levant Company in December 1625,[1] having then served for them faithfully four yeares, and spent industriously eleven of my best tyme among Infidells, not much to my proffitt, yet I repent not the tryall of God's great favour in so many and so crooked wayes. I professe ingennously to your Grace I have not advanced £1,000 in this imployment, and yett the Company have extended such liberalityes to mee, as for honesty I cannot complayne, nor for shame, knowing the poverty and weakeness of their trade exact more upon them. This is not a Residence wherein to make a fortune, for it must then rise by unjust wayes upon the Merchant or by enterteynment. They are able to give no more, and there depends no hope of preferment after it, because it is disesteemed in England. I have fallen upon many extraordinary charges in his Majestie's particular service, of which I dare not presume to aske recompence; it is enough if it bee accepted. Butt having fullfilled Dec. 9.

[1] The Ambassador at Constantinople was paid by this Company.

1624. Dec. 9. my tyme, my humble suite to his Majestie and your Grace is, that I may with good favour, retorne as soone as it shall conveniently stand with the commodity of the Company, of whose good I have great cause to bee respectfull. I have sett in order all their affaires and revived their trade, in such sort that I hope it shalbee both beneficiall to the Kingdome and to them, and in advance of his Majestes customes. I have settled the Peace with Barbary, if it bee not shaken againe by want of small liberalityes to maynteyne it. It shalbee to mee a comfort to have such a successor as may bewtify and build upon these my poore foundations. Heerein only I can doe them the last service, which is no yll one to His Majestie, to enforme Your Grace (upon whom they depend) rightly their estate and what manner of education is convenient for them. The Company are allready in debt, and the remove of an Ambassador is to them a charge they cannot recover in 4 yeares, all their Consulage abroad beeing not sufficient to defray the ordinary. It is not every man (though of great parts) that can fitt this place. It requires one well acquainted and tender of the affaires of merchants, one that hath experience and practicque with all nations: For though this imployment is slighted in England, yett (if it were not a kind of vaynglory in mee to presse it) I can showe good reason that to discharge this duty well doth require as much sufficiency and honesty as any other whatsoever, and there is as much dishonor and danger in any miscarriage. Here are many Ambassadors Resident, many Extraordinary, and these with their Princes of greatest estimation, having bene formerly tryed in England, Spayne, France and the Court of the Emperour, before they are trusted here. I am most assured that your Grace hath nothing equall in your care to a generall good. Nowe trade is a litle revived, if you please to conferre that grace upon the Company, or if I have any meritt upon mee to recommend a man qualified for the place, one that may comport with the merchants and these people, I shall esteeme myselfe too much honored by so great a mark of your Grace's favour. Herein you shall give life to a dead plant; for the Company having the power to present one, they can make their owne condition with him and save £1,000 in the remove. This is the cause of my presumption and I am confident in myne owne integrity, that your Grace will rightly enterprett my faithfull meaning to his Majestie's service and your owne honor. If his Majestie or your Grace have any other purpose or designment upon any, I am silent and aske pardon for my ignorance, only in all humility desyring then myne owne liberty that I may retorne to live under your Grace's shadowe, so poore a man that meat, drink, and myne owne cuntry cloth is all I can have and all my ambition. I beseech your Grace accept mee still for your servant. I have no such unworthy hearte to dissemble for any end. I honour and love your virtues, and, if you would vouchsafe to make tryall of mee, I will prove my devotion to your Grace to bee more zealous then I knowe howe to promise. If in the meane tyme you wilbee pleased to continue your mediation to his Majestie that I may have at least the comfort of his good opinion, I will repay your Lordship the beggar's reward, to pray for you, as I think all good Englishmen doe and is all I can doe, 1625. Dec. 9.

Your Grace's most humble Servant,

THO. ROE.

Constantinople, 9/19 December, 1624.

No. CLII.

CHRISTIAN DUKE OF BRUNSWICK TO THE DUKE OF BUCKINGHAM.

[Autograph signature.]

Monsieur. Je scay qu'aveque l'affection que vous avés au bien public, vostre bonté conduit tellement vostre disposition à la courtoisie, que me sentant deja plus obligé à vos faveurs qu'homme du monde, j'attendray avec supplication celle dont je requiers très instamment Vostre Excellence. C'est qu'il vous plaise avoir agreable Feb. 16/26.

1625. Feb. 16/26. de commander de vostre plein et propre pouvoir que six navires de sa Majesté, à tout le moins ceux qui sont à la Rade de Sandwidge se rendent icy au retour de ce Gentilhomme, l'attente desquels nous arreste encore icy, sur tout apres la perte de trois navires du Roy tres chrestien, en la tourmente de ces jours passés, et le debris des navires Holandois destinés pour escorte. Je supplie bien humblement Votre Excellence, puis que mon honneur en despend, que l'execution de sa volonté ne soit retardé en un fait de telle exigence, la Cavalerie Françoise la plus belle qu'il se puisse voir commençant à s'embarquer. Ainsy je m'advanceray, quant et elle, sans recevoir de destourbier en chemin par ceux de Dunkerk, qui avec quinze navires de guerre, et autant de Frey-buiters, nous attendent en intention de nous attacquer, à faute d'escorte suffisant. Ceste obligation augmentera grandement celles que je vous ay deja. Dont je seray tant que je respireray de Votre Excellence,

Monsieur,

Le tres humble et tres obeissant serviteur,

CHRISTIAN.[1]

De Calais, le 16/26 de Febvrier 1625.

Indorsed : Duke of Brunswick to my Lord.

No. CLIII.

THE MARQUIS OF EFFIAT TO THE DUKE OF BUCKINGHAM.

[Autograph signature.]

Feb. 17/27. Monsieur. Le Courier que Monsr de Brunzvik envoye à Vostre Excellence m'a dit que la tempeste avoyt esté sy furieuze qu'elle avoyt non seullement retardé nostre Cavallerie, mais fracassé tous noz vaisseaux de guerre quy la doibvent escorter, et l'on m'escrit par une qu'il m'a apportée que j' envoye à Vostre Excellence affin qu'elle voye comme ilz craignent ceux de Dunkerke, quy se preparent à

[1] He was to conduct French cavalry to join Mansfeld's force, which was at that time destined to march through the Low Countries to the Palatinate.

empescher leur passage. Cest pourquoy ilz ont recours à demander assistance de six ou sept de voz gardes costes et navires de guerre à ce passage et faire, s'il vous plaist, que le commandement soyt donné sur le champ, afin qu'il ny aye plus de temps perdu, car cette Cavallerye a tellement mangé la Picardie depuis deux mois qu'elle y est qu'ilz ny trouvent plus rien, et ont peur qu'ilz se desbandent, Cest pourquoy je supplie Vostre Excellence d'ordonner le plus promptement qu'il se pourra que l'escorte soyt donnée, affin que suivant son desir ilz puissent estre bientost joinctz avec Mons. de Mansfelt que le passionne, en cette consideracion estant,

1625. Feb. 17/27.

Monsieur,

Vostre tres humble et tres obeissant serviteur,

D' EFFIAT.

A Londres ce xxvij. Febr. 1625.

Addressed: Monsienr le Duc Bukingham Grand Admiral d'Angleterre.

Indorsed: Fr· Ambr to my Lo: 27 Feb. 1624.

No. CLIV.

THE LORD KEEPER THE BISHOP OF LINCOLN TO MR. JOHN PACKER.

[Holograph.]

Feb.

Sir. I returne you very heartye thankes for that accompte you have allreadye made of some parte of my remembrances, and hope you give me to heare (in time) of the rest. Judge Crooke[1] his election is received with the greatest applause that ever I knew any action in this kinde, and my Lord (to whose grace I doe appropriat the worke) much blessed and commended for the same.

The Warrant for Sergeaunt Richardson[2] wanted forme, and that for Sir Thom. Crewe[2] beinge. I send you therefor both, hopinge

[1] Sir George Croke, Justice C. P. February 11, 1625.

[2] Serjeants Richardson and Crewe succeeded Croke and Ranulph Crewe as King's Serjeants.

1625. Feb. that my Lord's Grace will supplie these two vacant places (of Justice Crewe[1] and Justice Crooke) with these two persons, either whereof hath beene a Speaker of the House of Commons. Sir Thom. Crewe hath been a very good servaunt to the Kinge in this last Session, and very ready (upon all occasions) to serve my Lord Duke. Thoughe he be relligious and of an humble spiritt, yeat is he very sensible of the least neglect, and (as my Lord Elsmer was wont to terme him) a very waspe, if he be angred.

I finde by my Lord Treasurer's extraordinary good intentions to me, that my Lord Duke hath settled my pension[2] better then his Grace promised unto me, and I heare from all men that his Grace powres favowres and respectes upon me to the Kinge upon all occasions. I pray God to blesse him for it, and to make me as able as I am willinge and cordially disposed to serve his Grace upon all occasions. And soe I doe (for this time) recommend you to God's protection and rest

Your very lovinge freynd,
Jo. Lincoln. C.S.

Addressed: To my very lovinge freynd Mr. John Packer Esqr at the Courte these.

Indorsed: Lo: Keeper to me.

No. CLV.

The Marquis of Effiat to the Duke of Buckingham.

Mar. 3/13. Monsieur. Je n'ay jamais songé à demander une choze sy publicque comme on la voullu faire entendre à Votre Excellence, me contentant de ce quy a esté accordé et non pas davantage, et avoir la lettre de Monsr l'Archevesque D'York, ou celle qu'a demandé Mons. le Garde des sceaux comme plus utile et moins scandaleuze,

[1] Ranulph Crewe, Ch. J. K. B. January 26, 1625.

[2] Of 2,000 marks. Sir J. Coke to Buckingham, January 1625, S. P. Dom. clxxxii. 79.

et que Monsr Conovay m'avoyt promis quand il alla à Neumarquet de m'envoyer dans le Jeudy ensuivant de son partement Et sy j'en suis encores là, tant il s'est peu soucié des parolles qu'il m'en a donnéez. Mais ce discours est de trop longue haleine pour en importuner V. E. par escrist; c'est pourquoy je le remetteray quand j'auray l'honneur de la veoir, esperant que ce sera dans un jour ou deux pour le plus tard, croyant que dans ce temps là il arrivera quelque courier de Paris quy apportera quelques bonnes nouvelles, quy serviront de passeport à cette importunité, ne dezirant pas incommoder es responses de V. E. auparavant, ce quy m'oblige d'en demeurer là: c'est pourquoy je quitte ce discours pour supplier V. E. de voulloir envoyer un mot de lettre par lequel elle permet de prendre les navires[1] dont son secrétaire ma donné le memoire, quy est sy zelé à nostre contentement par le commandement que V. E. luy en a faict, qu'il prend la peyne d'aller à expréz à Thiboldz pour luy faire entendre ce quy en est. Le Sr Burlamaki en a escrit un memoire que j'envoye à V. E. quy monstre la necessité q'uil y a d'en uzer ainsy, ce quy me force de supplier V. E. de voulloir envoyer ceste lettre, affin de parachever cette affaire que le Roy mon Maistre presse sy fort, passionnant de recevoir les fruyctz de la bonté du Roy de la Grande Bretaigne, à quoy V. E. a tant coutribué qu'elle a obligé toutte notre nation à se dire comme moy de Vostre Excellence, 1625. March 12/22.

Monsieur, tres humble et tres fidel serviteur,

D'EFFIAT

A Londres, ce xxij. jour de Mars 1625.

Addressed: A Son Excellence Monsienr le Duc de Bukingham, Grand Admiral d'Angleterre.

Indorsed: French Amb[r] to my Lo: 23 March, 1624.

---

[1] The ships which were ultimately taken against La Rochelle.

No. CLVI.

Sir Thomas Dutton to the Duke of Buckingham.

[Autograph Signature.]

1625. March 22.

May it pleas your Excellency. If my fortunes proves never so crose in my profession, yet the many bountys of your Grace's favores, must comand my life, when you ples. I am sorry your Grace's great desiers to have this army prosper[1] has had so bad success, which is wholy to bee imputed to the cruelty of the wether, and so remote a place as Giteringberke[2] assigned for our randevowes at this tyme of the yeare: and now wee are marched to our quarters at the Sprange[3] wee finde them all plundered and spoyld of all forrage and necessary provisions by the Princes of Orringes leauger, which has lyen in these partes all this yeare, and to speake truth our longe lyinge on shipboard, and the want of trancsport and provissions for our sicke men, which could noe wayes be gotten, has bine the meane cause of our great mortallity in generall.

Now, as wee are, it is impossible for the English Army to march into the feild with honore till the be supplyed with 5000 good men, well armed and clothed, and besides a present supply of sherts stockings and showes to refresh those nasty ill men wee have left, which have bine all poysoned for want of thes nesessarys: and in my judgement, the whole number now excedes nott the number of 6000 men of all sortes. I knowe not what reporte may come to your Grace's handes, of our noble Generall's usage of us, but in my pore oppinion, hetherto, considering all exstremetys, it could not be well mended: and I thinke without the Kinge resolve to suffer him to do some thinge here to ruenat the Kinge of Spaine's Army before Breda, our Generall wilbe able to doe nothinge in prose-

[1] Mansfeld's army.

[2] Geertruidenberg.

[3] Sprang, in North Brabant, where the Dutch under Prince Frederick Henry were watching Spinola's operations against Breda.

cutinge the Germayne Warres; the enemy beinge so powerfully possesed of all stronge places one the Rhyne: besides wee to leave to Spanish armey at our backes, and Tilli's armey and all the ill affected Germaynes to stope his passage, and starve him up without bloes, is to hazerdus in my opinion to adventure: but if wee fortune to give the enemy a bloue in these parts, in Godes name wee may hereafter march where wee liste. I most humbly crave your Excellency to pardon the errore of these my dutys, because I preferre your honore above my life: And so rest in all dutyes 1625. March 22.

Your Grace's humble servant,

Yoo^rs [?]

THOM. DUTTON.

Good my Lord, as I ever found your Grace kinde to me, so see my wife receave my meanes and what is dew to me in Ierland, to keepe her and my children and to pay my debtes in my absence, and God will reward you for it.

Frome the Sprange, 22th [1] of March 1625.

Addressed: To his Excellency the Duke of Buckingham in all dutye, these at the Court, England.

Inclosed: Sr Tho. Dutton to my L:

No. CLVII.

THE EARL OF CARLISLE TO THE DUKE OF BUCKINGHAM.

[Autograph.]

My most noble deare Lord. I grieve to heare that your Lordship dothe grieve so muche, and I feare, not onely out of my personall respects to your Lordship as your most faythfull humble servant, but for my love to the publiquee, that your immoderat April ?

[1] Originally written 18, 22 being written over the figures in paler ink.

1625. April. passion may be prejudiciall to our great Master's service. Your comminge hither is infinitly longed for by me for my owne particular contentment and desire to wayt upon your Lordship quickly, and more for the infinit use there would be of your Lordship's presence here, that by your vysdome authorety and dexterety the affayres might be managed with more advantage for his Majestie's honor and service. I consider allso that in the present conjuncture your Lordship's presence may be of excellent use at home, so as I could wishe since your presence is so necessary in bothe places that yow would borrow so muche of ubiquity as that your persone could be in the severall places where your sufficiensy is so necessary, but since that cannot be I will leave the choise to his Majestie's pleasure and to your owne infinit wysdome. If yow resolve to cum hither I shall have my longinge and your Lordship shall have my faythfull service. If yow shall take an other resolution I will not fayll to mak an offer unto yow of all that my Industry and Knoledge can collect submittinge all my proceedings and endevors to be censured and directed by your Lordship's wysdome, In which resolutione yow shall ever fynd

Your Grace's most faythfull frend
and most humble servant,
CARLILE.

Addressed: For your Grace.
Indorsed: E. of Carlisle to my L.

No. CLXIII.

ELIZABETH TITULAR QUEEN OF BOHEMIA TO THE DUKE OF BUCKINGHAM.

[Holograph.]

April 11/21. My Lord. I have sent this bearer Nethersole to the King my deare brother to condole with him our common loss, and to wish him a happie raigne, which I hope shall be more glorious then anie of his ancestors. I can say no other to you then that you have lost a good maister, and I a deare and loving father: what greef I feel for it you may easilie judge by your self. My affliction would be much more but that I ame confident of the King my brother's love, in whose favour I intreat you still to help to continue me. You shall understand by Nethersole how all goeth heere, and other particulars which I will faithfullie tell you. He is so honest as I ame sure you will trust him, which I intreat you to doe, and allso beleeve me ever 1625. April $\frac{1}{11}$.

Your most affectionat frend

ELIZABETH.

The Hagh, this $\frac{1}{11}$ of April.

By George Goring I made request for this bearer that he might succeed Sir Dudlie Carleton heere, I intreat you still about the same, and in the meane time that his allowance and place of Agent may be continued him, which he had by your favour you did to him for my sake; and he is your true servant for it.

Addressed: To the Duke of Buckingham.

No. CLXIV.

Count Mansfelt to the Duke of Buckingham.

[Autograph Signature.]

Monsieur. Votre Excellence scait si bien quelle puissance elle s'est meritoirement acquise sur moy qu'elle ne peut douter que la moindre de ses intentions ne me serve de loy, et que si parfois elle n'est accomplie, la faute en doibt estre plustost imputée à mon impuissance ou à l'indisposition du sujet sur lequel elle desire de m'employer qu à manquement de volonté, comme à la verité il arrive au faict des officiers du Regiment de Monsieur le Comte de May.

1625. May. Lincolne,[1] car estant reduict à deux cens et quelques compagnies à cinq ou six hommes, il m'estoit impossible de tenir tous les officiers en pied sans le deservice de sa Majesté. J'ay toutesfois pour le respect du dict Sieur Comte, et pour me conformer au desir de Votre Excellence, retenu les compagnies du Lieutenant Colonnel, Sergent Major, et la plus forte qui restoit en estat sans faveur ou acception de personnes, quoy que soubz d'autres Colonnels, veu qu'il m'estoit force de reformer le leur, ce que je m'asseure Votre Excellence ne trouvera mauvais pour les raisons portées cydessus, et si je n'ay peu en ceste occasion satisfaire de tout point à sa Volonté qu' elle ne lairra pour cela de se servir de moy en toutes autres humainement possibles, professant qu'il ne scauroit arriver plus d'honeur[?] et de contentement que m'employer à l'execution de ses commandements, dont je la supplie m'honorer de temps en temps. D'une chose la supplie-je tres humblement, qu'elle ne se lasse point en sy beau chemin, et que, nous procurant en temps les moiens de poursuivre un si grand et important affaire, elle se conserve la gloire et l'honneur de l'avoir entrepris et la volonté tres ardente que je luy ay vouée de me monstre à jamais,

Monsieur,
De Votre Excellence
Tres humble et tres
obeyssant serviteur,
C. E.[2] MANSFELT.

Au Camp de Donghen le—

Addressed: A son Excellence Monsieur le Duc de Bukingham, &c.

---

[1] "Mansfeld," wrote Carleton to Conway on the 14th of May (S. P. Holland) "hath reformed the Earle of Lincoln's regiment." A letter from Mansfeld himself in the same collection is dated from the camp of Dunghen, May 16.

[2] *i. e.* Comte Ernest, if I read the letters rightly.

No. CLX.

Elizabeth, Titular Queen of Bohemia, to the Duke of Buckingham.

[Holograph.]

My Lord. You may easilie imagine how welcome this bearer was to me, having brought so kinde a message from the King my deere brother. It is an infinite contentment to see my self so much in his love as both his letters and yours assures me I ame, besides this honest gentleman's relation, by whome I understand how much I ame still beholding to you for your forwardness in advancing all things that are for the good of my affaires, which hath made me intreat Sir Henry Vane to speake with you and acquaint you with some things that concernes me, and also about Sir Dudley Carleton, to whome I ame so beholding as I cannot but recommend his business to you. I have desired this bearer to acquaint you with all things, which I assure my self he will doe faithfullie. I will onelie end this letter with assuring you that you bound me by the manie obligations I have to you to be ever 1625. May 31. / June 10.

Your most affectionat frend

Elizabeth.

The Hagh, this 31 of May.

My Lord. I must intreat your favour for my servant Ashbournhame, who long and faithfullie served me. I onelie desire you to favour him to my brother that he may see his good service to me shall in some fashion be recompensed, though I have not the means; I have desired this bearer to solicite you for him.

Addressed: To the Duke of Buckingham.

No. CLXI.

Charles I. to Prince Rupert.

[Holograph.]

Boconoke, 3 Sep. 1644.

1644. Sept. 3. Nepueu. Since my last, it hath pleased God to give me an unexpected victory, and you will fynde by the particulars (which I leave to others) that God's protection of a just cause was never more aparant then at this tyme, for had our success beene ether deferd, or of an other kynde, nothing but a direct miracle could have saved us, and certainly nothing could be so unlooked for as that Essex in Cornwall should imitate (and outdoe) Meldrum at Newarke. Goring is now hemming in the Rebelles' horse which broke from us, they lying neere about Plimouth, and I have sent Sir Richard Grinefeeld with 1500 foot to assist him (who I hope is there by this tyme), following myselfe as fast as I may, intending[1]

l i s c a r and t a
to bee the morrow at 27: 30: 57: 11: 14: 64: 81: al: 78: 15:
u s t o k the n e x [t]
74 : 58 : 79 : 44 : 41 : nz: 48 : 1 : 71 : 80: and so on till wee joyne. The Rebell Midleton is said to bee about Bastable ; now I
to m a r
propose to you whether you will not thinke fitt nl.: 24: 16: 64:
c h with s e e d e unto d o r s e t shire
12: 38: p5: 60: 1: 3: 7: 2: ol: 5: 45: 65: 59: 3: 8: 378:
t o w a r d s h e r b o r n e
78: 46: 55: 16: 66: 6: 82: 60: 40: 4: 64: 21: 47: 64: 46: 4:,

[1] *i.e.* Intending to be the morrow at Liscard and Tavistock the next, and so on till we join. The Rebel Middleton is said to be about Barnstable ; now I propose to you whether you will not think fit to march with speede unto Dorsetshire towards Sherborne, the case being altered with us both since my last, I not knowing then ye were at Bristol ; yet by this I do not alter the main design, which [is] for you to join with me.

the case being altered with us both since my last. I not knowing 1644.
i doe n o t Sept. 3.
then, ye were at Briston, yet by this 33: e2: 50: 44: 80: 83:
a l t e r the m a [i] [n] designe which for
14: 27: 78: 2: 66: nz: 26: 17: 30: 46: 148: p6: c5:
Rp. to i o y n e with me
352: 21: 31: 45: 32: 50: 1: p5: i4: but as then, so now, I
refer it to you to do as you shall judge best for my service. So I rest

Your loving Oncle and most
faithfull frend
CHARLES R.

Indorsed: No. 20 Kg after Essexes defeate.

INDEX.

WESTMINSTER:
PRINTED BY J. B. NICHOLS & SONS,
25, PARLIAMENT STREET.

www.ingramcontent.com/pod-product-compliance
Lightning Source LLC
Chambersburg PA
CBHW032137230426
43672CB00011B/2366
* 9 7 8 3 3 3 7 2 6 8 0 5 3 *